China from Mao to Deng

China from Mao to Deng

The Politics and Economics of Socialist Development

Edited by the
Bulletin of Concerned Asian Scholars
with an introduction by
Bruce Cumings

M.E. SHARPE, INC., ARMONK, NEW YORK
ZED PRESS, LONDON

First published in the United States in 1983 by M. E. Sharpe, Inc.
80 Business Park Drive, Armonk, New York 10504

First published in Great Britain in 1983 by
Zed Press, 57 Caledonian Road, London N1 9DN

China from Mao to Deng, except for the introduction, was first published in the *Bulletin of Concerned Asian Scholars* (Vol. 12, no.4; Vol. 13, nos. 2 and 3; Vol. 15, no. 1).

Library of Congress Cataloging in Publication Data

Main entry under title:

China from Mao to Deng.

Includes bibliographical references.
1. Communism—China—Addresses, essays, lectures. 2. China—Politics and government—1976- —Addresses, essays, lectures. 3. China—Economic policy—1976- —Addresses, essays, lectures. I. Bulletin of Concerned Asian Scholars.
HX418.5.C47 1983 335.43′45 82-19668
ISBN 0-87332-240-1
ISBN 0-87332-244-4 (pbk.)

British Library Cataloguing in Publication Data

China: from Mao to Deng.

1. China—Politics and government—1976-
I. Bulletin of Concerned Asian Scholars
320.951 DS777.55

ISBN 0-86232-163-8
ISBN 0-86232-164-6 PbK

Printed in the United States of America

Contents

Acknowledgments

The current Editors of the *Bulletin of Concerned Asian Scholars* would like to acknowledge the collective contributions of the Editorial Board and of previous Editors. As has always been the case with books originating from the *Bulletin*, this volume represents the inspiration, insight and just plain hard work of a large number of dedicated people. It is due to their combined effort that these pathbreaking essays on China from the *Bulletin* will now be reaching a wider audience.

China from Mao to Deng

Introduction

Bruce Cumings

Events in China since 1976 have bred a certain humility among those who study this vast and fascinating country. It is rare now to find people who will sally forth to say anything with certainty, about almost any aspect of China; just as rare are political activists who still feel a strong pull from Beijing. The image of something new, unique, progressive, diabolical, fascinating, attractive, loathsome captured the minds of foreign observers of all stripes for four decades, roughly dated perhaps from the publication of Edgar Snow's *Red Star Over China*. Surely there was something coherent there that could be loved or attacked, admired or reviled. We thought we knew what that image was. Now, much if not all of it seems to have been illusion.

The Chinese revolution was never as liberating as progressives thought, as threatening as Cold Warriors thought, as dynamic as developmentalists thought. It did not change nearly as much in China as we thought. Perhaps it did not change all that much, it is possible to hear people say today. Perhaps it was as bad, if not worse, as its enemies said.

So, we live in a quieter time, but also a sadder time because the results of this century's greatest revolution now sit tarnished. The harsh glare of reality has revealed China to be human: a big, poor, proud country buffeted by internal and external forces that often are beyond its control; a country with immense developmental problems about which very little can be done in the "short run" that most of us spend our lives in. And it is, of course, not just China. We live in a time of lost mastery, when no nation stands as a beacon of hope and progress, when all nations wrestle with seemingly intractable problems. What is remarkable is that a sober, conservative mood should strike nations as diverse as China and the United States at about the same time, just as radical currents came simultaneously in the 1960s.

Sober reflections and quiet moods carry over into scholarship as well, of course, and so it perhaps is not a surprise that the field of contemporary China studies, in its mainstream, has been struck dumb by events since Mao Zedong's death. It still is impossible to find a single book that does much more than narrate the events of the past seven years, let alone seeks to relate them to what went before, and above all what scholars *said* about what went before. It is much more common to hear remarks about chucking out hundreds of books, now rendered irrelevant by events. Some of the major figures in the field have had virtually nothing to say. There have been, of course, varieties of I-told-you-sos written by people in whom the Chinese revolution awakened little sympathy or reflection. But we are talking about people who connected in some way, for good or ill, with four decades of events in China suffused with awe, mystery, fundamental change, and the deepest human emotions.

This book is not silent about post-Mao China. Just as scholars are now discovering a "Three Line Struggle" in China, so there are three broad interpretations in this collection of essays, all of them written by people who *did*, in greater or lesser degree, connect with the Chinese revolution. One interpretation argues for an abrupt change in 1976, carrying China away from what we can call for shorthand the Maoist vision. A second interpretation posits, with greater or lesser vehemence, that indeed an abrupt change occurred and it was all for the better: the Maoist vision was an unmitigated disaster, says one of our contributors, and others say it was a lot less than it was cracked up to be; they generally applaud the policy changes that have come under Deng Xiaoping. A third and heavily qualified position is that the post-1976 changes have not been so great, just as the differences between Deng and Mao were not so vast.

"Seek truth from facts," Deng tells us, but the reader of this volume will find that injunction to be a weak reed to hang on. The same facts—about plans and markets, about village life—look very different in the interpretations placed upon them by our various authors. There is no consensus, just dissensus. Aristotle wrote in the *Nichomachean Ethics* that "with a true view, all the data harmonize, but with a false one the facts soon clash." This is an improvement on Deng Xiaoping. This volume does not have a "true view" on the meaning of the Chinese revolution, and so we cannot harmonize the data. The reader will have to live with that, which means she or he will have to think it all through. If there are not true views, still there may be false ones, something else to look for. But Aristotle's meaning is not clear. Perhaps, implicitly, he suggests that a true view accommodating all the facts is an illusion, like our illusions about a China none of us knew very well, but which did provide us with a truth that seemed to harmonize those facts that we did know. More likely, he meant that amid the welter of events there is a logic that can be discerned by people, and then tested and retested against the facts; and that, at least in social life, there are no facts that appear irrespective of some logic, no facts that do not need to be interpreted according to some frame of reference.

Truth emerges from facts colliding with theories, and from theories colliding with each other. That is a good position, and most of us can agree that it is not far from what Mao had in mind. His epistemology, unlike many others, can accommodate and even thrive upon a book that comes to no fundamental agreement. He would also find wholly predictable, if not entirely enjoyable, an essay that loads most of the blame for China's problems and disasters on his shoulders. More than his followers, he knew he would be cursed in his grave. So, at any rate, this is the method of the volume: a mini-three-line struggle, a dose of facts, and the reader (as well as the introducer) feeling free to come to his/her own judgements.

It might be best to go to the comfortable middle first. The articles by Victor Lippit, Mitch Meisner and Marc Blecher, and Victor Nee all carefully examine various post-Mao policies relating to the Chinese countryside. James Nickum might also be included in this group, although for somewhat different reasons. His essay demonstrates that when an effective comparison is made between Chinese and Taiwanese development—that is, two areas with relatively comparable history, population, and developmental progress, Shanghai and Taiwan—the mainland's program does not look so bad, even during the "ten lost years" of the Cultural Revolution.

Meisner and Blecher take us through a most useful recapitulation of the role of county administration in rural affairs during the first three decades of the People's Republic of China, and also argue for continuity. In fact, they say that the best place to go to sort out contemporary policy debates is back to the 1950s, and particularly to Franz Schurmann's discussion of different modes of decentralization. Since Peter Van Ness and Satish Raichur also use Schurmann's typology, it appears that *Ideology and Organization in Communist China* is one book that stands the test of time better than most. Meisner and Blecher find a general and increasing restriction on the administrative role of counties, and a downgrading of the key role of the county Party leadership. They note increasing autonomy at the production team level. In a fascinating footnote (no. 48) Blecher tells us that time and again in interviews stretching over a year he heard from Chinese informants that the skilled, better-educated people in the villages he studied tended often to come from the "old bad classes," landlords and rich peasants. This evidence came after the Cultural Revolution decade had ended and reminds us that whatever may be said for the methods of the Cultural Revolution, its goals aimed at the continuing problem of an entrenched elite, deeply resistant to change and capable of perpetuating itself through generations. Deng Xiaoping, of course, has now reached out to this old and much-abused elite, seeking to mobilize it for the "Four Modernizations."

Victor Lippit and Victor Nee also assert continuity between the Maoist and post-Mao periods. Lippit finds that the commune system "remains an intrinsic part of the new development strategy" and provides a detailed description of various phases in the evolution of the commune system since the Great Leap Forward. He calls attention to problems that may result from Dengist policies: agricultural mechanization may aggravate unemployment; material incentives may hurt the collective ethos. But on balance Lippit expects such changes to raise levels of output, and not at the long-term expense of the values of the Chinese revolution. His conclusions, although carefully qualified, tend to support the general thrust of the post-Mao changes: "China's new development strategy is both necessary and viable. Although problem areas do exist, the leadership is aware of these for the most part and has taken measures to minimize the problems." Unlike some of our other authors, Lippit does not seem perturbed that material incentives, a bigger scope for private plots and the market, the attentuation of the revolutionary committee structure, etc., might leave the Dengists subject to charges of revisionism, of making China look more like the Soviet Union. China will continue having "a unique development strategy," he says, and the recent changes will pay off in increased output and heightened efficiency.

Victor Nee would probably agree, even though his article deals with just one village. His research benefits from the rich possibilities for fieldwork and scholarly exchange that have developed in recent years. At the same time, Nee demonstrates that library research also has its virtues: many of the conclusions he had arrived at earlier about this remote Hakka village proved accurate once he got the chance for on-the-spot fieldwork. In his visit in 1980 he found an optimistic spirit, good morale, and a generally liberalized climate of thinking, all of which were in contrast to informant reports on the village during the early 1970s. There had been a recent and "very sizeable" increase in modern inputs used in agricultural production. The situation of women, especially in access to education, also seemed to have improved markedly after the Cultural Revolution ended.

Thus far our authors seem to be in general agreement: there have been important changes since 1976, but not terribly abrupt ones. Lippit and Nee either argue or imply that the general thrust of Dengist policies is correct. Ralph Croizier might be added to this group, for he delights us with a series of cartoons that both benefit from the recent liberalization and show that the critical thrust is directed not just at Mao, but at the current leadership as well. Cartoon number three, however, raises a more fundamental question that tends to be begged in several of these articles. It shows one comrade standing ramrod straight, meant to represent the current leadership. Another comrade, inclining severely to the left, has had his perspective distorted. From his position, the other comrade seems to bend to the right. But if such terms retain any meaning, and if a generation of scholarship on China should not simply be thrown out, then the cartoon should be redrawn. It would show the one comrade inclining to the right, the other to the left, and each viewing the other as deviant. For there can be little question that the Dengist leadership has opted for policies long identified with the "right." That does not necessarily make them incorrect, but it does fit them more properly into the Chinese landscape.

It is absolutely essential, in my view, that we retain a dialogue between the Maoist past and the Dengist present in our work. China could not skip freely into the post-Mao period, but carried a host of previous problems and conceptions with it. So should our analyses of contemporary China. At any rate, this seems to be the assumption of Edward Friedman, Peter Van Ness and Satish Raichur, and Peer Christensen and Jorgen Delman. All of them would, I think, say that the changes since 1976 have been a major departure from those of the Mao period; Friedman would disagree sharply about whether this departure has been good or bad. But they all tell us, in one way or another, that the differences between the Maoist vision and the Dengist vision were sharp and fundamental.

Peer Christensen and Jorgen Delman treat what is now nearly a buried subject, not just in China but in Western scholarship as well. This is the developing theory of socialist transition spawned by the "Gang of Four" and the Shanghai School, not to mention by Mao himself. The authors caution us against uncritical acceptance of contemporary verdicts on these matters, especially ones "offered by people in power." Basing themselves in several Shanghai School manuscripts that have not been discussed before in the literature, they argue that Mao, Zhang Chunqiao, and others developed a "generative class theory" that represents China's "most significant contribution to socialist theory"; it also was in the Marxist tradition of critical theory, which is one reason the ideas had so much trouble in emerging as *praxis*. In essence, the theory states that the socialist stage *does* have material conditions that produce and reproduce antagonistic classes, or what the "Gang" called a new bourgeoisie. This theory would explicitly deny that Maoist ends can be reached through non-Maoist means; instead the means that one uses to distribute wealth, mobilize people, or stimulate production carry within them the ends that you seek. Thus socialist means must be maximized and capitalist means ("bourgeois right") "can only be restricted." Tang Tsou, Paul Sweezy, and others have written about this theory with insight,[1] but Christensen and Delman have come up with materials that do seem to prove that the "Gang" needs another member added to it—Mao Zedong.

In the discussion of how power in a socialist state may be usurped, according to the theory, it is clear to me, if not to the authors, that the "Gang" came close to Trotsky's argument about how socialist revolutions may be reversed. It is a question of political control at the commanding heights, precisely because the very newness of socialist relations of production means that there can be no automatic conditioning of the superstructure by the base for a long period of time.[2] Given that this is by nature a transitional period, the relationship between base and superstructure must be different than in a mode of production that has evolved over centuries: the base, as the authors quote Mao saying, may thus at times become subordinate to the superstructure. Political control of the superstructure by "revolutionaries," as the "Gang" or Trotsky would define them, is therefore critical.

Now, of course, this formulation in practice opens a Pandora's box where political struggle at the top is not only likely, but essential. Furthermore, and here I think is the real problem and the nub of Mao's failure, by arguing that there is no automatic conditioning of superstructure by base a vast realm for voluntarism is opened, a realm where man's will may become supreme over the materialism at the heart of Marxism. If there are no materialist or scientific "laws" that govern this relationship at a certain stage, then who is to decide what policies promote socialism, or when a state structure is in the hands of revisionists? This can only be an arbitrary and inherently ambiguous project.

Mao was an honest and committed revolutionary, willing even to sacrifice the Communist Party itself if it could not be a vehicle for realizing communism. Yet I think that he went to his grave steeped in ambivalence about these matters. His ambivalence, in turn, derives from the fundamental indeterminacy of Marxism as a guide to action at a particular time. Roberto Unger, in a stunning passage,[3] remarks that Marxism and the dialectical mode of thinking are superior to liberal or modern doctrines about unilinear evolution, and about the separation of ideas and events, theory and practice, or the segmentation of knowledge into arbitrary compartments (political science, sociology, etc.). Marxism posits that thought and action, and all social knowledge, must be combined into a unified entity if life is to be comprehended in its fullness.

Dialectics thus improves on simple, linear, cause and effect reasoning and seeks to marry thoughts and events. It gets us closer to the truth, but yet it does not produce truth. For if everything is opposition and unity, unity and opposition, what is it that cannot be proved by the dialectic? "We easily delude ourselves into thinking that we are masters of a method that is in fact little more than a mystery." Here, I think, is the most cogent reason at the level of theory for why Mao was unable to find successors or to opt unambiguously for a Zhang or a Deng. His sincerity in following the logic of his understanding of Marxism was matched, as Stuart Schram once remarked, by a firm conviction that he knew better than his peers. Therefore, who could carry on his inevitably voluntarist, even personal, project of realizing "true and correct" socialism in China?

Carl Riskin, in an article that appeared with the others originally, but which could not be included in this volume,[4] makes clear, I believe, that post-Mao economic reforms do represent a sharp break with past policy, whether the command economy of the 1950s or the Maoist system of 1958-76. Mao's understanding of economics, plans, and material incentives was "in principle . . . incompatible with a major market role in organizing and motivating economic activity." Market socialism, which we can call the Dengist reforms, is a largely uncharted terrain, and for socialists there *is* a distinct risk that the method of achieving socialist goals through capitalist means may someday throw the baby out with the bathwater; that is, "such a path risks capture by capitalism's powerful gravity." Yet this "does not seem to worry" China's reformers; on the contrary, Riskin finds a remarkable naiveté about the market in China, one that is just as voluntarist in seeking panaceas for backwardness as Mao's alternative Great Leap Forward. The "new flying leap" of the immediate post-Mao years, calling for a "war of annihilation in capital construction" among other things, brought to China droves of multinational corporation managers and billions of dollars in foreign plant and technology; almost as soon as this began, it ended amid a welter of unforeseen consequences, not the least the inability to pay for it all in the hard currency of the market. Riskin is quite right to point out that "the most elementary kinds of errors have been committed," especially when these very leaders now excoriate Mao for one error after another. Riskin develops a true dialogue between the past and the present, and takes seriously but without an ounce of cant the analytical problem of when socialism in fact becomes capitalism; he ends quite rightly by saying that the outcome of all this is "quite unpredictable," a dissonant note if there ever was one amid the rosy expectations that with "the moderates" at the helm in China, the ship of state will steer a steady course.

Edward Friedman's essay must be placed in a separate category from the others, both in method and in his judgments. The withering honesty with which he faces up to the evidence we now have about the costs of the Cultural Revolution, and the very considerable emotion with which he condemns the Maoists, cannot be understood solely with reference to China. For these are essays on Sino-American relations as well, about China and about those Americans, like Friedman and the rest of us, who did connect with events in China in the 1960s. He likens current policies to dreams full of hope, and Maoist policies to nightmares full of dread, stultification, violence. The metaphor is apt, I think, at least in one sense. If someone had happened along in 1968 and had told us that in 1980 Mao and his thoughts would be reviled and cursed, that the Cultural Revolution would number its victims in the millions, that the new Chinese leadership would look first to an American administration for support, that Chinese citizens would have a certain wondering euphoria about America, and that all this would be grouped under the rubric of a "modernization" program—that paradigm that most of us spent our graduate educations criticizing—that would indeed have been a nightmare, an unbelievable and threatening window on the future.

Yet this is the world we live in in the 1980s. A certain sort of romanticism circa 1968 thus gives way to a certain sort of moral condemnation in the 1980s. This is one response to the changes in China that has the great virtue of being honest, courageous, dedicated to truth, and willing to start again at the beginning and ask, what do we really know about China? Friedman's answer—and this must be his answer—is that we knew nothing: "How little we knew about China!" Of course, saying this immediately raises a second question: how do we know that what we know now is the truth? I think it is fair to say that Friedman does not appear to be bothered by this second question, but it bothers me. In a country with a billion people, ruled by an authoritarian system, with a new line dedicated to uncovering only a certain relevant portion of past crimes, and an old tradition of telling foreigners what the regime wishes them to hear, to be in step with current received wisdom in Beijing may be to be in step with the truth, but past experience suggests that it may not as well. Any of us can conjure up another dream, or nightmare: China in 1990, where a new leadership speaks of the "ten great years," 1966 to 1976, and the "lost decade" 1976-86, when revisionists and traitors usurped power, trampled on the rights of the workers and peasants, imprisoned and executed true revolutionaries.

There is also a certain poverty of language when an allegedly socialist regime can also simultaneously be described as "feudal," "fascist," a "serfdom," or when unnamed "proto-fascist" forces remain ready to pounce on China and turn it once again from reality to nightmare. I say this among friends who are long used to sharp criticism. These terms, which are uncomfortably close to those used by China's current ideologues, should either be justified for their social science aptness and content (no mean task), or dropped for their inevitable role in simply cutting off debate.

Friedman's sincerity in facing up to China's crimes, in being able constantly to keep before him the visage of a person struck dumb by torture during the Cultural Revolution, is something from which we all must learn. At the same time, we have to find some way to get beyond toting up dead bodies and horror stories. The crimes of the Cultural Revolution do not make the Maoist vision empty of content, just as the blighted lives of millions of minority people in the United States do not make American democrary nothing more than a cruel and empty promise.

The essay by Peter Van Ness and Satish Raichur is different from all the others in one important respect: they explicitly relate China to the world beyond it, something I want to come back to later on.

Van Ness and Raichur are unique in yet another way: after surveying three development strategies (the command system, the Maoist system, and market socialism), they find all three of them to be failures. In some ways, as the authors acknowledge, it can be said that China has pursued three strategies within a single paradigm, that paradigm being a more-or-less centralized command economy, the model for which was pioneered in the Soviet Union. Another way of saying this is that whereas socialist revolutions may or may not have been Marxist, after coming to power they have everywhere been Weberian. Modern states, whether socialist or capitalist, are in this sense alike. The paradigmatic figure is not a charismatic revolutionary, but a stodgy bureaucratic manager. The calling of the tribune of the people is replaced by sets of offices and roles, which can in theory be filled by anyone with the requisite training. And the goal of human liberation recedes as the typical Weberian demand for efficiency advances. The leadership appeals not to theory or truth for its legitimation, but to "effectiveness."[5] Reading the Van Ness/Raichur essay and thinking of socialism in these terms allows us to see how, for better or worse, Maoism was an onslaught against precisely this Weberian telos.

It was also, as David and Nancy Milton have argued, an onslaught against the Soviet Union. With the failure of Maoism, there is also the passing of those fundamental issues of principle which lay at the root of the Sino-Soviet conflict. The current Chinese definition of socialism, discussed in the Van Ness/ Raichur essay, clearly includes the Soviet Union: state ownership of the means of production and payment according to work.

In their discussion of Mao's theory of knowledge, the authors speak to some of the points I raised earlier about the inherent indeterminacy of dialectical reason. They also pursue the logic which is particular to each of the three development paths—an exercise that, as I said at the beginning, is essential if we are indeed to "seek truth from facts." One truth that emerges from the logic of China's current policies is that they demand some degree of integration with the world capitalist system. Van Ness and Raichur are the only authors to mention this other, and critical, dimension of China's experience. Each path in domestic policy carries with it a logic for foreign policy: alliance with the USSR in the 1950s, self-reliance in the 1960s, a developing relationship with world capitalism in the 1970s. This is an important insight; here again, Franz Schurmann's work stands out in our field. This time, it is his *Logic of World Power*, which probes the intimate links between domestic and foreign policy in China, the U.S., and the USSR.

As analysts like Schurmann and Immanuel Wallerstein have shown, the international system (both the world market and the system of states) has its own structuring effect on the choices that states make at home. Critical policy shifts in China since 1949 cannot be understood apart from it. Furthermore, the timing of what we might call a nation's insertion into the world system is also critical.

Looked at in this light, it is not so surprising that China's most rapid development came in the 1950s. Whatever else one may say about it, the Stalinist command system has proven effective in rapid industrial development in a followership mode, that is, industrialization that is "late" in world time. The resources of a strong state, combined with the advantages of learning from or copying technology from more advanced industrial nations, may substitute for domestic developmental disabilities, mobilize available resources, and "catch up" with more advanced states. Or so it appears for a time; in the 1950s there was thus an intimate link between China's industrialization strategy and its alliance with a more advanced industrial power, the Soviet Union. Such a strategy seems to have inherent limits, however; it may compress the time in which the first and second industrial revolutions occur, but it does not allow "leaps" ahead of the more advanced industrial powers. Instead, there is a hierarchy of industrial nations that seems to remain relatively fixed for a long time.

China's "natural" evolution, therefore, might have been from exhausting the potentialities of the Soviet alliance in expertise and technology transfers, to a turn toward the West and Japan (that is, a trajectory that would mimic that of, say, Poland, Hungary, Yugoslavia, and Rumania in going to the West for plant and equipment, and for capital). What is truly remarkable about China, however, is that there was a third path, "strategy B" for Van Ness and Raichur, that intervened —with dire foreign policy consequences. China's attempt to go it alone in the 1960s, taking on both superpowers at once, was extraordinarily courageous, if not foolhardy. It led to palpable threats by both superpowers to launch preemptive nuclear strikes on China. This can only be explained, in my view, by Mao's judgment that the Soviet Union had joined in a condominium with the United States at China's expense and implicitly had given up seeking to build an alternative socialist market system to compete on a global scale with the capitalist system, and by the inhospitability of the advanced industrial states (meaning the United States, but not France) to bringing China into the system.[6]

Without belaboring these points, it should be apparent that a global perspective can account for two of the three developmental failures discussed by Van Ness and Raichur. The 1950s command system did not so much fail as run its course, to the point of diminishing returns for China at home and abroad. The Maoist path, it now seems, not only failed but sounded the death knell for any truly self-reliant path to development in our time. Most developing countries now recognize that they must cut deals with world capitalism, usually not on their own terms, or eventually end up as a Burma or an Albania. Again, this expresses the great remaining strengths of the world market system in the late twentieth century, whether we speak of access to resources, expertise, technology, or markets. And, as Wallerstein has argued many times, this fact must raise the question whether there can be an authentic socialism in our time. Of all the recent cases, the Chinese turn outward would seem to be the most decisive support for this view. Yet it still is rare to find a China specialist with such a perspective —the only thing rarer being a China specialist who predicted China's intermeshing with the world market.

At the empirical, as opposed to the analytical, level there is also support for the structuring effect of the international system on Chinese choices. In my view the critical years in the Sino-American relationship were not just 1971 and 1972, but also 1977 and 1978. Until early 1978 the Carter administration had not decided to deepen the relationship with China; indeed in 1977 there was backsliding. During 1976-78 China thought that its extraordinarily ambitious heavy industrialization schemes could be paid for by ever-increasing petroleum recovery, which could be exported to Japan and elsewhere. But by the end of 1977 the first evidence came in that China's onshore recoveries might soon peak or plateau, unless it had access to technologies available mostly from multinational oil companies. In the spring of 1978 the Chinese took their first major initiatives to welcome technicians from the oil majors and to discuss the exploitation of offshore oil reserves. This was coterminous with the opening of "backchannel" communications between Washington and Beijing, and with the basic decision in Washington to normalize relations with China and to involve China directly in the Soviet-American confrontation. Two individuals whom we might call America's "oil gang," analogous to what Parris Chang has called China's "oil gang," journeyed to China: Senator Henry Jackson and Energy Department Secretary James Schlesinger. Jackson returned from China in February 1978 saying that China wanted to buy our oil technology and had a "new openness to the outside." Schlesinger led a delegation to China in November 1978 that discussed the transfer of petroleum drilling and exploration technology, while having pseudonymous articles appear arguing for a flourishing of the China card vis-à-vis the Soviet Union.[7]

Jackson and Schlesinger along with Zbigniew Brzezinski were intimately involved with the politics in Washington that led to normalization at the end of 1978. So what is the point? The U.S. government, and more particularly the Central Intelligence Agency,[8] were acutely aware that (1) American multinationals possessed superior oil recovery technology, whether for offshore platforms or onshore deep drilling equipment; (2) Soviet oil supplies were tightening and might even plateau in the early 1980s; and (3) this would give tremendous leverage for the United States to order the behavior of socialist states—if not the USSR, then China. In November 1977, just as China's onshore supplies gave evidence of plateauing, an official was quoted as saying about oil and its effects on Soviet bloc countries, "this could mean a reorientation of these countries' whole economies. . . . It could force the countries to become Western-oriented, and that's not bad politically."[9]

To the extent that China accepted such judgments on its oil capacities and its technology needs, it would inevitably spell out sharp changes in China's orientation to the United States. Specifically, the plateauing of domestic recovery would mean that anticipated foreign exchange earnings from oil exports would not reach expected levels, perhaps not for the two decades needed to bring offshore fields onstream, and therefore another means of earning foreign exchange was necessary: light industrial exports, on the model of Taiwan and South Korea. This is precisely the advice that the World Bank and U.S. government officials gave to China, and it is a key explanation for the extensive reorganization that occurred in 1979 and for the turn toward emphasizing light industry in 1980 and 1981.

In the event, the period 1978-1981 witnessed a virtual identity in American and Chinese strategic views, a close parallelism in mutual interests not just in regard to the USSR but around the world, and an increasing complementarity in economic exchange: American technology and grain for Chinese light industrial exports. That this identity seems to be far less certain in 1982 owes both to internecine struggles in the Reagan administration and to China shedding some of its illusions about the market and about the value and the implications of an ever-deepening relationship with the major capitalist world power.

This interpretation needs far more space and documentation to be defended adequately. It is offered merely to demonstrate the potential of an approach that situates China in the world of the late twentieth century and that probes the structuring of Chinese domestic policy choices by international forces. Obviously this would not account for all or even most of the variance. But it can no longer be assumed that Chinese politics can be grasped from a purely domestic, internal inquiry.

Notes

1. Tang Tsou, "Mao Tse-tung Thought, the Last Struggle for Succession, and the post-Mao Era," *The China Quarterly*, no. 71 (September 1977); also Paul Sweezy, "Theory and Practice in the Mao Period," *Monthly Review*, v. 28, no. 9 (February 1977); also Bruce Cumings, "The Political Economy of Chinese Foreign Policy," *Modern China*, v. 5, no. 4 (October 1979).

2. Leon Trotsky, *The Revolution Betrayed* (New York, Pathfinder Press, 1937), pp. 249-250.

3. Roberto Mangiaberra Unger, *Knowledge and Politics* (New York, The Free Press, 1975), p. 9.

4. Carl Riskin, "Market, Maoism and Economic Reform in China," *Bulletin of Concerned Asian Scholars*, v. 13, no. 3 (July-September 1981), pp. 31-41. Also published in Mark Selden and Victor Lippit, eds., *The Transition to Socialism in China* (Armonk, N.Y., M. E. Sharpe, 1982), pp. 300-323.

5. Alasdair McIntyre, *After Virtue* (South Bend, Indiana, University of Notre Dame Press, 1981), p. 25.

6. See Cumings, "Political Economy," pp. 444-445.

7. Justin Galen (pseud.), "US' Toughest Message to the USSR," *Armed Forces Journal International* (February 1979), pp. 30-36; see also Bruce Cumings, "Chinatown: Foreign Policy and Elite Realignment," in Thomas Ferguson and Joel Rogers, eds., *The Hidden Election* (New York, Pantheon Books, 1981), pp. 196-231.

8. See in particular U.S. Central Intelligence Agency, *China: Oil Production Prospects* (Washington, D.C., 1977).

9. *The New York Times*, November 21, 1977.

A Theory of Transitional Society
Mao Zedong and the Shanghai School

by Peer Moller Christensen and Jorgen Delman

Introduction

The coup d'état in China in October 1976 struck most of the Western world with astonishment. Within a couple of months political power relations in China seemed to be reversed, as was its most recent history. Taken aback by the Chinese explanations and disoriented by the suddenness and finality of events, public opinion in the West tended to accept the reasons for the coup d'état offered by the victorious conspirators.

It is, however, highly problematic to accept immediately new explanations—as well as old—just because they are offered by people in power. Beneath current accusations against Mao Zedong and the "Gang of Four" for "sabotaging," "undermining," etc. the socialist economy and the socialist system, one finds substantial evidence that doing away with the Cultural Revolution is not just a question of legal justice. Real political and theoretical contradictions between factions within the Chinese Communist Party (CCP) leadership certainly existed and formed the basis for recurrent power struggles. Therefore we still find it worthwhile to study the decade of the Cultural Revolution—not to "acquit" Mao Zedong or the "Gang of Four" of whatever mistakes or crimes they may have committed, but to gain a more sober and realistic understanding of that tumultuous decade.

In this respect it is necessary to consider the theory or theories lying behind the Cultural Revolution as a basis for analyzing actual policy-making. In this article we intend to present an outline of the theory of transitional society developed during the period 1949–1976 by the radical wing within the CCP, notably Mao Zedong and the Shanghai School, economists and politicians in Shanghai who cooperated with radical politicians within the CCP leadership (such as Zhang Chunqiao and Yao Wenyuan).

This theory was presented as a "political economy of socialism" based on, but critical of, Soviet Marxism. In its final version it came close to contemporary Marxist theory propagated by members of the New Left in Europe such as Charles Bettelheim and Rossanna Rossanda. One of the interesting features of this Chinese theory was its ability to gradually free itself from Stalinist dogmatism and the straightjacket of Soviet Marxism and to reach new insights concerning the nature and structure of China as a socialist society.

Our article is divided into five parts: First, we present a theory we call the "system theory" which was developed under Stalin's auspices in the Soviet Union in the forties and early fifties and later exported to China. Part two is a brief digression introducing the development of a theory of market-socialism in China in the late fifties and early sixties. Part three traces Mao Zedong's development of a "generative class theory," and in part four we analyze the theory of what we call the Shanghai School which was developed in the early and mid-seventies. It is presented here for the first time outside China. In our final remarks we shall offer some comments on the applicability of this theory as well as on its self-contradictions and obvious limitations.

The "System Theory"

The political economy of socialism was not introduced in China on a wider scale until the early fifties, and then in the form of the Soviet "system theory"[1] which found its way to China as part of the superstructure of Soviet economic and political assistance after Liberation in 1949. The "system theory" was presented as *the* Marxist theory on the political economy of socialism and was expounded by Soviet manuals on political economy, primarily in *Political Economy; A Textbook* published in 1954.[2]

Before this book came to China, Chinese economists already had a notion of the nature and ideas of the "system theory" from Stalin's small pamphlet: "Economic Problems of Socialism in the USSR" (1952), which was meant as a guideline for the authors of the "Textbook," themselves distinguished Soviet economists.[3] Stalin's participation in writing the "Textbook" and final approval of it made it the most authoritative work of the "system theory." It later appeared in second and third editions, but the theoretical substance remained identical.

We do not know to what extent the "Textbook" was used in China before 1959, when an official translation of the third edition appeared.[4] But we do know that Mao Zedong followed the translation of the third edition with intense interest and that he criticized it in his "Reading Notes"[5] immediately after its publication.

Most of the ideas and concepts of the "system theory" came from the classical writings of Marx, Engels and Lenin, from Stalin, and from various Soviet economists. They were well-known beforehand, but this was the first attempt to present socialist political economy as a coherent entity and a scientific system. The "Textbook" was divided into chapters covering all known modes of production from tribal communism to as-yet-unrealized communism. The aim was to elaborate on Stalin's rather sketchy theses and concepts, to present a scientific understanding of the evolution of society, and to bring order to the chaos of history.

One basic concept in the "Textbook" is that social development is determined by two qualitatively different categories of objective laws. One category of laws consists of *general laws* operating through *all* known modes of production, as for example the law determining that production relations (which Stalin defined as comprising the ownership system, mutual relations within production and the distribution system) will invariably, and almost automatically adapt to new economic imperatives and will follow developments in social productive forces. The other category of laws are *specific* to one or some, but not all modes of production, as for example the law of value, which is the basic law of commodity production, as in capitalism.

The "Textbook" defines *socialism* as an independent and relatively stable social formation with its own set of objective laws. At the core is a *"fundamental law of socialism"* determining that socialist production produces not for profit, as in capitalist production, but to satisfy the ever-increasing material and cultural needs of the working people in the process of building socialism.

Around the "fundamental law" there are a series of mutually interrelated *non-fundamental laws."* They are all subordinated to the "fundamental law" and serve to fulfill its demands. The most important "non-fundamental laws" are: (1) The law of planned and proportinate development guaranteeing correct relations among the various sectors of the economy and of production; (2) the law determining that there will be a constant heightening of labor productivity guaranteeing a constant and swift development of material production; (3) the law of distribution according to work guaranteeing everybody who works an income in correspondence to his/her productive efforts; (4) the law of value (itself the "fundamental law of capitalism") guaranteeing that products are exchanged at equal value.

These laws are defined as objective and incontestable. They are independent of man's will. They gradually extend their sphere of influence after the establishment of socialist production relations, and at the same time they replace the specific laws of the previous mode of production.

The "Textbook" follows Stalin in asserting that the law of value still exerts its influence under socialism because commodity production and commodity circulation still exist. But it is emphatically stressed that it operates in a "purified form," controlled by public ownership and socialist planning and consequently having only a regulatory function. Even though socialism is considered to be an independent social formation, there still exist categories such as money, commodities, value etc. known to be vital to capitalist economies. Theoretically they are identified as concrete expressions and manifestations of the objective laws governing socialist society, but it is asserted that they too exist in a "purified form," *free of capitalist content.*

According to the "Textbook," as long as these laws are understood and applied correctly, socialist production will be able to develop smoothly and at a rapid pace. Consequently, socialist society will experience a corresponding fulfillment of the ever-increasing material and cultural needs of the people. Political economists, therefore, have it as their task to identify and study the objective laws in order to provide a basis for rational economic policies.

Even though the "system theory" presents itself as a logically coherent and scientific theory of socialism, it contains a series of more or less obvious self-contradictions and unsolved theoretical problems which tend to neutralize its analytical potential altogether. To mention but a few:

- The "system theory" defines objective laws as part of the *object* of political economy. However, when reading the "Textbook" it becomes apparent that these laws have all been defined *beforehand,* not detected by analyzing real social problems, relations and contradictions in the USSR. Thus the method tends to become tautological, and the conception of socialism mechanistic.
- Secondly, the entire theoretical complex has been put together from bits and pieces taken from the writings of Marx, Engels, Lenin, Stalin, and various Russian economists without taking into consideration the original textual and historical context. The intention of Stalin and the authors obviously was to substantiate a preconceived theory of socialism and to construe a system of thought, a "genuine" and "scientific" Marxist theory, only in order to explain economic policies and beautify harsh social realities.
- Thirdly, the "system theory" is a closed system of thought which precludes the possibility of identifying new laws. This tends to neglect the allegedly dialectical method of analysis of the "Textbook."
- Fourthly, the *critical* dimension so prevalent in Marx's criticism of bourgeois political economy entirely disappeared in the "system theory." The "Textbook" reduced political economy to a science of legitimization more geared to the needs of economic policy-making than to the needs of obtaining knowledge about the nature and structure of socialist society.
- Finally, the "system theory" purported to be a science for and of the working people. It maintained that anything done by the leaders and the Communist Party was done "in the interests of the working people." This idea based itself on the assumption that, due to the nationalization of the means of production, the working class had become masters in socialist society. Furthermore, class-struggle would die out because there was no more private ownership to form a basis for continued exploitation of the working people. The obvious intention was to ideologize a non-existent social harmony within production relations. It is a well-known fact that production relations in the USSR were imbued with contradictions. The violent suppression of opposition under Stalin bears testimony to this. By ideologizing production relations, the "system theory" precluded itself from becoming the critical theory and instrument of class-struggle which Marx's original theory had been.

The political economy of the "system theory" was the subject of several articles in the Chinese economic magazine *Jingji Yanjiu* (Economic Studies) from its inception in 1955.[6] But most articles concentrated on specific topics, primarily the question of objective laws under socialism. The "system theory" was not presented officially in its entirety until the appearance in 1959 of the translation of the third edition of the

"Textbook." The Chinese version of the "system theory" was basically identical to the Soviet original,[7] but it had to be applied in an entirely different social and historical context. Therefore, it quickly met with opposition, notably from market socialists like Chen Yun and Xue Muqiao, and from Mao Zedong, who was at that time starting to develop a theoretical platform of his own.

The Theory of Market Socialism

We shall not dwell long on the topic of market socialism here,[8] but only briefly give an introduction to the theoretical platform of its foremost protagonists, Chen Yun and Xue Muqiao. For them the key problem left unsolved by the "system theory" was the question of how to interpret the function of the law of value* under socialism. They claimed that the law of value should be allowed to play an independent and active role in developing and controlling the market in a socialist economy, thus contending the idea of the "system theory" that the law of value only had a regulatory function and was controlled by economic planning.

Chen and Xue maintained that large sectors of a planned economy could be substituted by a market economy controlled by the law of value, i.e. primarily the supply-demand mechanism. They acknowledged the qualitative difference between the laws governing a planned economy and market economy, and consequently the contradiction between the two. But, nonetheless, they believed that a market economy could still cure some of the maladies of a planned economy, such as overcentralization of economic decision-making, bureaucratization of the planning apparatus, ineffectiveness in creating overall balance, and extensive waste of raw materials and labor. These were all problems which had arisen in the course of the first five-year plan based on Soviet planning principles and the ideas of the "system theory."

The inspiration for working out a Chinese theory of market socialism came from various sources, primarily the Yugoslav experiment, but also from debates on economic reforms then current in East European countries.

Mao Zedong's "Generative Class Theory"

Mao Zedong was a most radical critic of the "system theory." During the fifties and early and mid-sixties he developed a stand of his own on several aspects of political economy, in opposition both to the "system theory" and to the theory of market socialism. Mao's formulation of a "generative class theory"[9] (a theory on the growth of new classes within socialist society with a socialist economy as the material foundation) was undoubtedly his most significant contribution to socialist theory.[10]

The "generative class theory" saw the light of day in the mid-sixties as the result of a long and rather complex development running through at least three phases: (a) before 1958; (b) 1958–61; (c) after 1961. Here we shall briefly summarize the main points in this development, in order to provide the Chinese theoretical and conceptual background to the theory of the Shanghai School.

Before 1958 Mao's most important theoretical contributions were his assertions that class struggle continues in socialist society even after the transformation of the ownership system,[11] and that revolutionizing production relations is a necessary precondition to promoting an extensive development of social productive forces,[12] i.e., economic growth. Furthermore, Mao revived the concept of revisionism which was excluded from the "system theory," identifying revisionism as a bourgeois tendency within the communist party having its roots in socialist society itself. The protagonists of revisionism "dream of a restoration of the capitalist system," stated Mao.[13]

In the second phase Mao criticized Soviet theory directly. In two criticisms (1958 and 1959)[14] of the above-mentioned pamphlet by Stalin and in his "Reading Notes" of 1960, Mao presented a series of new ideas. All three articles were criticisms of Soviet texts, and therefore do not present themselves as consistent theoretical works. They were sketchy commentaries and critical notes by means of which Mao reached new insights concerning the nature of socialist society.

In these works Mao broke away from the idea that socialism was an independent mode of production. He found socialism to be a transitional social form, a society on its way between capitalism and communism. It is not—as claimed by the "system theory"—characterized by harmonious and peaceful development (provided objective laws are correctly interpreted and applied). On the contrary, Mao found that socialism is dominated by contradictions between economic base and superstructure, between productive forces and production relations, and—most importantly—within production relations themselves. Thus he still considered social contradictions and class contradictions to be the motivating force in social and economic development.

Mao acknowledged the existence of objective laws, but stressed that they are, after all, only man-made and that one cannot allow oneself to become a slave of them as did the protagonists of the "system theory." Mao favored a much more voluntarist approach in his recurrent stress on the primacy of production relations over productive forces. It was stated several times by Mao that major developments in productive forces always come after changes in production relations. The process of constantly revolutionizing production relations is a process of simultaneously changing all three aspects of these relations: the ownership system, mutual relations within production, and the system of distribution of the social product. The direction of the process is from private to collective to state ownership and finally to ownership by the whole people; from one person management to party committee control and other forms of democratic management; and from individual consumption to collective, from pay according to work to recompensation according to need.

By stressing the need for simultaneous revolutionization of all three aspects of production relations, Mao discarded the evolutionary and mechanistic beliefs inherent in the "system theory" and stressed the revolutionary potential of socialism instead. This approach manifested itself in many respects. First of all, Mao saw the Great Leap Forward in 1958 as a conscious attempt to evade the inherent logic and implicit social consequences of the law of value as identified by Marx in *Capital*. The Leap did not justify its costs economically speaking, but it was necessary in political terms in order to satisfy new

*The law of value was identified by Karl Marx as the law governing commodity production. Roughly speaking, the law of value determines that all exchange in a commodity economy is carried out at equal values, measured in terms of socially necessary labor spent in producing a specific economy. In capitalist society the law of value has a wide range of economic, social and political implications and consequences manifesting themselves in a very competitive and anarchic production leading to waste of raw materials and labor force.

demands of production. Secondly, the always incomplete process of continually revolutionizing production relations will exert its influence on the economy, which will move forward in leaps and bounds and will constantly suffer from imbalances. Mao disagreed with the "system theory" that regarded balanced and proportionate development as an objective law. He argued that it can only be regarded as a political imperative. Consequently, development is wave-like, leaps are followed by stagnation, maybe even retrogression, until followed by new leaps. Finally, Mao argued that planning can by no means be meta-historic, always securing proportionate development and correct coordination between supply and demand. The role of planning is to maintain a certain equilibrium, but this can only be done temporarily. Planning is a process of learning and planning can only be perfected by studying leaps and bounds, disproportions and imbalances, whenever they occur. Therefore, plans do not belong to the economic base—as claimed in the "system theory"—but to the superstructure, as a form of consciousness.

On the question of the existence of the law of value and of a commodity economy in socialist society, Mao basically agreed with Stalin's viewpoints. But he did dispute Stalin's assertion that the means of production are not commodities simply because they are produced by state-owned enterprises and transferred within the state-owned sector. Mao argued that as long as there are two ownership systems, collective and state, means of production will still be exchanged as commodities. Therefore, the only way to finally do away with commodity production is—given the necessary stage of development of productive forces—to carry through the transition to ownership by the whole people within all spheres of production, to go from exchange of commodities to exchange of products and from exchange of value to exchange of *use-value*.*

During the third phase Mao again focused on China's internal problems, and especially on the nature of class struggle. This led finally to his formulating the "generative class theory" around 1964–65. This process can be traced in the development of Mao's vocabulary during the period, but let us first summarize the preconditions. In the mid-fifties Mao had pointed out that the turbulent class struggles of the past had come to an end. But at the same time he asserted that the bourgeoisie still existed, and that the contradiction between the bourgeoisie on the one hand and the proletariat on the other would continue to exist for a considerable period.† Class struggle was by no means over and might even evolve into a state of violent clashes between antagonistic classes and political groups.[15] This posed the question of whether the struggle came from the old, now socialized, bourgeoisie or a new one generated within socialist society. Mao was far from clear on this point. In "Reading Notes" he did, however, argue that there are "vested interest groups" and "conservative strata" in socialist society trying at each new phase of social development to exert their influence to consolidate development and prevent further changes in order to protect their own vested interests and privileges.

Basing himself on these theoretical observations, Mao quickly moved towards new insights when combining them with actual developments in China during the period 1961–64/5. In early 1962 he argued that in socialist society the working class is confronted with "new bourgeois elements" generated within the given social framework and that these are also to be found within the Communist Party, thus opposing socialism from within.[16] In August 1962 he stated that class struggle most importantly was aimed at new non-socialist forces, i.e., new bourgeois elements and "people walking the capitalist road." Here Mao for the first time used the concept of "capitalist roader." He furthermore stated that China might change color and become revisionist or even fascist if these people were allowed to make policy.[17]

Later in 1962 Mao advocated the policy of continued class struggle in the essay, "The Party's Basic Line For the Historical Period of Socialism," but this was only a summary of theoretical concepts presented previously.

During the period 1961–65 Mao more than once criticized the leadership's desire for privileges and warned people in leading positions against trying to protect their vested interests. All these points were summarized and further elaborated upon in "On Khruschev's Phony Communism and Its Historical Lesson For the World" (1964), which presented an analysis of "capitalist restoration" in the Soviet Union and attempted to identify the material basis for a new privileged layer taking over power in a socialist society. This analysis was primarily made for foreign policy reasons, and Mao never applied this analytical approach in detail to China. But he obviously thought a similar restoration possible in China.

Even though he would not admit to the existence of new classes of social layers in China (specifically a "new bourgeoisie"), he said that it was important to focus on "people in power within the communist party."[18] They were identified later in December that year as the protagonists of capitalist policies and branded "people in power within the communist party walking along the capitalist road."[19] Thus Mao had formulated the basic analytical concept of his "generative class theory."

In May 1967 he commented further on the issue of "capitalist roaders." He stated that they were old revolutionaries who had stopped with the democratic revolution. They did not want to make socialist revolution, and consequently propagated capitalist policies.[20] By identifying the Communist Party as the nodal point in the overall social process whereby the new bourgeoisie is generated, and by pointing out the need for continued class struggle, Mao not only presented a new conception of socialist society; he also provided a guideline for future political struggles in China. As Mao was not willing directly to admit to the existence of a new bourgeoisie as a class, but only as a "stratum," "elements," etc., it may be argued that his "generative class theory" was at most a sociological theory. Apparently he never succeeded in combining his insights in the political economy of socialism with his new theory of classes and class struggle. But with the publication in 1976 of his "Instructions" (which we shall deal with later on), he may have reached new understandings, especially during his last ten years while cooperating with the new cultural revolutionary theoreticians such as Zhang Chunqiao and Yao Wenyuan.

* Whereas Marx saw a close connection in the contradiction between exchange value and use value within commodities under capitalism and the existence of class struggle in capitalist societies, Mao did not draw the same conclusions concerning class struggle under socialism. To him the law of value was a purely economic phenomenon.

† According to *Mao Zedong Xuanji*, vol. V, p. 65, Mao, as early as 1953, had already identified the main contradiction in socialist society as being that between the bourgeoisie and the proletariat. It has to be borne in mind, however, that vol. V of the Xuanji was published *after Mao died* under the auspices of Hua Guofeng. It has been proved that some of the texts were revised, crucial words were changed and paragraphs inserted or omitted. So this short quotation from 1953 may be an invention of the editors made for political reasons.

The Shanghai School and "Political Economy of Socialism"

After the many tumultuous events of the Cultural Revolution and its many programmatic and organizational reforms, a theoretical summary had to be made—a summary which could draw theoretical conclusions from the practical experiences and put them into a theoretical framework. After the de facto suspension of the most radical cultural revolutionary reforms from 1967 and onwards, the "cultural revolutionary" wing within the CCP had to try to maintain at least the theoretical perspectives of the Cultural Revolution.

From 1970 to 1976—especially after the fall of Lin Biao in 1971—an intense effort was made to develop a comprehensive, independent Chinese theory on socialism. The result was the manual "Political Economy of Socialism" (PES), which was based on the cultural revolutionary experiences and Mao's interpretation of the nature and structure of Chinese society. This work was mainly carried out by a group of economists from Shanghai, many of them connected with the Institute of Political Economy at Fudan University. (We shall call this group the "Shanghai School.") The purpose of writing the manual was to summarize and develop the theoretical basis of the actual policy propagated by the "cultural revolutionary" wing within the CCP.

We do not know the exact nature of the relationship between the "Shanghai School" and the "cultural revolutionary" wing, but without doubt Zhang Chunqiao and Yao Wenyuan took active part in the work and Zhang Chunqiao played an especially important role. After their arrest in October 1976, the "Gang of Four" and the Shanghai School were accused of having planned to canonize "Zhang Chunqiao Thought."[21]

The final edition of "Political Economy of Socialism" never appeared. The printing press was stopped by the coup d'état on October 6, 1976. The book was confiscated and a year later it was condemned as a work intended to create "the theoretical basis for the counterrevolutionary program of the 'Gang of Four.' "[22] Later we shall present a rough outline of the theoretical content of the final edition of "Political Economy of Socialism." As the process of writing this book, however, ran through many stages and phases and took the form of a constant and thorough-going revision and development of the theory, we have chosen also to describe the different manuscripts which were written during the process.

It is a general rule that discussions and decisions concerning important political matters in China occur behind closed doors. Solutions and documents are not presented to the public until an agreement has been reached. Apart from the more chaotic periods of the Cultural Revolution this has been the main pattern of political life in China ever since 1949. But this procedure was *not* followed during the process of writing "PES," even though it was of considerable importance to the policymakers of the "cultural revolutionary" wing within the CCP. All the manuscripts were published in limited numbers in order to give people an opportunity to make comments on the manuscripts and thus contribute to the constant improvement of the theory. In this way there are rich opportunities for comparatively open discussions on the theory. It is remarkable to see how thorough were the changes made during the relatively short period from 1971 to 1976. Original self-contradictions were gradually solved and the final edition of "PES" presented a comprehensive and consistent theory. This theory analyzes the social basis of class contradictions in Chinese society. In contrast to the above-mentioned Soviet "system theory," this theory could not be used to legitimate the Chinese social structure: it was a "critical" theory.*

The Starting Point

When writing a manual on the political economy of socialism during the '70s, Chinese economists could base themselves upon Mao's conception of socialism as well as on the Soviet "Textbook" and a manual written in Shanghai in 1961.[23] But at the same time it would be necessary to further develop Mao's theory of socialism by incorporating criticisms of what was considered to be the "capitalist restoration" in the Soviet Union as well as the experiences from the actual class struggles during the Cultural Revolution. Therefore a manual on political economy of socialism would have to provide answers to the following questions:

- How could the Soviet Union have turned capitalist?
- Can China turn capitalist as well? If so, how could this happen and what could be done to prevent it?
- Can a bourgeoisie be generated in China that might eventually usurp political and economic power? If the answer is positive, what will this bourgeoisie be like, and will it be able to initiate and promote a capitalist development?

The following description of the development of the theory elaborated by the Shanghai School will emphasize those elements in the different manuscripts representing phases in the criticism of the Stalinist "system theory." In this connection we particularly want to examine how the books answer the above-mentioned questions. In our opinion the answers provided to these questions gradually burst the dogmas and formulas of the "system theory." Therefore, we do not intend to give a total and complete picture of the books and manuscripts, but only intend to describe the main theoretical development.

The First Manuscript

From 1971 to 1976 five versions of "Political Economy of Socialism" were written. The actual work started in June 1971 when Zhang Chunqiao approved the plans for writing such a book. The first manuscript was presented in September 1972.[24] According to that manuscript, the main feature of socialism is the abolition of private ownership of the means of production. Socialism is a coherent social system basically different from capitalism. The socialist system determines the character of the various elements within the system, which, therefore, *a priori* are different from their capitalist counterparts.

In describing socialism the manuscript used China as an example—as a concrete manifestation of the conception of socialism. Apart from the fact that this brought the theory close to becoming a theory of legitimation, it also implied that certain phenomena in Chinese society *a priori* are defined as socialist and therefore fundamentally different from similar phenomena

* Peer Moller Christensen had access to the 1972 and 1975 manuscripts when he was a foreign exchange student at Fudan University in Shanghai in 1979. As for the unpublished 1976 manuscript, we have only had access to selected quotations from it published by the Chinese press after the coup in 1976. The rest of the manuscripts have been unavailable to us, but fortunately the Shanghai School customarily printed popular versions of the *PES*, thereby making it possible for us to analyze the main trends of thought in the unavailable manuscripts. The popular versions were published in greater numbers and were more widely distributed than the originals.

inside capitalist societies. Economic categories such as commodity, money, wage, capital, profit, etc. found to be objectively existing within Chinese society are not equivalent to their capitalist counterparts. On the contrary, only the form is the same. In socialist society these phenomena are *socialist*. This way of conceiving economic categories was a legacy from Stalin, and for a long time it was an obstacle to making a realistic and concrete analysis of actual problems in Chinese society.

According to this manuscript, the abolition of private ownership to the means of production has made comprehensive economic planning possible. Introduction of conscious planning has in itself caused a change in the nature of socialist production that is basically different from private production. Socialist production is, fundamentally speaking, directly social production, and labor in socialist production is therefore no longer private labor but directly social labor producing directly social products. As exchange within socialism, however, takes the form of commodity exchange, the products of socialist production also contain "value." Therefore socialist production is a unity of a directly social-working process and a value-creating process.

This conception originates in the Soviet textbooks on the political economy of socialism. In our opinion it is a theoretical misconception, an ideologization of reality. According to Marx, directly social labor is work which does *not* have to use the value form to realize its social content. All commodities are a unity of use-value as well as exchange value, and this unity is actually what the manuscript describes. When distribution of products in China has to take the form of commodity exchange, it really shows that Chinese economic planning is insufficient to make production directly social and work directly social labor.

In the 1961 manual from Shanghai all production under socialism had been described as commodity production, but still as a form of commodity production which is basically different from commodity production under capitalism. According to the 1972 manuscript of "PES," all commodity production under socialism is not only basically different from its capitalist counterpart, but a part of production under socialism is simply no longer regarded as commodity production. Exchange within the state-owned sector of the economy is not called "commodity exchange" but "product exchange." Product exchange is not realized through a market but through state allocation based upon economic plans.

In this way the 1972 manuscript adheres to ideas propagated in "Economic Problems of Socialism in the USSR," where Stalin wrote that the reason for the objective existence of commodity relations within socialist society is the existence of two forms of ownership, collective and state-ownership. According to Stalin, exchange within the state-owned sector of the economy (primarily exchange of means of production) can no longer be called commodity exchange.[25] Similarly the 1972 manuscript asserts that socialist product exchange as well as commodity exchange are basically different from all other forms of commodity exchange known down through history. With these new forms of exchange, elements of a direct distribution of means of production and goods for consumption emerge, elements pointing forward towards communism.

All in all, the conception of socialism presented by this manuscript is a mere duplication of Stalin's basic ideas and concepts. It contains the implicit conclusion that, due to the abolition of private ownership of the means of production, the bourgeoisie has lost the social basis for exerting its power, and consequently the bourgeoisie will never reemerge. Therefore there is no longer any risk of a "capitalist restoration." The most important aim in socialist society is, therefore, to develop productive forces through planned production. This will lead socialist society to a gradual transition to communism.

The most apparent self-contradiction in the 1972 manuscript is between the authors' repetition of the fundamental concepts and ideas propagated by the "system theory" on the one hand, and the incorporation of Mao's critical viewpoints and his rejection of the conception of socialism of the "system theory" on the other. A few examples should suffice to show this:

—Even though the authors of the manuscript considered the change in the system of ownership the constituting factor of socialism, they also stated that the question of ownership has not been completely solved in China; a major part of the Chinese economy is still collectively owned and, therefore, only socialist to a certain degree. Furthermore, there is still a problem with the leadership in the state-owned sector of the economy. If power slips from the hands of the working class and "true marxists," the "bourgeoisie and its agents inside the party, walking the capitalist road," may transform the enterprises into capitalist ones. In this way the bourgeoisie may usurp power and lead the country in a capitalist direction. This, states the manuscript, was what had happened in the Soviet Union.

—The 1961 manual had also come to the conclusion that the collective sector might change character and turn capitalist if the leadership-power of the *collectively owned units* was usurped by rich peasants and higher middle-peasants. In the 1972 manuscript the question of leadership-power was extended to include relations within the *state-owned sector*. In this way the first step was taken to reject the schematic division inherited from Mao, of the relations of production in three elements: (a) the ownership system; (b) mutual relations within production; and (c) the distribution system. Mao had inherited this schematic *tripartition* from Soviet Marxism and it had been part of the Stalinist legacy adhered to by the CCP. Conceiving the problem of leadership as a constituent element of the ownership system, however, makes this tripartition analytically inapplicable. As long as the relations of ownership were synonymous with formal, legal relations, there was no problem. But when interpreting leadership-power—which belongs to the category of mutual relations within production—as being a constituent element of the ownership system, the demarcation line between the aspects of the relations of production is blurred. Consequently, you have to approach the relations of production as a *totality*.* On the one hand, the transformation of the relations of production is not simply a legal transformation of the ownership of the means of production. On the other hand, transforming the relations of production is a necessary prerequisite for developing the productive forces. In this respect this manuscript adopts Mao's idea from "Reading Notes" that "A change in the relations of production always precedes a major development of the productive forces."[26]

* Despite this new recognition, the 1972 manuscript still takes the tripartition of production relations as the basis for the description and analysis of socialist society. Furthermore, this apparent self-contradiction was never dealt with by the Shanghai School in later manuscripts.

—Even though it is stated that planning changes the nature of production, the manuscript adheres to Mao's idea on the incompleteness of planning. The authors of the manuscript state that a plan can never guarantee a development with complete sectoral balance:

Nothing in the whole world develops in complete equilibrium. Equilibrium is temporary and relative, disequilibrium constant and absolute.[27]

—The manuscript attempts an analysis of a "new bourgeoisie" which might take the lead in a "capitalist restoration" by introducing two concepts, "those inside the party taking the capitalist road," and the "bureaucratic monopoly bourgeoisie." But the manuscript does not identify the material basis for the emergence of this "new bourgeoisie" or for a possible capitalist development. It only points out illegal, "system-external" factors in this process: the ideological influence from the bourgeoisie, "capitalist traditions and birthmarks," and the illegal sprouts of capitalism such as black market, corruption and the like.

—This manuscript describes economic categories under socialism as fundamentally different from their counterparts in capitalist economies, thus making it impossible to explain how the same economic categories and phenomena may become constituents in a capitalist process of production.

—Furthermore, the 1972 manuscript describes exchange within the state-owned sector as a form of exchange which can no longer be called "commodity-exchange." What would then be the precondition for transforming this "product-exchange" back into capitalist commodity-exchange?

It can be seen that this manuscript contained a lot of self-contradictions and inconsistencies, which had to be solved in the following process of rewriting and revision. After its publication in September 1972, the Shanghai daily, *Wenhuibao,* published a number of articles under the headline "Study Some Political Economy." They presented the most important ideas and concepts from the manuscript in a more popular form and subsequently compiled and published them in November 1972 in a small pamphlet again called "Study Some Political Economy."[28] The book carried the same introduction as the manuscript, an essay by Fang Hai originally published in the Magazine *Hong Qi*.[29] The purpose of publishing the book seems to have been to start a broad public study campaign and discussion on the political economy of socialism.

The Second Manuscript

When the first manuscript was finished in September 1972, Zhang Chunqiao and Yao Wenyuan left Beijing for Shanghai in order to arrange a meeting to discuss the problems which had arisen in the writing.[30] The meeting took place in October and Zhang Chunqiao presented some new "directives" on the basic theory and line of argumentation presented by the book. The directives suggested the following themes to be elaborated upon and they were to provide the theoretical nuclei of the book:

—1. There are capitalist factors *inside* socialist relations of production.

—2. The question of ownership is a question of power.

—3. Mutual relations within the working people are class-relations.[31]

The first thorough revision of the manuscript was made after this meeting, and the process of revision was finished and the second manuscript written some time during 1973.[32]

The manuscript itself is unavailable, but in May 1974 another popular manual on political economy entitled "Fundamentals of Political Economy"[33] was published in Shanghai. Even though the manuscript had been revised, the theoretical contents do not seem to have been basically altered. The three themes mentioned by Zhang Chunqiao at the meeting in October 1972 were not elaborated upon; for example, the concept "capitalist factors inside socialist relations of production" was not mentioned at all. (In fact it was not to reappear until the final edition in October 1976.) The self-contradictions so manifest in the first manuscript remained, and the authors still adhered to the fundamental ideas of the "system theory" which excluded the possibility of a "capitalist restoration."

Mao's 1975 Instructions

Shortly after the Fourth National People's Congress in January 1975, the national media published a quotation of Mao's which started a mass discussion campaign, "The Campaign for Studying the Theory of Proletarian Dictatorship." Mao did not take part in the NPC session, and many China-watchers interpreted this as his way of showing disagreement with the decisions taken by the Congress. If this is true, the publication of the quotation and the following campaign might be an answer to the Congress made by him and his political allies.

In the quotation which was called "Mao's Latest Instruction on the Question of Theory," Mao states:

In a word, China is a socialist country. Before liberation she was much the same as capitalism. Even now she practices an eight-grade wage-system, distribution to each according to his work and exchange by means of money, which are scarcely different from those in the old society. What is different is that the system of ownership has changed. ——— *Our country at present practices a commodity system, and the wage-system is unequal too, there being the eight-grade wage-system, etc.; these can only be restricted under the dictatorship of the proletariat. Thus it would be quite easy for people like Lin Biao to push the capitalist system, if they came to power.*[34]

This quotation fits perfectly into the theoretical development of the Shanghai School. It solved one fundamental theoretical problem of the first two manuscripts, the contradiction between the Stalinist conception of socialism on the one hand, and the claim that a "capitalist restoration" could take place on the other. According to Mao, socialist economic categories such as commodity, money and wage are not basically different from their capitalist counterparts. On the contrary there is no qualitative difference, and they could, therefore, quite easily become functional in a capitalist production process.

In the same year, Yao Wenyuan and Zhang Chunqiao published articles, in March and April respectively.[35] They elaborated further upon the ideas presented in Mao's "Instruction" and on the framework and issues raised by the manuscripts of the "PES." The close connection between the start of the "Campaign for Studying the Theory of Proletarian Dictatorship" and the theoretical work done by the Shanghai School is made clear by the fact that Yao Wenyuan and Zhang Chunqiao's articles as well as Mao's "Instruction" initiated the campaign. Yao Wenyuan and Zhang Chunqiao, who were both in the "Cultural Revolutionary" wing of the CCP, were directly involved in the theoretical work with the "PES" in Shanghai. Nevertheless, it has to be underlined that the campaign was not only a part of the theoretical development of the Shanghai School; it was also the starting point of a new and very intense political struggle in China.

In their articles Yao Wenyuan and Zhang Chunqiao used the designation "the Lin Biao clique" as a synonym for "the new bourgeoisie." Apparently, the articles were not directed at Lin Biao and his political allies. They were attempts at analyzing the material and social basis for the appearance of a "new bourgeoisie" and the possibility of a "capitalist restoration." No doubt, the object of the analysis was a much broader social group than the group around Lin Biao. According to the articles the problem with the "new bourgeoisie" had not been solved by purging Lin and his group. The "new bourgeoisie" was still to be found in powerful positions in China.*

Taken as a whole, Mao's "Instruction" and Yao Wenyuan's and Zhang Chunqiao's articles presented a solution to the most conspicuous weaknesses and self-contradictions of the second manuscript of the "PES": the first being the absence of an analysis of the material basis for the emergence of a "new bourgeoisie"; and the second the contradiction between the interpretation of economic categories and mechanisms under socialism as fundamentally different from those under capitalism, and the supposition that a "capitalist restoration" is a possibility under socialism.

In their articles Yao Wenyuan and Zhang Chunqiao pointed at "bourgeois right" as the material basis for the emergence of capitalism and a "new bourgeoisie." They rejected the views presented by the first two manuscripts of "PES," where "bourgeois right" was regarded as a phenomenon closely connected with the "three major differences" (i.e., the differences between city and countryside, between worker and peasant, and between intellectual work and manual work) and as a principle primarily functioning within the sphere of distribution. Yao and Zhang regarded "bourgeois right" as a more general concept, as *exchange at equal values* with its roots in commodity-production, and playing a role within all aspects of relations of production. In accordance with Mao's "Instruction," they stressed that it is possible for a "new bourgeoisie" to promote a capitalist development because socialist economic categories and mechanisms are not basically different from their capitalist counterparts.

The Third Manuscript

After the publication of Yao Wenyuan and Zhang Chunqiao's articles, the second major revision of the manuscript of the "PES" was started. The revision resulted in the third manuscript.[36] This manuscript incorporated the theoretical viewpoints contained in Mao's "Instruction" and in Yao and Zhang's articles. But at the same time, the concept "product-exchange" was still used to describe exchange within the state-owned sector of the economy. The idea that socialist commodities are not basically different from their capitalist counterparts did not include products produced and exchanged within the state-owned sector. Even though Mao's "Instruction" and Yao and Zhang's articles were an enormous inspiration to the Shanghai School's theoretical clarifications, the "PES" still contained ambiguities and self-contradictions in 1975.

The Fourth Manuscript

The fourth manuscript of the "PES" was written during the period from June 1975 to December 1975, when Zhang Chunqiao corrected the draft himself. Unfortunately, we have not had access to this manuscript, but in December 1975 a revised edition of "Fundamentals of Political Economy" was published.[37] As it can be presumed that this manual was written on the basis of the fourth manuscript, it is possible to attain a fairly clear picture of the theoretical contents of the fourth manuscript.

The "Fundamentals" goes even further than the earlier manuscripts in two respects: in the analysis of the role of state under socialism; and in the analysis of commodity production under socialism.

—*1. The analysis of the state*. The manual states that the socialist state is—in Lenin's words—a "bourgeois state" because it has to protect "bourgeois right." Consequently the transformation of private ownership of the means of production into state-ownership is *not* tantamount to a transformation of the system of ownership into a "non-bourgeois" form. Thus "Fundamentals" rejects the identification of socialism with state-ownership of the means of production, an idea which was still present in Zhang Chunqiao's article[38] and in the third manuscript. In this way the road had been paved for a more reasonable and logically consistent explanation of Soviet "state monopoly capitalism."

—*2. The analysis of commodity production*. The manual rejects the concept "product-exchange" used in earlier manuscripts. According to the "Fundamentals," all exchange under socialism is commodity exchange, and this goes for exchange *within* the state-owned sector as well. This is a complete rejection of Stalin's idea concerning production within the state-owned sector. Actually, this had already been the case in the 1961 manual from Shanghai[39] which had stated that all exchange under socialism is commodity exchange. But whereas the 1961 manual considered commodity exchange and commodity production under socialism to be fundamentally different from commodity exchange and commodity production under capitalism, "Fundamentals" stated that commodity exchange under socialism is not very different from its capitalist counterpart.

In these respects the 1975 edition of the "PES" represented a step forward both in rejecting Stalin's analysis of socialist commodity production and his general concept of socialism, and in the theoretical clarification of the Shanghai School. But it still contained a fundamental self-contradiction inherited from earlier manuscripts, i.e., the idea that production under socialism is a unity of direct social production and value creating production. This self-contradiction was not solved until the writing of the fifth and final manuscript of the "PES," which was to have been published in Shanghai in October 1976.

* Seen from a theoretical point of view, it is difficult to understand why the Lin Biao group was used as a target, but it has to be borne in mind that Lin Biao was the most recent victim of inner-party struggle in China, and following the rules and traditions of political strife in China, theoretical criticisms and analysis frequently are made as criticisms of the most recently degraded political opponent, regardless of actual political viewpoints.

The Fifth Manuscript

When the fourth manuscript of the "PES" was ready in December 1975 Zhang Chunqiao wrote a new "directive," which started the last major revision of the manuscript. In this "directive" he wrote:

> *We must criticize revisionism. Criticize Liu, Lin and Deng.*[40] *Criticize Trotsky, Bukharin and the like. Political economy can not be written properly, if revisionism is not criticized.. We must understand that the influence from Stalin's mistakes is still very strong.*[41]

The result of the revision was the fifth manuscript of the "PES."[42] The authors had planned to publish the book in October 1976, but, as noted, when the book was still in the press, the coup d'état of October 6 occurred and the manuscript was confiscated. After the coup the Chinese media heavily criticized the unpublished book and a similar one written in Tianjin in close cooperation with the Shanghai School.[43]

The critical media articles contain quite a few quotations from the two "PES" books, which were considered to be the result of the theoretical work of the "Gang of Four" and their supporters. (For a list of critical articles, see the Appendix.) Even though we have not had access to the two "PES" manuscripts, it has been possible—by means of the many quotations in newspapers and magazines—to get a fairly comprehensive picture of the theoretical contents of the manuscripts. In the following we shall present the manuscripts as one theory of political economy of socialism elaborated by the Shanghai School immediately before their political defeat.

According to the Shanghai School's theory, socialism is a transitional society consisting of both communist and capitalist factors and elements, existing simultaneously within socialist relations of production. The capitalist factors are not simply surviving elements of capitalist structure but are factors reproduced through the social and economic processes in socialist society. They are found within all spheres of socialist economy. The existence of capitalist factors and elements within socialist relations of production implies that capitalism and a bourgeoisie are constantly produced and reproduced in socialist society. "The new bourgeoisie" emerges within the ranks of the working people and especially inside the Communist Party. The material basis for the emergence of a new bourgeoisie is to be found in the incompletely transformed structures of socialist society—i.e., in the above-mentioned capitalist factors and elements such as commodity, money, wage-relations, the exchange of equal values as a regulating principle in the economy and, finally, the continued existence of a division of labor inherited from the old society.

Division of labor leads to the development of an "intellectual aristocracy," which deprives the workers of the real right of leadership to the means of production. In this way the system of ownership will gradually change its nature. Within the enterprises there will emerge a system of intellectual workers ruling over manual workers. According to the final stand of the Shanghai School, such a system has to a certain degree already developed in China. Therefore the proletariat is already being ruled over and exploited by the "new bourgeoisie." Consequently the "new bourgeoisie" will be the most important adversary of the proletariat in the class struggles during the entire socialist period, and the "new bourgeoisie" must be regarded as the most important object of the revolution under the dictatorship of the proletariat.

The contradiction between the proletariat and the bourgeoisie is therefore the most important contradiction in socialist society; and class struggles, which are outcomes of this contradiction, will first of all be struggles for the extension or limitation of "bourgeois right," i.e., the capitalist factors and elements *within* the socialist relations of production.

The collectively-owned economy is an incompletely transformed structure within the ownership system. The means of production as well as the results of production are private property owned by individual collective units: production is, in that sense, *private* production. Furthermore, the question of the leadership of collective units as well as within the state-owned sector plays a very important role, with the decisive question being which class really controls the means of production. If the power structure of the leadership of an enterprise is changed, the *"ownership"* of the means of production may change accordingly. Socialist enterprises may change their nature and become the property of a bureaucratic monopoly-bourgeoisie if the workers are deprived of the leadership-power, i.e., the right to manage the enterprise or the collective unit. When the "new bourgeoisie" has the means of production in its hands it may be able further to promote a capitalist production process, because capitalist factors and elements already exist in all spheres of socialist production.

Socialist production, moreover, is the production of commodities. The existence of commodities and commodity production is not just due to the coexistence of the two forms of ownership, ownership by the state and collective ownership. Within the state-owned sector alone, an equally important reason is the relative independence of individual accounting enterprises such that the mutual relations *between* the enterprises will in fact be relations between individual "owners," and production even within the state-owned sector will again be *private* production.

The circulation of commodities under socialism can also be transformed into circulation of capital. If this transformation is carried through, labor power may again become a commodity and money can be transformed into capital. This transformation may come about if the necessary realization of value becomes the aim of commodity exchange instead of the realization of use-value. This is important because the law of value is the law of commodity production and here it is identified as playing an important role in the socialist economy. In other words, according to the 1976 "PES" manuscript, the law of value under socialism is not basically different from the law of value under capitalism. By letting the law of value regulate production the bourgeoisie can subordinate the production of use-values to the production of values. When one uses money and prices, the price of a commodity may be higher than its value. Production of this kind of commodity will earn a bigger profit than the average item, and therefore it may become attractive for certain enterprises to maximize their profit by producing that kind of commodity rather than less profitable (but socially useful) ones. Production aimed at realizing surplus-value may thus, under given circumstances, distort overall production and the allocation of occasionally scarce resources in a socialist society.

As mentioned above, a capitalist restoration may take place first and foremost because of the existence of this commodity circulation carried out by means of money. Furthermore, the "funds" of the various enterprises are only incompletely transformed forms of capital, thus being still very similar to capital in the old society. Therefore, it would not be necessary to change fundamentally the form or contents of such funds to have them performing the function of capital. The same goes for wages. The socialist principle, "To each according to one's work" is not basically different from wage labor. No fundamental transformation of the form and content of wages would be necessary to make labor power a commodity once again.

According to the 1976 manuscript, the ideological form of a "capitalist restoration" in China might well be like the "theory of productive forces" and "the four modernizations," both of which express the ideology of the "dying out of class struggle under socialism." To make sure that socialist society advances towards communism, then, it is said to be necessary to stage many "cultural revolutions," the aim of which will be gradually to limit and eliminate capitalist elements and those factors defined as "bourgeois right" within the relations of production, including the division of labor inherited from the old society. In this way the material basis for the emergence of a "new bourgeoisie" and capitalism can be eliminated.

The old division of labor has to be eliminated by the workers taking active part in and exerting control over the management of the enterprises and by forcing intellectual workers to take part regularly in manual work. The contradiction between intellectual and manual labor should be eliminated through these means and through a restructuring of the educational system, which gradually must eliminate the boundaries between production and education. The material privileges of the "new bourgeoisie" must gradually be eliminated through a reform of the wage system. The reform must aim, first, at discarding the use of "material incentives" as the most important means of raising the enthusiasm of the workers, and second, at establishing a more even distribution of wages. Bonuses and piece-rate wages would be abolished and society as a whole would gradually leave the principle "to each according to one's work." Finally, production must be planned, in accordance with use-value criteria and, conversely, the influence of value categories must be limited.

Comments on the Final Theory

The 1976 manuscript of the "Political Economy of Socialism" was the final result of a long process of theoretical development, which was suddenly and involuntarily cut off. It presents, if not a complete, then at any rate a consistent answer to the questions left unanswered by Mao, specifically how can a capitalist restoration take place in China or in any other socialist country, and which social forces will promote such a development?

Even though this final theoretical position solved most of the self-contradictions inherent in the earlier manuscripts of the "PES," it still contained a number of unclarified points and weaknesses. As mentioned above, the basic issue in the theoretical development of the Shanghai School seems to have been how capitalism can develop in a socialist society. But Mao and the Shanghai School never formulated a clear and consistent definition of capitalism. They described China before 1949 as "semi-feudal and semi-colonial" as well as "much the same as capitalism." Because of this ambiguity it is difficult to see why the difference between the Soviet Union and China is so great that China deserves to be called "socialist" while the Soviet Union is described as "capitalist." They did not say which structures within China's "socialist economy" have to be changed before it might be called one producing surplus value as in capitalist production.

Another weak point is the class analysis. The "new bourgeoisie" is defined as "the bureaucratic monopoly bourgeoisie" and "those performing intellectual work in production." How does this fit with the idea propagated by the manuscripts that the Communist Party is the main "hotbed" for this "new bourgeoisie"? This problem was left unsolved, because the Shanghai School lacked a critical analysis of the functions of the Communist Party in China.

Describing the specific measures which must be undertaken to prevent a "capitalist" restoration, the Shanghai school failed to make clear *who* the agents of these measures might be. They implicitly assign the Communist Party a central role in this process. This seems problematic after defining the party as the most important "hotbed" for the new bourgeoisie and capitalist tendencies. It seems that the members of the Shanghai School were able to criticize and abandon Stalin's economic ideas and theories, but when it came to practical political measures and their implementation they could get no further than clinging to Lenin's ideas and the theory of a vanguard party. This seems paradoxical when one recalls that the Shanghai School had its roots in the cultural revolutionary wing of the CCP which advocated replacing this very same party with other political structures.

Mao Zedong's theory and that of the Shanghai School emerged amidst factional struggles within a Communist Party which had inherited much Stalinist dogmatism and which was without political democracy. Within the political and theoretical traditions of either the CPSU or the CCP, it has been common practice to barrage opponents with abuse rather than conduct serious political debates. The eventual aim was always to purge opponents, not to come to terms with them. In this connection, the term "bourgeois," for example, has been one of many useful words in the treasury of abusive vocabulary. It might be argued that it should be unnecessary to pay any serious attention to one faction calling a competing faction "bourgeois" in its quest for power, because this is what the political culture demands.

In our opinion, however, this would be too hasty a conclusion. Even though Mao and the Shanghai School *were* influenced by rigid Stalinist dogmatism, it would be erroneous to write off the analytical potential of their theory. When looking at the entire theoretical process developed by Mao and the Shanghai School we find sufficient proof that their angle and analytical method were new. They showed an astounding desire to do away with the somewhat metaphysical conception of socialism prevalent in the "system theory" and to adapt a more realistic attitude towards some of the problems of Chinese society. They eventually worked out a platform for analyzing the incompletely transformed social and economic structures in so-called socialist societies. It is, after all, remarkable that a critical theory such as this could be conceived by leading political figures within the party and state of an allegedly socialist country.

But does the theory of the Shanghai School have real theoretical validity? What are the implications for understanding modern China? Does this theoretical platform in any way contribute to the still evolving theories on transitional society? These are extremely important questions that remain open, and we hope that further research may provide answers to them.

Notes

1. This is our own designation for this specific theory. It is meant to describe a theory regarding socialism as a social system governed by a set of objective laws. The "system theory" is regarded as a scientific system in itself.

2. Danish ed., Copenhagen 1955.

3. Another source has been: Mi Fei Sibilidunnuofu (M.F. Spiridonov), *Zhengzhi jingjixue jiangyi, I-II* (Lectures on Political Economy), Beijing: Gaodeng Jiaoyu Chubanshe, 1954. We found this manual in a second-hand bookstore in Shanghai in 1979. As it was published *neibu* (internally) in a limited number of copies it has—to our knowledge—never been listed in an official bibliography. Consequently, we did not know of its existence until accidentally buying it. Basically, its theoretical substance corresponds to that of the "Textbook," and we shall still consider this the most authoritative and influential work in the Chinese context as it was written under Stalin's auspices and later criticized by Mao personally.

4. *Zhengzhi jingjixue. Jiaokeshu (disan zengding ben) I-II* (Political Economy: Textbook [Third Enlarged and Revised Ed.]), Beijing: Renmin Chubanshe, 1960. This is yet a revised edition of the third revised edition published in January 1959 (Reviewed by Li Yun in *Hongqi* (Red Flag) no. 15, 1959). An East German edition of the "Textbook" is available: *Politische Ökonomie in der USSR*, in Martin (see note 5), pp. 124-129.

5. The *Reading Notes on the Soviet Text 'Political Economy'* is available in Mao Tsetung, *A Critique of Soviet Economics*, annotated by Richard Levy and with an introduction by James Peck (N.Y.: Monthly Review Press, 1977). German ed.: Helmut Martin (ed.), Mao Tse-tung, *Das Machen wir anders als Moskau*, (Hamburg: Rowohlt, 1975). The Chinese original is available in two slightly different versions (both published in Taiwan): *Mao Zedong sixiang wansui* (Long Live Mao Zedong Thought), 1967, pp. 167-247, and *Mao Zedong sixiang wansui*, 1969, pp. 319-99. Hereafter: *Wansui*-67 and *Wansui*-69 respectively.

6. For the indices and subjects of *Jingji Yanjiu* see: James Nickum, *A Research Guide to Jingji Yanjiu (Economic Studies)* (Berkeley: University of California, Center for Chinese Studies, 1972).

7. A good introduction is given in an article by Yu Ding: *Xuexi zhengzji jingjixue xuyao zhuyi de jige wenti* (Some Problems to Pay Attention to When Studying Political Economy), Renmin Ribao (People's Daily), July 27, 1959.

8. The issue of market socialism in China is still virgin soil. Here we can only give a few tentative references: G.W. Lee, *Current Debates on Profits and Value in Mainland China*, Australian Economic Papers, June-Dec., 1965, pp. 72-78; Charles Bettelheim, *Die Preispolitik und die Rolle des Profits*, in Bettelheim et al., *Der Aufbau der Sozialismus in China*, München, 1972, pp. 103-74; *Jianguo yilai shehuizhuyi shangpin shengchan he jiazhi guilü lun wenxuan, I-II* (Selected essays on the theory of socialist commodity production and the law of value since the founding of the PRC), Shanghai: Renmin Chubanshe, 1979. Unfortunately, this collection of essays excludes material from the Cultural Revolution including that of the Shanghai School.

9. A designation introduced by Bill Brugger in Brugger (ed.), *China, The Impact of the Cultural Revolution*, Croom Helm, 1978.

10. In "On the 'Restoration of Capitalism'—Mao and Marxist Theory," (*Modern China*, vol. 5, no. 1, pp. 41-78), Joseph W. Esherick traces the roots of the analytical concept "Restoration of Capitalism" in Marxist literature and in Mao's writings. He sees Mao's contribution to socialist theory as being the development of the analytical concept "capitalist restoration." But it becomes apparent from Esherick's article that Mao's contribution in this respect cannot be identified by explicit reference to his own works, but only by induction. Therefore, we find it more fruitful to trace Mao's "generative class theory," which can be substantiated by references, and which is, actually, a blueprint for the theory of the Shanghai School, which expounded the concept of "capitalist restoration" by taking Mao's "generative class theory" as one of its starting points.

11. *"Guanyu zhengque chuli renmin neibu maodun de wenti"* (1957) (On the Correct Handling of Contradictions Among the People), *Mao Zedong xuanji* (Selected Works of Mao Tse-tung), vol. V, Beijing: Renmin Chubanshe, 1977, pp. 363-402, p. 389.

12. *"Guanyu nongye hezuohua wenti"* (1955) (On the Co-operative Transformation of Agriculture), *Mao Zedong Xuanji*, vol. V, pp. 168-91, where Mao argues that cooperativization precedes industrialization on a big scale and consequently mechanization of agriculture.

13. *"Guanyu zhengque . . . ,"* p. 392.

14. *"Guanyu 'Sulian shehuizhuyi jingji wenti' yi shu de jianghua"* (1958) (Speech Concerning "Economic Problems of Socialism in the USSR," in: Mao Tse-tung, *A Critique . . .* pp. 129-134), Wansui-69, pp. 247-251; *"Dui Sidalin 'Sulian shehuizhuyi jingji wenti' de piyu"* (1959) (Critique of Stalin's "Economic Problems of Socialism in the USSR," in: ibid., pp. 135-137), Wansui-67, pp. 156-166.

15. *"Guanyu zhengque . . . ,"* p. 389.

16. *"Zai kuoda de zhongyang gongzuo huiyi shang de jianghua"* (Talk at the Enlarged Work Conference of the Centre), Wansui-69, pp. 399-423, here pp. 406-407.

17. *"Zai Beidaihe zhongyang gongzuo huiyishang de jianghua"* (Talk at the Central Work Conference in Beidaihe), Wansui-69, pp. 423-429, here pp. 424-428. The manuscript for this talk is probably the most important source for identifying Mao's theoretical stand in this period.

18. *"Zhongyang gongzuo zuotanhui jiyao"* (Summary of the Central Work Conference), Wansui-69, pp. 578-97, here p. 582.

19. *"Zai zhongyang gongzuo huiyishang de jianghua"* (Talk at the Central Work Conference), Wansui-69, pp. 598-602, here p. 599.

20. *"Dui Arbaniya junshi daibiaotuan de jianghua"* (1967) (Talk to the Albanian Military Delegation), Wansui-69, pp. 673-679, here p. 677-678.

21. *Renmin Ribao* (The People's Daily), November 24, 1977.

22. Ibid.

23. *"Zhengzhi jingjixue jiaocai" (Shehuizhuyi bufen)* (Teaching Material on Political Economy. (Socialism-part)), Shanghai, 1961.

24. *"Shehuizhuyi zhengzhi jingjixue" (Zhengqiu yijian gao)* (Political Economy of Socialism). (Manuscript to be commented) Shanghai 1972. (Hereafter "PES," Shanghai 1972).

25. Stalin: *"Economic Problems of Socialism in the USSR,"* 1952, Beijing, FLP, 1972, p. 53 ff.

26. "PES," Shanghai, 1972, p. 120.

27. Ibid., p. 164.

28. *"Xuedian zhengzhi jingjixue,"* Shanghai, 1972.

29. *Hongqi* no. 7, 1972.

30. *Guangming Ribao*, January 16, 1978.

31. Ibid.

32. *"Shehuizhuyi zhengzhi jingjixue" (Modinggao)*, "PES" (Final draft), Shanghai, 1973.

33. *Zhengzhi jingjixue jichu zhishi*, Shanghai, 1974. It has been translated into English and published by M.E. Sharpe: *"Fundamentals of Political Economy*, ed. by George Wang (New York, 1977).

34. *Peking Review*, February 28, 1975.

35. Yao Wenyuan: *On the social basis of the Lin Piao-anti-party-clique*. *Peking Review*, March 7, 1975. Chang Chun-chiao: *On exercising all-round dictatorship over the bourgeoisie*. *Peking Review*, April 4, 1975.

36. "Shehuizhuyi zhengzhi jingjixue" (Modinggao dierban), "PES" (Second edition of the final draft), Shanghai, 1975.

37. *Zhengzhi jingjixue jichu zhishi* (Fundamentals of Political Economy), Shanghai, 1975.

38. See Bettelheim: The Great Leap Backwards.

39. See note 23.

40. Liu Shaoqi, Lin Biao, Deng Xiaoping.

41. *Renmin Ribao*, November 24, 1977.

42. *Shehuizhuyi zhengzhi jingjixue* (Political Economy of Socialism), Shanghai, 1976.

43. According to the *Guangming Ribao*, April 17, 1978, contact was established between the Shanghai School and a group from the Nankai University in Tianjin, also working on a manual on the political economy of socialism, in July 1975. The cooperation between the two groups was continued until 1976. The book written by the Tianjin group was published as late as November 1976 (*"Political Economy" (Socialism part) (Revised Edition)* (Tianjin, November 1976) and later it was criticized alongside the book written in Shjanghai. We consider the Tianjin group as belonging to the Shanghai School. In reconstructing the theoretical contents of the final manuscript of the "PES" we have, therefore, also used quotations from this book, as they both are criticized for being "Gang of Four"-theory.

Appendix

Chronological list of articles in Chinese magazines and newspapers criticizing the Shanghai School.

Nov. 24, 1977, *People's Daily (PD):* "A book which creates the theoretical basis for the counterrevolutionary program of 'the gang of four,' " by Dong Fureng and Tang Zongkan.

Dec. 5, 1977, *Guangmin Ribao (GR):* "On socialist wages and their concrete forms," by Wu Jinglian, Zhou Shulian and Wang Haibo. (Continued in *GR* Dec. 12, 1977).

Jan. 16, 1978, *GR:* "A completely counterrevolutionary 'Political Economy,' " by Hu Naishi and Wang Yongzhi.

Jan. 20, 1978, *Jingji Yanjiu (JY)* no. 1, 1978: Leading article: "Lead the struggle to expose 'the gang of four' in the fields of economics to the end."

Feb. 20, 1978, *JY* no. 2, 1978: "Refute the theory invented by 'the gang of four' on 'the double character of socialist relations or production,' " by Hu Ruiling. And: "Will money inside the socialist economy necessarily create a bourgeoisie?" by Zhang Wenxiao.

March 20, 1978, *JY* no. 3, 1978: "A reactionary theoretical system," by Dong Fureng. And: "An example of how 'the gang of four' distorted the character of socialist commodity production," by Yang Dongqing.

April 5, 1978, *PD:* "Condemn a 'Political Economy,' " by Zhang Chaozun and Hu Naishi. And: "Refute the theory of the socalled 'two factors' of socialist relations of production," by Xing Hua.

April 17, 1978, *GR:* "Examples of phenomena pretending to be left but actually right, inside the political economy," by Ma Piao. And: "A bad book propagating the reactionary viewpoints of 'the gang of four,' " by He Wei.

April 20, 1978, *JY* no. 4, 1978: "Criticize the idealistic economic theory of 'the gang of four,' " by Hu Ruilong, Zhao Renwei and Duan Ruofei. And: "Refute the theory of the socalled 'two factors' inside the socialist relations of production," by Wei Xinghua. And: "Is the contradiction and struggle between the proletariat and the bourgeoisie the concentrated expression of the fundamental contradiction of socialism?" by Wang Qingbao.

April 24, 1978, *PD:* "Criticize the counterrevolutionary 'gang-book,' 'Political Economy of Socialism.' "

May 20, 1978, *JY* no. 5, 1978: "Are the socialist relations of production, relations between the proletariat and the bourgeoisie?" by Zhou Shyulian.

May 29, 1978, *GR:* "Socialist commodity exchange can not engender capitalism," by Li Guangzi.

June 20, 1978, *JY* no. 6, 1978: "A black example of historical idealism," by Wang Ruisun. And: "We will not allow the distortion of the present socialist common ownership system in our country," by Wang Changchun. And: "Are mutual relations between people in the socialist production process class-antagonistic relations?" by Wang Haibo. And: "Will the socialist commodity system necessarily produce capitalism and new bourgeois elements?" by Liu Gangdi.

July 20, 1978, *JY* no. 7, 1978: "On profit in the socialist economy," by Kuang Rian and Zhang Zhouyuan. And: "Criticize the false doctrines fabricated by 'the gang of four' concerning the law of value," by Wang Yongzhi. And: "The question of the relationship between the fundamental and the most important contradiction in socialist society," by Jiang Zhong.

Aug. 20, 1978, *JY* no. 8, 1978: "Why must this book be criticized?" by Tang Zongkan. And: "A bad book propagating the reactionary ideological system of 'the gang of four,' " by the critique-group of the Institute of Economic Research, Nankai University, Tianjin. And: "Reject the slogan 'Repudiate the slogan: All for the modernization,' " by Yang Shengming and Guan Bai.

Sept. 20, 1978, *JY* no. 9, 1978: "The category, profit, and the management of socialist enterprises," by Wu Jinglian, Zhou Shulian and Wang Haibo. And: "The fundamental difference between the circulation of funds and the circulation of capital," by Cheng Mujiu.

Sept. 20, 1979, *JY* no. 9, 1979: "The theory that 'classes exist from the beginning to the end' has brought confusion into the formulation of the political economy of socialism," by Dong Fureng.

Nov. 20, 1978, *JY* no. 11, 1978: "We will not allow the distortion of the character of socialist reproduction," by Wu Shuqing.

The Original Chinese Revolution Remains in Power

by Edward Friedman

The Chinese revolution fundamentally changed state and society. State power and control over much of the more industrial and financial economy were transferred to the hands of Marxist socialists dedicated to using the surplus to improve the life of the many. In the countryside, the landlord system was exploded.

A basis was set for future progressive developments. There was still much good and important work to do. But the revolution was over. There no longer was social dynamite to explode or a hated state to topple. It makes little sense to discuss what occurred afterwards as a second revolution, a revolution after the revolution. There is even less sense to the idea that in China people associated with a capitalist road have been struggling with those committed to the socialist road. Socialism is a rah-rah word in China among ruling groups. Therefore whoever is defeated is almost by definition a capitalist-roader, a bad person, someone who would have led society astray. But surely, the defeat of this or that faction is not a revolution. Revolutions are not everyday occurrences. They happen seldom, if ever, in the life of a nation. The forces that make for revolution take time and circumstance to accumulate, and have not been present in China since the establishment of the People's Republic.

Depending on which of numerous groups have temporarily seized hegemonic control of the levers of state power, different and contradictory policies have been described as anti-socialist. While outsiders may joke about it, there is nothing funny about being labelled a capitalist-roader in China. A person so labelled suffers the penalties associated with being convicted of subversion, of plotting to overthrow the government, of trying to return China to a people-eating system which devoured families and once brought misery and starvation beyond reckoning.

But none of China's ruling groups have opted for a landlord system, for private usury, for industry owned by a handful with a legal right to buy or sell such factories to enrich themselves, for laborers left to their own devices to sell their labor as a commodity in a market. The issues even in sum and even as caricatured by one's opponents never add up to capitalism as capitalists comprehend it.

The term capitalist roader, however, is more than a convention to give good conscience to China's victors in sending the vanquished to a Sinic Coventry. It is a poison which makes compromise and open politics impossible. Since defeat means defamation and worse, opposition groups secretly plot to undermine their opponents. To define Chinese politics as a Manichean combat between good and evil, socialism and capitalism, creates political dynamics where all politics are ploys toward coups and any means—slander, imprisonment, torture or murder—is legitimate since one is persuaded that one must do unto one's opponents before they do unto you. When state power holders use that coercive apparatus against adversaries defined as class enemies, they are not arm-chair social analysts making dynamic structural distinctions; they are executioners. Their words are weapons which silence and smash alternatives.

While I agree with those who argue that the socialist commitment could not be truly achieved without making political and economic democracy real, there was after 1949 in China no revolutionary movement promoting that needed change. But how should we understand an end to possibilities for revolutionary change? The conservative view of how revolutions the revolution ends. The conservative view of how revolutions end—best expressed by Brinton and premised on Pareto—is that revolutions restore normality. Nothing fundamental changes. Dangerous utopians, who understand nothing of reality except power aggrandizement, seek fundamental change. More recent embodiments of this conservative approach include the technological determinism, modernization and convergence theories. Be still, they say. Nothing better can be achieved by aroused, ignorant masses. The Chinese have come to their senses.

In the second view, classically formulated by Trotsky in an analogy between the French and Bolshevik revolutions, the revolution ends with betrayal. The ruling fraction that would continue the revolution is ousted by traitors to the revolution, a process identified with the month of its supposed occurrence in France, the Thermidorian reaction.

But there is no Thermidorian reaction. What occurs in a France or Soviet Union or China or Kampuchea is that, if a new ruling fraction tries to force society beyond what society desires or will bear, the new state must resort to terror. It is the use of terror that indicates that the revolution has passed what is progressively possible, that the revolution is over. The terrorists may be thrown out of power as the Jacobins were and the gains of the revolution consolidated or the terror may continue, as with Stalin or Pol Pot, thereby alienating the citizenry as the state imposes forms with even more inhuman content.

Understood in this light, there is only propagandistic nonsense to the notion that the death of Mao and the arrest of some of his left terrorist allies, labelled a Gang of Four, abruptly ended the revolutionary process in China. Discussions of this topic are confused not only by conceptual errors but by bald ignorance of the facts.

People say that the stories of terror now coming out of China are exaggerated to serve selfish political purposes, that, in fact, there were but a few excesses, mostly of a minor nature. I remember during the Cultural Revolution when it was possible to believe that bloody noses of a few Red Guards was the extent of the violence. Even the known deaths—as when unarmed soldiers were murdered by Red Guard factions in the soldiers' attempts to restore order—seemed to prove that the excesses were few. After all, the soldiers were sent in unarmed. The state's goal clearly seemed to be to minimize violence.

Nonetheless, it is now obvious that the terror and suffering were mammoth, mind-boggling in the extreme. In fact, the reports in the post-1976 Chinese press grossly *understate* the brutal acts of violence. There is no campaign to reveal all. Many people are ashamed to describe the cruel humiliations their family members suffered, some not surviving the cruelty. Many protectors or precipitators of the violence remain in power or may return to power. People are still afraid to talk. Outsiders mistake this caution and shame for equanimity and no desire for revenge.

Although even in sum the printed words on the terror offer but a pale reflection of the blood that flowed, no one is qualified to deny the bloody reality until he or she at least reads Amnesty International reports, the Hong Kong patriotic journals, and books such as the Chinese literature of the wounded. But since silence and shame are the rule, there is no substitute for simply talking to as many Chinese as possible.

Facts on the horrors of the Cultural Revolution period leak out one by one, more by accident than by design. There is no campaign to reveal the whole, cruel truth. Someone visits the People's Publishing House and discovers that an editor is blind in one eye. Only later is it revealed that it was punched out in the Cultural Revolution. I visit a university and discover by happenstance about the scientist who was driven to suicide by drinking lye. A Chinese youth tells of visiting Nanning and seeking hundreds of dead bodies from a continuing carnage she swiftly fled. A foreign resident scholar hears about the two scholars whose heads were smashed in. An American of Chinese descent wishing to return home is informed that his elderly father, long unheard from, was killed in the Cultural Revolution, and has now been rehabilitated. Children of accused and jailed people were left to wander alone till they went mad. Others were left with their brains smashed and scrambled. One visitor listens to the story of the woman forced to beat with a whip her own frail father, and is told, after the whip breaks, to have another ready the next morning to continue the whippings. The zealots leave. The woman and her father hang themselves. Another visitor carries the tale of the high school students who beat their principal to death and then forced his closest colleague to carry the coffin in a supposed celebration of the death of a class enemy. Someone else recounts the beating to death of his elderly father, already exiled to the northeast because of free speech in the hundred flowers period, murdered by new zealots extirpating powerless, weak, defenseless victims a decade later.

The press carries some few tragic accounts, too: Xia Yen left a permanent cripple, Peng Dehuai sealed up in a room without light or sound, the slitting of wind pipes to silence opponents, the brutal degradation of Lao She driving him to suicide, the execution in 1970 of Yu Loke, the author of the Cultural Revolution essay opposing class inheritance by blood. The numerous accounts of sadistic degradation, of human brutality almost cannot be absorbed.

At first the accounts of murder, terror and torture seem endless. Then one realizes that the Chinese leaders and people are ashamed. They are not trying to expose all these horrors. Only a fraction of the ugly truth is seeping out. The real horror has to be much worse. We can only guess at how much worse. At an absolute minimum the number of dead is in the hundred thousands. There is no way the victims of incarceration, mayhem, torture and maiming can be less than millions. And the victims of verbal abuse have to be ten or a hundred times that. Anyone labelled or accused brought disgrace to friends and family. The accused walked with head lowered, looked no one in the eye. Children, neighbors, workmates, friends and family were abandoned or similarly branded and disgraced for association with the one beyond the pale. It was medieval cruelty in the extreme.

Some people brush all this aside as accidental or incidental, but the terror should have told us that the revolution was over. Ignoring the real world of flesh-and-blood, ravaged, crippled and scarred Chinese population, these foreign progressives claim that what really matters is that those who believed in the continuing revolution have been ousted by people who lack that faith. It is then argued that China has abandoned self-reliance for subordinate integration into world capitalism, that China has abandoned the peasantry and levelling up for a policy of primarily benefitting the already privileged urban minority, that China is allowing a separate strata of intellectuals to rule over the people. In sum, the Maoist attempt to continue the revolution after the revolution, the only real second revolution, has lost power.

But even a perusal of the record proves that this lament has no factual base. What it does is measure the claims of a previous faction of the future they hoped for against a worst-case description of some present policy tendencies. It does not compare what is in progress with what was in process. We should.

There is no evidence, beginning with 1955–1956 collectivization, that any levelling up of the peasantry occurred. Even scholars previously sympathetic to the vision and claims of the Shanghai faction now agree that those claims were bogus. The Japanese economist Kojima Reiitsu[1] even declares that that faction lost power precisely because it couldn't improve conditions in the countryside, the rural areas being the heart-beat of the decisive Chinese military. Ben Stavis finds that malnutrition was close to 15 percent.[2] Nick Lardy finds that inequality grew with anywhere from 100 to 200 million left short of food.[3] The imposed irrational policy of grain self-reliance destroyed more suitable crops, reduced protein available and denuded the soil in large regions of the north, northwest and southwest. In Yunnan Province, for example, grain production per capita had decreased by 94 jin from 1956 to 1978. The post-Shanghai faction government rapidly and radically tried to grapple with the inherited disaster.

> *During the spring festival of 1977 . . . our country was confronted with many problems: the reserve grain . . . could last only ten months, many warehouses were empty, and our foreign exchange was almost exhausted. At that point we in a gamble still appropriated reserve grain and used up all our foreign exchange to buy sugar, to import edible oils and flour. Why did we do this? . . . [T]he task of the greatest urgency was to solve that [food] probblem, and, at a Politburo conference, the Party Central Committee decided to distribute the reserve grain and buy grain and sugar abroad to make sure that the people would have enough food for the Spring Festival. When that major task was settled, the production work could be continued. . . .*[4]

Deng Xiaoping and the other leaders who were victimized by China's ultra-left and punished by being sent to poor villages were shocked that such poverty and misery could persist in "socialist" China. Appalled by China's failure, they have resumed power with a primary commitment to eradicating the causes of persistent misery in rural China. Not to comprehend this fact, not to understand that levelling up had not occurred, not to put that at the center of one's comprehension of Chinese dynamics after October 1976 is among the largest errors—if not the largest error—one can make in misunderstanding China today.

The economic extremes in China's countryside are much greater than the 4:1 or 5:1 ratio claimed in official government statements and reproduced in the scholarly literature. But in the one commune on the North China plains where I have done work the gap is already larger. And outside of Beijing in Red Star commune where I have stayed, the wealth is four times that of the richest village in the commune where I have worked. In addition, rich suburban communes in the south are more than twice as wealthy as Red Star, while poor mountain villages often have less than half the wealth of even the poorest village of that North China commune. In short, I have seen differences of over 100 to 1.

A long essay would be necessary to do justice to the large number of changes intended to benefit the rural poor that have been instituted by the Marxist materialist coalition headed by Deng Xiaoping since taking power in the autumn of 1976. They have begun to turn around a previously regressive rural tax system. Tax holidays have been declared for especially poor regions. Whereas all rural China has been given much higher prices for its farm products, an additional price premium is paid to poor regions. More bank loan money (which is subsequently written off as a gift when used productively) has been earmarked for such regions. The price the state charges farmers for production inputs has been cut. Specialists are being sent out all over the countryside to help peasants move into high value production. The state is investing in the infrastructure that will make this pay off. The new government holds out the promise of having previously poor Chinese areas specialize in particular foods—e.g. meat or fruit—and then win good money when the state pricing policy wins profits from prices charged wealthier urban dwellers on such items. In 1979–80 value was transferred to the countryside while city people suffered from 15% inflation. For the first time since the forced collectivization of 1956, a dent may have been made in the rural-urban gap. The government is persuading poor peasants that, in contrast to the previous period, if they act to enrich themselves, they will no longer be denounced as capitalist roaders.[5]

An official "Commentator" claimed in a July 4, 1978, *People's Daily* essay, "Transforming Poor Production Is an Urgent Task," that

> *leading cadres in many prefectures have not paid attention to the urgent demands of the masses of poor production teams or listened to their appeals. Some leading cadres have not visited these poor production teams for years to examine their work and solve problems. They simply let these masses live in misery and allow problems to accumulate.*

The "Commentator" urged regional leaders to involve themselves with "poor production teams and help change their features and catch-up with well-to-do production teams as soon as possible." The "Commentator" concluded that that kind of leadership and social change "is a matter of great importance which affects the general situation." Taking 50 yuan a year per capita income as the definition of a poverty line, the new policies led to a decrease in the number of poor rural Chinese work teams from 18.6 percent of all teams in 1978 to 10 percent in 1979.[6]

Perhaps the most startling aspect of recent revelations is just how much the Maoist policy never was carried out. Contrary to claims of having put more stress on the peasant and agriculture, in fact, the percentage of investment in the Mao era that went into heavy industries such as steel and electronics for the military actually increased. This is because Mao opposed balanced development and emphasized campaign economics. Steel and defense came first. They were the priority items. The rural sector was slighted. It was a residual concern. Peasants may have been first in Maoist hearts but they were last in the budget.[7]

The poor peasants pouring into Beijing in 1979 carried heart-rending tales of how previous ruling groups slighted their needs. The new ruling group's demotion of steel from its position as a priority product tells us a story which many of us were not ready for. Mao, with his continuing stress on heavy industry, steel and grain slighted the necessary investments in and price arrangements for light industry, foreign trade and economic crops needed to raise the rural poor. Others among ruling groups would have broken—and have now broken—further from the Soviet Stalinist model than Mao.

In fact if we but go back over the political history of the People's Republic of China we discover that one major outstanding story is that all the Marxist materialist opponents of China's Marxist ideologues contended, and not without some good reason, that they would do better for China's tillers of the soil than would Mao. In the years before Mao on 31 July 1955 instigated rapid collectivization, these people worried about the material losses such as the slaughter of animals and morale losses from mere uncomprehending obedience that would accompany coerced collectivization. Their concerns were justified.

Mao tried to extract himself from the dilemmas he caused by premature collectivization by initiating in 1958 a Great Leap Forward linking an impossibilist promise of "to each according to self-defined needs" with mass mobilization of labor. The resulting destruction of production and of labor incentives took rural China but one step from mass starvation. Minister of National Defense Peng Dehuai's subsequent critique of Mao's Great Leap policy and interventions on behalf of suffering villagers were, if anything, constrained and understated. He was nonetheless denounced by Mao as a "rightist opportunist." Is a rightist, in the view of China's Marxist ideologues, someone who puts at the center of policy the material needs of China's rural poor?

Deng Xiaoping, Chen Yun *et al.* readjusted policies in the early 1960s to re-woo country people through increased material rewards for production. This successful attempt to get the economy going again and to speak to village notions of equity was denounced in the Cultural Revolution period as the essence of taking the capitalist road. Consequently the ultra left could never win most of rural China to its side.

Once the Cultural Revolution ended, Zhou Enlai, Li Xiannian, Yu Qiuli and other economically oriented planners in Zhou's State Council networks organized an August 1970 agriculture conference to inaugurate a program intended to raise productivity and market value for the countryside. That program became the target of Zhang Qunqiao's ultra left pot-shots at alleged capitalist tails in the countryside. It is, however, still the program that defines policy in China today. Hua Guofeng's 1975 addition to Zhou's program sought to make richer villages and communes take responsibility for raising up poorer ones as a means of achieving equality in each county. The Jiang Qing group promised to raise the rural poorest by pushing distribution to larger geographical units so that more from production by richer areas would go to less well off units. That approach, too divorced from increasing the overall pool of goods and wealth produced, was experienced as levelling down and, seeming unjust and primitive, made little headway. Nonetheless, it is a fact that the Marxist materialists had since 1953 developed a critique of Marxist ideologues—Chen Boda, Zhang Qunqiao *et al.*,—in China and an alternative program which offered more to rural dwellers.

In short, there was nothing wrong with the values by which foreign progressives weighed Maoist China. It is just that the facts were often close to the opposite of the claims. This is true on the issue of factory democracy, too. Previous positive evaluations of the Maoist model were premised on analyzing data similar to a study of racism in the U.S.A. based on the Constitution, a reading of the Supreme Court's *Brown vs. Board of Education* decision and subsequent civil rights legislation, plus reports of progress and improvement toward the egalitarian goal. In other words, Chinese factory life in fact was undemocratic, alienating and unproductive.[8]

It is perfectly understandable that many progressives who were committed to the Maoist vision have suddenly grown cynical and rhetorical. Such people's transformation is a mirror image but a few years later of a similar process which occurred among people in China following the Lin Biao clique's coup attempt. Chinese who had worked hard to see the world such that Lin was Mao's only true successor to continue the revolution which was being betrayed by Liu Shaoqi *et al.* suddenly were informed that Lin and Liu were in fact similar kinds of people. This was too much to take. Cynicism spread like a malignant cancer in China after 1971. Maoism was dead.

Now the same thing is happening outside of China. The source is obvious. The Cultural Revolution's rendering of China's political history to legitimize terror and stagnation as revolution was a fraud. Innocent victims who were fooled by the fraud must rethink everything, otherwise they cannot understand that the original Chinese revolution remains in power.

But this should not be surprising. It was, after all, a revolution which won power in 1949. Society was fundamentally transformed and that change was for the better. Such extraordinary events are few and far between. The social tinder of revolutionary dynamite cannot be manufactured overnight. There is no immediate new social misery to organize for yet another revolution tomorrow in China. For the state to insist on more revolution despite society is for the state to become terroristic against society. Those Maoist, statist terrors have split state and society asunder, erupting in fiery divisions, outrages and hates—but not revolution. Revolution is impossible.

The Deng Xiaoping regime has enacted a series of liberating reforms which promise a new and better day for most Chinese. The labels have been removed from families who previously had been put in "black" categories. This frees many times more than the millions of individuals directly labelled. Their family members, and not always merely immediate ones, also suffered disgrace and disability, isolation and ostracism. How cruel the days when family members did not dare even visit or speak or express concern for the other, when obloquy, pariah status and virtual internal banishment were the political reality for millions upon millions of Chinese.

In sum, Deng Xiaoping, Chun Yun and their allies, like the Maoists before them, cannot transcend the forces that both made and delimited the original revolution. Some of these forces are beyond Chinese control. China cannot repeat growth by the path taken by Taiwan, South Korea and Hong Kong starting a quarter of a century ago. The world market has changed. The U.S.A. is no longer so open to importing many products in which China is competitive. Given the costs of high technology, the soaring nature of international interest rates, etc., China has been compelled to abandon its optimum vision of leaping ahead by using the value earned on energy exports.

In like manner, the new government cannot simply order the lower officials to act on rational economic calculations. These people, usually veterans of the last years of the revolutionary civil war or the Korean War, now perhaps aged 55 or so, feel too old to learn these new skills. And they'll be damned if they'll abandon their new security, just having been rehabilitated after having survived the Cultural Revolution's vigilantism.

Similarly, the more than 10 million officials promoted in the Cultural Revolution decade are not enamored of the new policies. People in their regions are often afraid to act while that violent left remains entrenched in power. The post-1976 administration is constrained from launching an attack on so many people.

Thus as in the Maoist period there is a huge gap between the official promise and the day-to-day practice. In contrast to the friendly foreigners' fear that intellectuals now run China, in fact, Chinese intellectuals don't yet even run universities. The ex-military types in charge there refuse to budge. The original revolution remains very much entrenched in power.

Yet much of Chinese culture is bursting again with energy. Hundreds upon hundreds of journals have bloomed. How glorious to see Ding Ling returned from the Chinese Siberia to which Mao had sent her. How wonderful to be able to look forward to a new novel by that creator. How sad to hear that her persecutors ripped up and destroyed a previous draft.

For the first time in living memory China is beginning to confront openly some of its most serious problems. Previously China had been silent about its rape problem. Suddenly it is acknowledged. Newspapers run stories about the capture of murdering rapists. Their crimes are detailed. A trial of one such accused has been televised.

In like manner, there has been open acknowledgement of the pervasive abuse of power for petty personal, familial, or clique advantage. Some guilty parties have been punished and their crimes detailed in the local or national press. The government has launched a campaign requesting private letters to investigative agencies as a way of ferreting out and checking those who abuse their bureaucratic power. And to keep the campaign from turning scurrilous and libelous or a matter of settling personal grudges, stiff penalties are put on false accusers.

Lots of powerful people in China, especially at middle and local levels and in the military, do not like these changes. They proudly claim that they no longer watch the dirt on TV or read the corrupted press. They preferred the ultra-left period when the media was optimistic and romantic and the stress was on positive heroes. What they see these days is not liberation but a tearing down of an image of a pure China. These anxious people, fearful of losing the little they have, are cultural conservatives. They are like fundamentalists in West Virginia who are not easily won to the cause of gender equality by explaining the naturalness of lesbianism, and the artificiality of the family system. They too value families.

The Chinese Revolution has, among others, a familistic content. It was fought by people who had lost family. Its fruits included stable, secure families, marriage, children (and a population explosion) and government support for burial (which along with fuel, clothing, education for their children and food are guaranteed to the families of army veterans).

Already in the early 1950s Mao abandoned the politics of equality for rural women to hold the loyalty of male rural Party leaders who wished to enjoy the familial fruits of victory, marriage, children, family.[9] When Mao promoted the notion that under socialism a person was first a producer such that more people meant more productivity, not less for each to consume, he was very popular in the countryside. Big, male-run, three-generation families, the Confucian ideal, came closer to being realized for the majority of China's people under Mao's tutelage than at any other time in Chinese history. But Mao's population policy was a catastrophe for China. No doubt it was more than necessary by 1979 to do something drastic to reverse the tide. But a suddenly imposed population control system of disincentives could not help but be mammothly unpopular in China.

The same syndrome exists in many policy areas. What is popular is catastrophic; what is necessary is unpopular. The result has to be compromise and trade-off. The historical reality is that there is not and cannot be an over-all correct policy line. Any viable policy will also have costs, create problems and make enemies. It is a political issue and not a social science how one weighs and balances these complex and unpredictable reflexive relations. Consequently, an attempt to comprehend Chinese politics as a two-line struggle between good and evil is not merely Manichean nonsense; it also calls attention away from most of the decisive factors and forces which shape, limit and persist in continuing to define and deflect Chinese policy options.

In China familial items are naturally made the law of the land. Wives can be divorced if they don't bear children. Children have the obligation to care financially for parents in their later years. Factory workers can bring back a child from the countryside if they can retire and therefore legally make the child heir to the job. Traditional thought and behavior such as these give content to the Chinese government's universalistic policies.

Familism means that the Deng regime's stress on individual behavior today and in the future as a just measure of reward is not obviously authoritative to peasants, especially the major early beneficiaries of the revolution who have close ties to the army. Especially in early liberated areas—perhaps a fourth of rural China, no more—more committed to the collective and egalitarian path, the new economic policies often seem a perversion to steal from the revolutionaries the familial fruits of their revolution.

The entire period since the establishment of the People's Republic of China in 1949 starkly reveals the limits of the original revolution. The Maoist transition to socialism was claimed to be a transition to ever larger units of distribution until finally the state itself would distribute the wage pool equally to all. But "the state" is coercive power over others. What a wonderful faith to believe that it would not treat its own ruling stratum and related social base better than others. Marx assumed that democratic forms now given real content would preclude this. But the Maoist theorists of the transition to state planning accompanied by state distribution do not see why that broad democracy is necessary. They believe good people at the top—they themselves—will do good. But this often ignores the nature of bureaucratic reality: access to resources is conditioned by personal ties.

In bureaucratic societies, income obscures more than it reveals. Income disparities at an enterprise level often overstate inequality by not including subsidized health, education, housing, etc. On the other hand, income does not measure perquisites: for example, "work meetings" at resorts, travel money, access to special stores, priority to better housing and medicine, being in the know about what's available and how to get it, being part of networks which offer opportunities for kith and kin. The language of pure income, of the worker as commodity, the language of free capitalism—Marx's language—obscures the social structural dynamics and relations of bureaucratic and statist societies. It is an index of the irrelevance of Marxist idealist theorists that they focused on capital and defined bureaucracy in capital's categories and never did the opposite, the increasingly necessary work, of giving priority to statist and bureaucratic realities. Marxist theorists of the long transition and the Chinese Marxist idealists are of little help in addressing central issues of checking inequality of power, status and wealth as it takes on institutional form.

It was one entrenched grouping seeking with its allies to remove another such grouping which characterized the Cultural Revolution period. Fear, fawning and fierce fighting were foremost. All the struggles since 1966 brought to the fore resisting groups which benefitted from the original revolution, groups who feared they would lose out in attempts to expand and transcend the revolution's original social base. These are embodied in the politics of the military at the highest level of state power.

How can the new Chinese leadership win the military and its peasant base (tied to the military by the hope of jobs and the glory of higher status and shared memories) to the new cause of socialist democracy and market-oriented modernization? How can it win that peasant-military backing when it is in the process of carrying out a policy to end the special privileges of military service which had made an army posting once so attractive to so many peasant youth? The armed warfare of revolutionary strife in China brought a new army to power. The meaning of that decisive fact was clear in the villages as well as at the highest reaches of state power.[10]

Soon after liberation, one high party leader, Gao Gang, decided to move against the groups and policies linked to State Council leader Zhou Enlai and Party leader Liu Shaoqi. Gao's tactic was to appeal to the obvious fount of power in China, the liberation armies. Gao claimed that those of the military revolutionary base areas had had their revolutionary birthright stolen by such as Zhou and Liu whose people came from the areas not controlled by the new armies. Gao underestimated Zhou's ties to the army leaders and Mao's ties to Zhou, Liu and the army. But Gao surely well understood that that victorious army had the power to make or break groups and policies in the new China.

This became obvious to anyone with eyes to see during China's Cultural Revolution. Even Albanian strongman Enver Hoxha's writings then note in mock shock that it was the military which was the base of power in China. But all informed observers understood that Mao through Minister of National Defense Lin Biao had ousted competing military leaders such as Peng Dehuai, Lo Ruiqing, He Long and even Zhu De to assure his group and policies of military backing before launching the Cultural Revolution against Party power-holders.

Differences among military groups were revealed as decisive differences within Chinese politics. Ultra-left Red Guard groups hoped the army's Thirty-second Division would support and save them. Lin Biao would rely on the Air Force as the core of his coup plan. But the dominant center of the military in 1967 tried to call a halt to this destructive chaos launched by Beijing's ultra-left state power-holders. The renounced and well-connected author of "Whither China," Yang Xiguang, sadly commented:

> *A senior army cadre openly and arrogantly assailed the Central Cultural Revolution Group. This was their general policy in August and September [1967]. 'Does the Central Cultural Group still want the People's Liberation Army?' If it doesn't, then we will pack up and go home. The Central Revolution Group has so shifted the veteran army cadres that they are separated from their wives and children, their homes broken up and their kin lost!*[11]

Military leaders would see themselves as traitors to their family and their revolution should they let unreliable student rebels prevent them from passing on their heritage. Those student rebels, or at least a section thereof, had concluded that to keep power-holders in China from becoming a self-replicating ruling class, the Cultural Revolution would have to be carried into the military. But that the military powers would not permit.

Not to accept the military definition of the limits of the Cultural Revolution, Chairman Mao Zedong found, was to risk civil war, military coup and right-wing reaction. Mao conceded to them. The extension of the Cultural Revolution ended. Marshall Ye Jianying and other leaders of armed forces put an end to the quest for power of the Shanghai Group in 1976. This military may be opposed to the ultra-left but they are also attached to Mao, the peasants and their army heritage. This creates quite a problem for the Deng Xiaoping group.

The post-Mao rulers of China have set out to woo this military so that their democratic policies can go forward. This requires pushing the military out of politics, and explains why high-level Communist Party people are committed to democratization in ways that many top military people are not. Most importantly, the Party people in power were the victims of the capricious mass vigilantism of the Cultural Revolution whose ultimate meaningless, factionalized, ultra-left violence is sketched by Nancy and David Milton.[12] Not only these Party people as individuals but their closest friends of a lifetime of revolutionary endeavor and their family members were degraded, beaten, banished, tortured, even driven to their death. Precious few leaders lack painful scars.

This experience has left many such top Party people—as well as ex-Red Guards whom Mao used and tossed away—passionately committed to never allowing such things ever to happen again in China. Perhaps it is something akin to Europe's experience with religious wars, inquisitions, and pyres of intolerance which led many there to dedicate themselves to liberty. There can be no doubt that the deep identification with such as law, rights, constitutionality, due process and checking abuses of power is genuine. But so are the obstacles to it from sectors of the military. And the history of post-liberation China warns us that the military—while not in charge of daily affairs—regularly has the final say on large policy reorientations.

The new government is trying to attach its version of Mao to the peasantry's popular culture. It welcomes happy celebrations of the traditional New Year. It explains that the ultra-left distorted Mao's activities to injure the peasantry's cultural identities, wrongly denouncing the popular as the feudal. Former Chief of Staff Lo Ruiqing wrote a letter dated 27 February 1968 explaining that some people, fearing that it would dim Mao's shining image, hid from everyone Mao's actual thoughts and deeds such as his 1959 visit to Shaoshan where he climbed a hill to visit his parents' burial place and laid a bundle of pine twigs on their tomb. When Mao climbed down the hill, he said,

> *We communists are thorough-going materialists. We do not believe in ghosts or deities. But we must acknowledge the fact that we owe our birth to our parents . . . The next time I come back I will pay them another visit.*[13]

The post-Mao Party democratizers are likewise trying to hold the loyalty of the military elite to their cause. They have called attention to those few top generals—He Long, Lo Ruiqing, *et al.*—who did suffer from the forces of Lin Biao and the ultra-left. The indignities heaped upon the martyred dead, He Long and Lo Ruiqing, have been described in vivid detail. The restored Fu Qiongbi has described the injustices he suffered because of illegality, frame-up and lack of a system of justice.

But the most important figure is Peng Dehuai who already in 1959 stood against Mao's left excesses which so wounded the Chinese people. His speeches confronting Mao then have recently been exhumed. Early in 1979 the military paper, *Liberation Army Daily,* published a long memoir by Peng's nieces and nephews titled "Tearful Recollections in Memory of our Uncle Peng Dehuai." The article treated Mao as merely a misled emperor. It focused on the evils of the "empress" (their term, not mine), Mao's wife, Jiang Qing, and the terrors Peng faced starting with the Cultural Revolution. You

> *. . . were thrown down to the 18 depths of hell. They . . . paraded you through the streets and beat you with fists; people wearing boots kicked you in the groin. . . .*

His relatives' homes were sacked. They were investigated and labelled "alien class elements." The decree was, of course, on the family as a whole: "No matter how well they behave, they must not be admitted to the party."

The purport for the army leadership and their familism is clear. It is underscored by the rest of the tale. Peng's niece, Meiguei, was allowed to visit her uncle in a hospital on April 23, 1973. She found the windows covered with newspapers so that no light could get in. Confined to bed, her uncle was denied not only light but also writing material and sound. His jailers had broken his radio. "I am not even allowed to see the view outside," Peng commented. No one would speak to him. Peng requested of Meiguei: "After my death, send my ashes to our native place. Bury me there and plant an apple tree on my grave so that my ashes can make the tree grow."

But when "uncle's heart ceased beating" at 3:35 in the afternoon of November 29, 1974, only his niece Peng Qang was allowed to go to the hospital to try to make final arrangements. Since officials only allowed her 20 minutes off from her factory job, she found no way to bring the ashes home. The enemies of Peng, those who mistreated him are then described as "black-hearted people who put on red hats," people who lacked "any humanitarian sense and who enforced their fascist despotism."

The lengthy piece concludes:

Uncle, you may rest now. The Party's Central Committee headed by Comrade Hua Guofeng has smashed that newspaper-covered window to let in the sunshine and the colors of spring. Rest in peace.

But the future is not safely assured. Reading the Chinese press, controlled in the main by people friendly to the Party democrats, modernizers or Deng, creates the misleading impression of stable power. People in 1975 and 1976 over-rated the power of the ultra-left when their allies dominated China's media. The ultra-left was easily quashed in 1976 because it had virtually no military base. But that is not true about the opponents today of socialist democratization. They are led by soldiers. One cannot even rule out the possibility of civil war or a straight military take-over or a "left" alliance of anti-intellectual, anti-market nativistic blood and soil types which takes China to fascism. The continuing clash is real. The military may have to be bought off and appeased with new, expensive weaponry and strong policies on Taiwan or Vietnam. The future no more than the past will be made at will by a few civilians at the center of state power. The revolution entrenched powerful, legitimate interests both at the levels of state and society.

While we cannot be certain of the role of China's military in shaping China's future, the Shanghai Group's push to ever more left policies did not benefit China. Twenty years ago the Cuban government too promoted a slogan "Always to the left." In retrospect, the policies behind that slogan boomeranged. By going economically too far to the left, a situation was created that fostered a backlash, the increasing imposition of a system similar to the Soviet Union's, even including the secret police. The renowned socialist thinker, E. P. Thompson has exposed the cant hidden in the notion "No enemies to the Left!" Thompson wrote:

how is it possible to say there are no such enemies, after the experience of high Stalinism, after Budapest 1956, after Prague 1968? . . . what possible meaning is attached to "the Left" when it teaches lessons of anti-moralism, anti-humanism . . . ? . . . Does the suppression of reason and the obliteration of the imagination have any place on "the Left"?[14]

There are enemies to the left, and people who write of the dynamics of the socialist project in the People's Republic of China must come to terms with the new evidence of wasted efforts, cruelty, and death. One no more learns if the USSR under Stalin was on the way toward communism by a brilliant explication of the rules of Soviet collectives—while remaining silent about the struggles among rulers and about the death toll—than one learns where China was going by examining the rules of factory management while remaining silent about a deterioration of housing, transportation, education, culture, productivity, and the damage to truth-telling, trust, honor, decency and all that makes life secure and hopeful. We must deal with the reality of the splitting of families, the torture, forced suicides, beatings, degradations in the tens of millions, and things such as people, for lack of space, cooking in the bathroom and keeping their baby under the bed. China has meant no contraceptives, and marriage delayed into the thirties because there is no place to live. Fear and rage, depression and cynicism; these are an integral part of the legacy of Maoism.

And for what? Regional inequalities did not decline. The rural-urban gap did not decrease. What fell was both faith in Marxism and belief in a socialist future. In such systems, Thompson wrote,

"Marxism" performs the function of an "Ideological State Apparatus," and Marxists are alienated, not in their self-identity, but in the contempt of the people.[15]

It is to the credit of the post-Mao rulership that it is trying to end what previously had won the contempt and cynicism of the people, and that it is re-examining and rethinking the meaning of Marxism and Leninism and Stalinism and Maoism and Titoism and many other approaches to the problems of our time. Everything affecting China's real problems—overpopulation, limited land, weak infrastructure, powerful military, traditionalist peasantry, high cost of extracting resources, and so on—is under scrutiny, including the Party, the relation to the world market, other nation's socialisms, etc. Just how much democratization and demilitarization is possible when the Chinese revolution remains in power and very much entrenched in power? That remains an open question to be decided not in the abstract here but in real struggle in the People's Republic of China.

Notes

1. Kojima Reiitsu, an unpublished paper presented at a panel of the 1980 session of the Association for Asian Studies.
2. Stavis, "The Standard of Living in Rural China," forthcoming.
3. Lardy, "Food Consumption in the People's Republic of China," August 1980. (unpublished ms.)
4. "Chang P'ing-hua's Speech to Cadres on the Cultural Front," *Issues and Studies* 14:12 (December 1978), p. 102.
5. This does not make for a free peasant market as Cuba has where the sky is the limit on prices. In China, the state keeps prices within a controlled band of possibilities.
6. *Hong qi,* 1980, No. 6, p. 39.

7. In other words, foreign progressives who welcomed Maoism as an alternative to Stalinism were in no small part misled. The critical alternative to Stalinism in China from the early 1950s on has always rested more with the Chen Yun, Sun Yefang group. Cf. my "Maoism, Titoism, Stalinism," in *The Socialist Transition in China* (Victor Lippit and Mark Selden, eds.; forthcoming).

8. Cf. Andrew Walder, "Some Ironies of the Maoist Legacy in Industry," *Australian Journal of China Studies*, January 1981.

9. Kay Ann Johnson, *Feminism and Chinese Socialism*, forthcoming.

10. In her magnificent, albeit flawed novel, *The Sun Shines Over the Sangkan River*, (Beijing: Foreign Languages Press, 1954) China's great feminist writer, Ding Ling, described a late 1940s landlord out to escape the worst pains of pending land reform and power change. His escape is to have a son join and fight in the revolutionary army. An army family, he could see, was specially privileged in the new China.

11. *The Revolution Is Dead, Long Live the Revolution* (Hong Kong: The 70's, 1976), p. 190.

12. *The Wind Will Not Subside* (New York: Pantheon, 1976).

13. *Renmin Ribao*, 23 March 1978.

14. *The Poverty of Theory and Other Essays* (New York: Monthly Review Press, 1978), p. 189.

15. Thompson, *The Poverty of Theory and Other Essays*, p. 25.

The Thorny Flowers of 1979: Political Cartoons and Liberalization in China

by Ralph Croizier

Nineteen-seventy-nine was a vintage year for both artistic and political experiments in China. In the arts the continued revival of traditional plays and paintings almost entirely replaced the stereotyped political art of the Cultural Revolution. Even more remarkable, growing contact with the West brought Brecht to the Chinese stage, Beethoven at the Beijing symphony, impressionism in art exhibitions. Foreign travellers were treated to the vaguely art nouveau nudes of the Beijing airport murals. Chinese readers were exposed to a new "realism" in literature which went beyond recounting the "wounds" of the Cultural Revolution period to frank exposure of defects in contemporary society.

Not all of these innovations were unambiguously welcomed by the political leadership. After much controversy over possible insults to the Dai minority people whose females were shown not only nude but also "unrealistically" elongated in the celebrated airport murals, the more offensive portions were screened off from public view. But nudes have not disappeared from Chinese art schools or art magazines and, even more significantly, both Chinese ink and oil painters pushed closer and closer towards abstraction. Similarly, the exposure literature touched off a backlash calling for positive stories to "praise the virtues" of socialist society. But the ensuing debate during the summer and fall came down generally on the side of further exposure in order to correct defects. Finally, at the Fourth National Conference of Writers and Artists in late October, Deng Xiaoping called for a continuation of the hundred flowers atmosphere, albeit with certain provisos about supporting socialism and promoting the four modernizations.

The political front was no less active and, of course, intimately related to these artistic questions. Tighter control over the Party's center by Deng Xiaoping's moderates after the Third Plenum of the Central Committee in December 1978 gave further impetus to liberalization in two ways. First, the Party leadership wanted the intellectuals' support in discrediting and weeding out surviving Cultural Revolution leftists in the State and Party bureaucracies. Second, the intellectuals' best efforts were needed to spur the somewhat flagging drive for the four modernizations upon which the new leadership had staked so much. These considerations were at least partially behind many of the most prominent political developments in 1979. The rehabilitation of erstwhile rightists (both political and intellectual figures), the identification of Lin Biao and the Gang of Four as leftist deviationists rather than closet rightists, continued exposure of Cultural Revolution crimes along with reassurances of socialist legality, the growing movement against the cult of Mao—all served to reassure intellectuals that their security lay in support for the Party moderates. Similarly, Deng Xiaoping's call for an "emancipation of the mind" and his widely publicized dictum that "practice is the sole criterion of truth" were slogans designed to appeal to intellectuals just as his economic policies gave them greater importance in leading the four modernizations.

This is not to say that Chinese politics in 1979 were made solely by or for the intellectuals. The struggle within the Party, both over issues of principle and over paying off old scores, had its own causes. Nor did the ascendancy of the "moderates" make for smooth and unambiguous liberalization. Apart from stubborn rearguard action by remaining leftists and ordinary cadres' qualms about rapid abandonment of so many key Maoist policies, there were misgivings among Party administrators about too much freedom and diversity of opinion, especially when it led to criticism of their own position and privileges. So the politics of liberalization acquired a complex three dimensional character. The Party administrators appealed to the intellectuals, especially writers and artists, for support against the left. The creative intellectuals carried their attacks on leftist authoritarianism over to authoritarianism in general. The new power holders then felt threatened and retracted some of the newly extended freedoms. Thus, early in the year Deng Xiaoping defended "democracy wall" but by the fall it was shut down and the most outspoken dissidents were silenced. "Exposure" literature was welcomed when it attacked leftists and rooted out irrationalities in the system but was restricted when it questioned the system itself. Airport nudes were covered, uncovered, and covered up again. Despite more freedom of expression than at any time since 1957, intellectuals and artists were not making Chinese politics, but they were an important part of the process.

No other art form so directly reflected this connection between art and politics as did the political cartoon. The genre was hardly new in the People's Republic. Since 1949 political cartoons have been a regular feature of the Chinese press, supporting Party policies and attacking enemies both foreign and domestic. But the kind of social and political satire associated with political cartoons in the West, the ridiculing of those in power and exposure of serious problems in society, has usually been absent. As a result, Chinese cartoons have lacked the sting or bite of the pre-liberation left-wing cartoons and woodblock prints. When the cartoonist cannot draw the Emperor without clothes he becomes more propagandist than satirist. This has generally been his role in the People's Republic, although the first two "hundred flowers" campaigns showed that the talent for sharp political and social criticism had not disappeared. But neither 1957 nor 1961 saw cartoons with so much bite and so much topical relevance as the crop in 1979. The special political circumstances of that year—struggle within the Party leadership, appeals to the intellectuals, encouragement of at least a certain amount of criticism, the sense of liberation from the artistic tyranny of the Gang of Four—provided specially favorable conditions for this most irreverent of political art forms.

Starting early in the year national and regional newspapers increased their publication of cartoons both by professional and amateur artists. The former, from older artists such as Hua Junwu and Liao Bingxiung, often expressed the frustrations of creative intellectuals with political controls. The latter, from workers and students, often expressed popular complaints about living standards and work conditions. Some newspapers, such as the *People's Daily* and the *Workers' Daily*, expanded their cartoons into special supplements. The most important was *People's Daily's* "Satire and Humor" (*Feng Ci Yu Yo Mo*), four pages of foreign and domestic cartoons. By fall, leading literary and art magazines carried articles explaining the healthy, democratic nature of this art form and by the end of the year exhibitions of cartoon art were held in such major cities as Beijing, Shanghai, Sian, and Guangzhou.[1]

This greater prominence for cartoons was noteworthy in itself. But more significant was the enlarged scope of their subject matter, their elevation to a vehicle for serious social satire. Amidst the hundred flowers of the new liberalization in the arts and thinking, these stand out as the most prickly species.

Not all, however, were critical or even serious. There was

改不了期的"约会"

1. "An unbreakable date," *Gungren Ribao* (*Workers' Daily*), August 8, 1979.

also more room for light humor, amusement, or entertainment in China than there had been at any time since 1957. After all, relaxation of political controls over culture and daily life was part of the reaction against the rigors of the Cultural Revolution and in itself an important political decision. Other non-prickly cartoons were political but carried a positive message supporting accepted government goals and policies. But even here they showed some interesting changes as in the *Workers' Daily* cartoon linking technological modernization with a boy-girl romance theme (Illustration 1). The title is, "A 'date' whose time could not be changed." In the upper panels the boy tells the girl he has something to do this evening and asks to change their date. She smilingly agrees because she has something to do, too. In the bottom panel, as they bump into each other at a meeting on science and technology, each exclaims "I'm still seeing you this evening!" Shades of the Soviet tractor romances of the 1930s! But in China personal romance had been a forbidden theme under the collectivist morality of the Cultural Revolution. Now art and literature recognize the legitimacy of personal life and interests, although ideally linking them to the general social purpose.

But it is the critical cartoons that arouse the most interest, for these "thorny flowers" are what prick the conscience of a society and most clearly reveal its problems and tensions. For the last five years the Gang of Four have been favorite targets for cartoonists' wit, and bile. Of course, this castigation of the fallen radicals has had official support but it has been more than a campaign orchestrated from higher up. It has also been a genuine catharsis for the resentment felt by intellectuals (and artists) over how they were treated during the period of leftist predominance and for their fear of its revival. The identification of the Gang as leftists and the campaign against their "remaining poison" allowed cartoonists to zero in on present-day leftists, not just the ghosts of the Cultural Revolution.

This anti-leftist campaign put some interesting new twists on the reversal of political verdicts from the Cultural Revolution. The radicals were now condemned, or ridiculed, not just for their tyranny, fanaticism, and impracticality but also for dogmatism and conservatism. In many of the cartoons it is the radicals who, by clinging to outworn dogmas and especially "textualism" (*benbenjuyi*), are the real conservatives who obstruct change and modernization. Ironically, the reverence for texts and neglect of practice with which surviving Maoists are now charged was one of Mao's favorite criticisms of his opponents. It shows that just who is a dogmatic conservative depends very much on the political point of view. In 1979 that viewpoint emphasized economic progress and a general loosening of collectivist restraints. Thus a favorite symbol of the leftist conservative mentality was the Party member with a pigtail hidden under his cadre cap. Lizo Bingxiung shows one blowing his top when exposed to a magazine with a picture of a couple kissing (Illustration 2). The issue of sexual morality, or prudery, was a good one for drawing attention to similarities in Maoist and traditional thinking. Other cartoons extended it to other spheres but it is worth noting that, compared to the vitriolic exuberance of the wall newspaper caricatures of the Gang of Four, most of these new anti-leftists cartoons were relatively restrained. For example, a smilingly complacent cadre in an "always leftist" revolving chair represented those opportunists who followed the left line through all the twists and turns of the Cultural Revolution decade. Or a boatload of earnest rowers all crowded to the left-side of a boat about to capsize from the imbalance satirized

2. Liao Bingxiung, "Explosion," Gwangzhou Cartoon Exhibition, December 1979.

the prevalent belief that it was safer to lean to the left rather than the right. Another cartoon, appearing in *Workers Daily* in early summer, raised some more sinister aspects of the leftist deviation (Illustration 3). It showed a dogmatic cadre who leans so far to the left he almost falls down but he refuses the hand of his straight standing comrade because, "You are leaning to the right." The upright cadre has a book clearly labeled "Marxism-Leninism" under his arm. The left deviationist has a worn-out volume without a recognizable title, but readers might guess whose writings it represents, particularly in the context of the campaign against cadres who insist that whatever Mao said was right and whatever he did not say cannot be right. He also carries a capitalist hat to "cap" his opponents as capitalists and the leftist club to beat those who do not agree with him.

The club became a frequent symbol for the violence and oppression of the fanatical left, something on which intellectuals were very sensitive. Huang Weichiang shows two of these animated clubs mourning their departed master, "The Soul of the Extreme Left" (Illustration 4). A more chilling and less humorous reminder of leftist oppression and the fear of leftist remnants waiting to get back at their critics came from the "explosive" pen of the older cartoonist Liao Bingxiung (Illustration 5). It shows a wild-eyed leftist fanatic going through "works that criticize Lin Biao and the Gang of Four" and recording the names and offenses of their authors. His copy book has the caption "Repay good for good; repay evil for evil; what still has not been repaid; the time has just not yet come." Behind him stands the "extreme left" club, broken but repaired for future use. On the wall hang pictures of Lin Biao and Jiang Qing. The "loyalty" of the red heart (the original is in color) can only remind viewers of the cult of loyalty towards Mao which the left had fostered.

For the intellectuals and artists who, like Liao Bingxiung, had suffered under the Gang of Four this was a crucial issue. How could the crimes and persecutions of the Cultural Revolution be understood, and how could they be prevented from reocccuring? Therefore, when the Party mounted a nationwide campaign over the particularly cruel persecution and eventual execution of an anti-leftist female cadre, Jang Zhisin, in Manchuria, it stimulated art which was not always limited to the approved purposes of attacking the Gang of Four and remaining

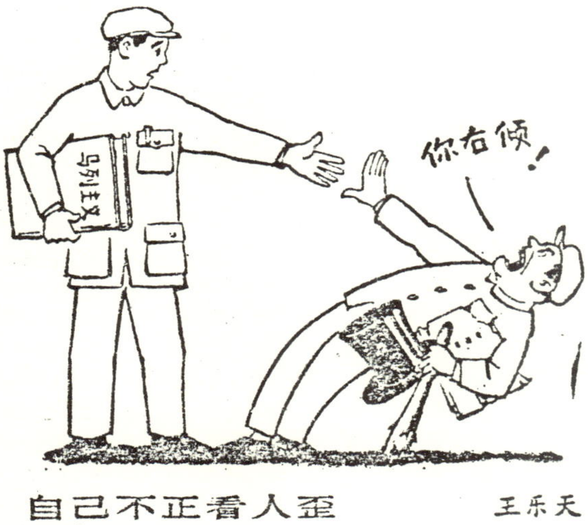

3. Wang Dungtien, "When you are not upright you see others as deviant," *Gungren Ribao* (*Workers Daily*), July 24, 1979.

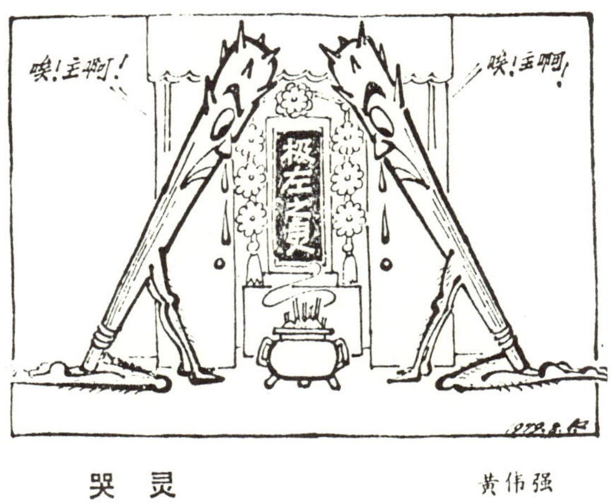

4. Huang Weichiang, "Mourning," Gwangzhou Cartoon Exhibition, December 1979.

5. Liao Bingxiung, "One more record," *Jian Hua* (*Sword Flowers*), Gwangzhou, November 1979.

7. Jang Kaisi, "Locked up," *Gungren Ribao* (*Workers Daily*), August 15, 1979.

6. Guo Changxin, "When she was alive we were friends," *Fung Ci Yu Yo Muo* (*Satire and Humor*), *Renmin Ribao* (*Peoples Daily*), August 20, 1979.

leftists. Much of the Jang Zhisin commemorative art was sentimental kitsch.[2] A wistful, rather delicate young girl fallen among flowers tinged with her blood. Or a martyr ascending through rose colored clouds to a Marxist heaven. But some of it was very moving and very powerful. In a woodcut which was reproduced in the *People's Daily* cartoon supplement, a shamefaced cadre wearing a black arm band for Jang Zhisin covers his face while the accompanying poems reads (Illustration 6):

Earth produces grains in abundance
Some people claim the credit
Now that things have taken a turn
They say when she was alive we were friends
If you seek the true face
Only heaven knows.

The message is plain, and embarrassing for those cadres who made the transition from the Cultural Revolution to the new era. Where were they when such crimes were being committed? Why didn't they speak out then, "when she was alive"? The woodcut itself in its stark black color and strong, simple lines is reminiscent of the Lu Xun inspired social protest woodcuts of the 1930s. It is not "funny paper" stuff.

So Jang Zhisin became a symbol for protest minded intellectuals, with implications for present authoritarianism as well as past crimes. The exhibition of cartoon art held in Gwangzhou in December was dedicated to the "memory of comrade Jang Zhisin" with a mock tombstone near the entrance. On the tombstone was a mirror with an invitation for all Party members to look in it and see how they measured up to her standards of truth and courage. The exhibition itself castigated present bureaucratic and authoritarian cadres as much as the discredited radicals.

Indeed, for artists and intellectuals authorized attacks on leftist autoritarianism led to issues of freedom and democracy in general. One area particularly close to their hearts was political control over the arts. More than one cartoon has shown the artist or writer as a caged bird, fed and protected by the Party, but not allowed his freedom (Illustration 7). Here his keeper says, "Release you? I think I am taking care of you!" In 1979 cartoonists were not alone in demanding less care and more creative freedom.

8. Tan Yungdao, ''Management,'' *Jian Hua* (*Sword Flowers*), Gwangzhou, November 1979.

9. Hua Junwu, ''What I say goes,'' *Chinese Literature,* 1979.

10. Hua Junwu, ''The tiger's rump,'' *Jian Hua* (*Sword Flowers*), Gwangzhou, November 1979.

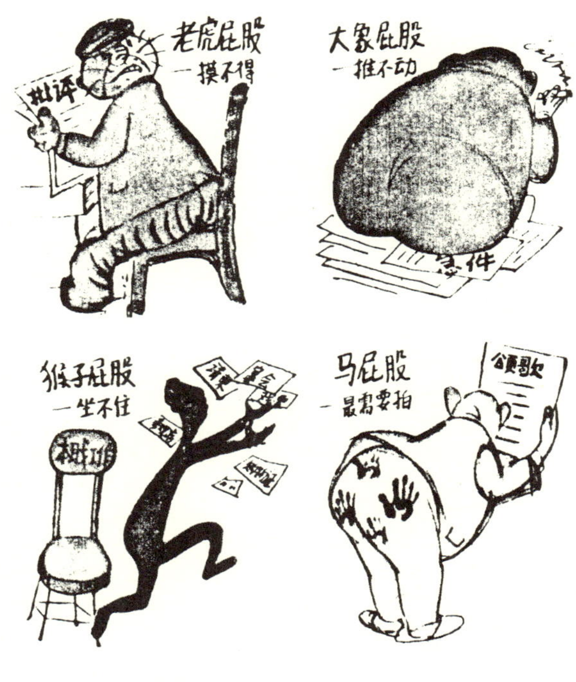

11. Wang Mi, ''Bureaucratic rumps,'' *Feng Ci Yu Yo Muo* (*Satire and Humor*), *Renmin Ribao* (*Peoples Daily*), November 20, 1979.

12. Hua Junwu, "Comparative Slowness," *Feng Ci Yu Yo Muo* (*Satire and Humor*), *Renmin Ribao* (*Peoples Daily*), November 20, 1979.

They also took up demands for more democracy and less authoritarianism from other groups in society. For instance, Tan Yungdao drew a four panel cartoon showing a Party boss' reactions to demands for factory democracy (Illustration 8). First he tears in half the worker's petition for democracy (in Chinese, "people as boss") saying, "You are people, I am boss." He continues, "You want democracy for the proletariat? Well, you represent the capitalist class." He puts a capitalist hat on the worker and concludes, "not going along with me is to oppose the Party."

Such unflattering portraits of Party administrators were numerous. Some of the most interesting might be called a bureaucratic bestiary or, because many drew on the common proverb about not daring to touch the tiger's rump, might be better termed a bureaucratic rumpology. The most famous of these cartoons by the Beijing cartoonist Hua Junwu shows a tiger in Party cadre uniform arrogantly strutting and defying anyone to criticize him (to touch his rump) (Illustration 9). Run in the *People's Daily,* this cartoon was known throughout China.[3] Interestingly, this phrase about the tiger's rump was used by Mao in criticizing Party bureaucrats. In the post-Mao era it is apparently still relevant. Hua Junwu brings out one of the reasons why in another cartoon lampooning the servile careerists who support bossism in the Party (Illustration 10). The long tongued smiling cadre says, "The tiger's rump cannot be touched, but it can be licked."

Extending this rumpology beyond authoritarianism to other defects in cadre leadership, in November Wang Mi published his "Bureaucrats' Rumps" in the *People's Daily* (Illustration 11). The tiger's rump can't be touched—he won't tolerate criticism. The hippopotamus' rump can't be moved—he sits on urgent work. The monkey's rump can't sit still—he abandons his own work to flit about with incidentals. The horse's rump needs a lot of patting—he wants praise from his subordinates. Hardly a flattering picture of Party leadership in action but the top leaders also have an interest in exposing these abuses and inefficiencies among cadres. Mao, himself, had tried a similar cure for bureaucratism, inefficiency and separation from the masses during the first hundred flowers campaign and had used very different medicine for the same ailments in the Cultural Revolution. These cartoons are evidence that the disease has not been cured. Although the post-Mao leadership seems to be less concerned with socialist principles than with economic results, it is trying just as hard to eliminate these obstacles to progress. To follow the bestiary a little further, Hua Junwu's tea-drinking, cigarette smoking and newspaper reading cadres on snail back represent the speed with which they get things done (Illustration 12).

From the workers' point of view, indolent bureaucrats not only retard modernization but pass more of the burden on to those who work. A *Workers' Daily* cartoon has three bosses supervising two straining workers (Illustration 13). It takes the Maoist injunction "Deeply penetrate to the front lines" as its ironic title. The frustrations of other sections of the population with bureaucratic inefficiency and leftist dogmatism are seen in Liu Yung's *People's Daily* cartoon "Preventing 'individual prominence' " (Illustration 14). This was one of the leftist pieties during the Cultural Revolution and apparently it has not entirely disappeared. The Party cadre here makes sure that all runners keep the same pace.

This theme of obstacles to modernization extends beyond criticisms of Party cadres to general social problems which are revealed in more graphic detail than ever before in the People's Republic. Laziness, sloppy work, waste, lack of public spirit, bad manners, crime and public indifference to it are all exposed. One cartoon that brings together exposure of social evils with criticism of bureaucratic inefficiency again comes from the sharp pen of Hua Junwu (Illustration 15). As a policeman leads away a criminal arrested for graft, a cadre squanders a bag of gold labelled, "National property, the blood & sweat of the people." The caption reads "Graft is a crime; waste is unstopped." This cartoon is in the context of several well publicized cases of Party cadres being involved in large scale embezzlement of public funds. Ordinary crimes and bad habits were satirized but the sharpest barbs seemed to be aimed at those in positions of authority.

For instance, there are innumerable cartoons on the prevalence of bribery and corruption in the bureaucracy. Some of the wittiest went back to the Party's guerrilla war heritage for ironic contrast (Illustration 16). In "storming the pass," representatives of one unit use a cigarette machine gun and liquor bottle grenades in their battle to get needed supplies or authorization from another unit. Another common tactic was to show the Party cadre as a traditional deity, the god of wealth, or in this case the multi-armed Buddha (Illustration 17), who can distribute the good things of the new society such as money, political power, job assignments, watches, T.V. sets. Of course, he must be prayed to and given offerings.

Beyond corruption and inefficiency as obstacles to modernization, there is the protest against favoritism and privilege. This may be the sharpest criticism of all in a society dedicated to equality. A *People's Daily* cartoon in October showed how the fish (in America, the "pie") is cut in China (Illustration 18). A large slice for relatives, a large slice for leaders, another for oneself, and one for delegates. Then when only the head and tail remain it is hung up with a sign offering fish for sale to the general public. Other cartoons show cadres enjoying the good life and its material goods. Television sets are especially prominent, along with food, cigarettes and liquor. But not all corruption is in material goods. The *Workers' Daily* ran a four-panel

13. Liu Kedung, ''Deeply penetrate to the front lines,'' *Gungren Ribao* (*Workers Daily*), August 10, 1979.

14. Lin Yung, ''Preventing 'individual prominence,' '' *Feng Ci Yu Yo Muo* (*Satire and Humor*), *Renmin Ribao* (*Peoples Daily*), August 20, 1979.

15. Hua Junwu, ''Corruption is a crime; waste goes unstopped,'' *Feng Ci Yu Yo Muo* (*Satire and Humor*), *Renmin Ribao* (*Peoples Daily*), August 20, 1979.

16. Jang Jungjin, ''Storming the pass,'' *Feng Ci Yu Yo Muo* (*Satire and Humor*), *Renmin Ribao* (*Peoples Daily*), September 20, 1979.

17. Hua Keguan, ''The many-armed Buddha,'' *Gungren Ribao* (*Workers Daily*), August 22, 1979.

18. *Feng Ci Yu Yo Muo* (*Satire and Humor*), October 20, 1979.

strip showing how proletarian fraternity breaks down in a hierarchical society (Illustration 19). At first two workers embrace each other, then when one returns to the factory as department head he still extends his hand to his comrade. But when he is section head he has only a cursory wave and a grunt for his former workmate. Finally, the worker remains silent as a sign announces the inspection tour of bureau chief Wang. Friendship and solidarity give way to power and position.

The importance of personal connections with those in positions of power for getting ahead is shown in another cartoon called "Three Faces" (Illustration 20). When a young job applicant brings a letter of introduction to a Party cadre and announces that, "My father is the Provincial Committee Secretary . . ." the boss rises from his chair to greet him with a smiling face. But as he goes on to add ". . . Provincial Committee Secretary's wife's colleague's fellow classmate," the smile fades and indifference replaces the warm welcome when he thought this youth well connected with those in high position. The cartoon resembles the play, "Supposing I Were Real?," which was something of a sensation in 1979 for it told how an imposter gained all kinds of favors and privileges by pretending to be the son of a high ranking Party leader. When finally exposed his only defense was, "What if I were real?" Would that have justified the favoritism?

Complaints about favoritism for friends and relatives of the elite, about getting ahead through personal connections or what the Chinese call "going through the back door," were not new but in the last few years they have surfaced with a vengeance. There is an ironic congruence here between these cartoonists, who were opposed to the former tyranny of the left, and the Cultural Revolutionaries' original complaints about privilege for Party autocrats. These artists may oppose the radicals in many areas, and they have been quick to note that in power the radicals also took care of their own, but on the specific issue of

19. *Gungren Ribao*, January 24, 1980.

20. *Da Gung Bao* (HK) reprinted from *Renmin Ribao*, December 1, 1979.

和尚与秃子对话

王树忱

——会念经吗？
——不会！
——能敲木鱼吗？
——不能！
——凭什么当和尚？
——秃头！
——怎么进来的？
——后门！

21. Wang Shukang, "Dialogue between a monk and a baldy," *Feng Ci Yu Yo Muo* (*Satire and Humor*), *Renmin Ribao* (*Peoples Daily*), October 20, 1979.

"the back door" dissident intellectuals and Maoist radicals share a common complaint. So does the new Party leadership, which does not want nepotism inhibiting the drive for modernization. Still, so long as the Party apparatus has a monopoly of power and so long as individual cadres are tempted to use that power for private ends, such phenomena as that satirized in Wang Shukang's "Dialogue between a Monk and a Baldy" will remain (Illustration 21). The monk asks "baldy" (a Party cadre also seated on a prayer mat with a shaven head like a monk) "Can you chant the sutras?" "No." "Can you beat the wooden fish?" "No." "On what did you get to be a monk?" "As a bald head." "How did you get in?" "The back door."

The boldest and most explicit warning about the net effect of all these abuses of power comes from Liao Bingxiung who in an article in *Fine Arts* commented that restoring feudal attitudes was a greater danger to socialist society than any surviving bourgeois influences.[4] He illustrated this in a cartoon for last December's exhibition in Gwangzhou (Illustration 22). A Party boss rides in a sedan chair born by cadres on poles reading "trumpeting praises and patting the horse's rump." They in turn are borne by lower cadres and all receive promotions, assignments and favors from higher up. The caption reads "Everybody very Happy." The accompanying text is in somber

皆大欢喜 廖冰兄

22. Liao Bingxiung, "Everybody very happy," *Jian Hua* (*Sword Flowers*), Gwangzhou, November 1979.

contrast to the amusing picture. "Because the leaders have to ride in a sedan chair, there are people who have to carry a sedan chair. Those who ride are happy, those who carry get the grease from it. Important people also carry, they also then ride in sedan chairs. One layer carries another layer. It seems like the old bureaucracy. If this kind of unhealthy phenomenon is not eliminated, the fate of the nation is in peril."

How seriously the leadership will take such warnings and how much it can do about the problems remains to be seen. The immediate question for Deng Xiaoping and company seems to have been how far they could let such criticisms go before they started to call into question the legitimacy of Party leadership and socialist society. By the end of 1979 the tentative answer was no further. As "Democracy Wall" was closed and the most outspoken dissidents put away, the tone of China's political cartoons started to change. Criticisms of inefficiencies and exposure of social problems continued. So did some digs at cadres but the attacks on cadres in general diminished in number and intensity. On the issue of democracy, the last issue of *The People's Daily's* "Satire and Humor" for 1979 ran a cartoon on "Two Authoritarians" (Illustration 23). One shows a bureaucrat telling his audience "What democracy? What I say goes." The second has a sloppy long-haired dissident in Western-style clothes writing a wall poster "What I say goes, only then it is democracy." The leadership was condemning both extremes and trying to find a road down the middle. But by early 1980, if the cartoons are any guide, they were veering away from open criticism in favor of order and authority. Dissidents labelled "anarchists" and "extreme individualists," were shown as selfish, bigoted, and irresponsible. The situation was summed up in a cartoon of a wrecker trying to tear down the gate of socialist democracy so that his two enormous bags of extreme individualism and anarchism could fit through. He is being stopped by a worker (Illustration 24).

Perhaps the gates of possible democracy in China are not wide enough to admit much more diversity of opinion or criticism of the system at present. The rehabilitation of Liu Shaochi and cancelling of wall newspaper type of mass criticism does not augur well for further experiments with freedom of speech and criticism. But the renewed Campaign against the Gang of Four makes the Party sensitive to charges of perpetuating the kind of authoritarianism and "cultural dictatorship" which was one of the fallen radicals' main crimes. More important in the long run, the present leadership will need the intellectuals and need to encourage more "emancipation of the mind" if China is

24. Wang Jeji, "Won't go in," *Feng Ci Yu Yo Muo* (*Satire and Humor*), *Renmin Ribao*, January 20, 1980.

23. "Two authoritarians," *Feng Ci Yu Yo Muo* (*Satire and Humor*), *Renmin Ribao* (*Peoples Daily*), December 20, 1979.

25. Tan Yungdao, "Thorny flowers," Cartoon exhibition, Gwangzhou, December 1979.

to have rapid technological and economic progress. Cartoons remain a potent weapon for stimulating thought and exposing abuses. There may not be another crop to compare with the "thorny flowers" of 1979 for some time, but they should not all wither. The society, and especially the Party, needs its internal critics. Some of the sharpest wield cartoonists' pens.

One final cartoon may best sum up the situation (Illustration 25). In it a genial Party cadre lifts various art flowers into the vase of "one hundred blooming flowers." Ink painting, oil painting, posters—all go nicely. But when he comes to pick up cartoons his fingers are pricked by the sharp thorns. The Party can, of course, cultivate thornless cartoons but they will lose their most important function in satirizing the worst defects in the new society. It might be better if the Party grew a thicker skin and endured some thorns among the new hundred flowers.

Notes

1. The author attended, and was allowed to photograph at, the Guangzhou exhibition in December. Held in a large hall at the Cultural Park, it drew large crowds.
2. A sample of these may be found in the leading art journal *Mei Shu Yue Kan* (*Fine Arts Monthly*), Beijing, September and October, 1979.
3. Another version of it was shown in the Guangzhou exhibition. In it a Party boss is bawling out a worker for putting up a cartoon about touching the tiger's rump. The bureaucrat is confounded when the worker shows him the same cartoon published in *Peoples Daily*.
4. *Mei Shu* (*Fine Arts*), Guangzhou, vol. 1, no. 1, December 1979.

Rural Development, Agrarian Structure and the County in China

by Mitch Meisner and Marc Blecher

Introduction*

In 1975, elements in the Chinese leadership attempted to establish a comprehensive policy line for rural development. Issued as a set of guidelines for setting up "Dazhai-type counties," the program, publicized most notably in Hua Guofeng's speech at the First National Conference on Learning from Dazhai in Agriculture, reinterpreted and extended on a general level a set of policies and "experiences" that had been in evidence in Dazhai and Xiyang since the Cultural Revolution, and had grown out of earlier experiments with collective economic forms since the formation of the people's communes. A close look at these documents, especially at Hua's six-point program for building Dazhai-type counties, shows a general policy that incorporated many on-going tensions of the turbulent Cultural Revolution decade and may be considered an attempted compromise among existing positions, though, in light of present perspectives, with a radical "lean."

The years since Mao's death have seen the rapid dismantlement of this program. Undercurrents of indirect criticism which began to appear in 1977 built gradually into open, direct attacks by late 1978, which in turn grew in severity through early 1981, by which time the Dazhai-Xiyang model had been almost fully repudiated. Criticism touched all of the substantive features associated with the Dazhai-Xiyang program: brigade-level accounting, its methods of allocating work-points and grain, collective cultivation of private plots, and collective provision of housing and various social services. Aspects of Xiyang's economic record were also called into question: it was accused of inefficient and wasteful planning and management of large scale infrastructure projects and industrial enterprises, and its falsification of grain production statistics from 1973 to 1977 was revealed. Chen Yonggui, the famous Dazhai brigade secretary who, in connection with the ascendance of Dazhai and Xiyang, catapulted to a Vice-Premiership, was accused of abuses like nepotism, favoritism and subjectivism, and was dismissed from all his posts.[1]

Dazhai's and Xiyang's own experiences in rural development since 1967, and the attempts to generalize them into a national program, involved a structural emphasis on the role of the county in the administration of and political leadership over rural development. In this article we will examine the reasons for this emphasis on the county, the various substantive aspects of rural development policy with which it was associated in the Dazhai/Xiyang model, the implications of its role for social (including class) relations and conflict in rural China, and its fate in the post-Mao years as the Dazhai/Xiyang model has come under attack. We will argue that the county continues to today to play a key role in rural development administration. But the scope for *political* leadership over rural development emanating from the county, especially from the county party committee, has been sharply circumscribed. The county is now to be strictly limited in its capacity to intervene in the economic affairs of the collective units at the commune level and below, especially in carrying out redistributive policies among them. This change resonates to the declining importance in post-Mao China of political considerations and power in almost all spheres of social cultural and economic activity, including socialist productive relations such as ownership, organization, planning, regulation, distribution, and redistribution.[2]

It is still an open question whether or not decreased leeway for politically-motivated decision-making by the county Party Committee and collective-sector allies (especially brigade party branch committees) implies a reversal in rural "class relations" in development, as might be suggested by analogies with earlier periods. In fact, to some persons in political power now, the relatively explicit attempt by the 1975 program of establishing Dazhai-type counties that would link a fairly strong class line to other redistributive elements was one of the problematical elements in that policy formulation, tying it fatally to the past.

Few Western scholars have examined closely the relationship since 1949 between modes of production in the local, rural economy and class relations. Managing a developing economy which is rooted in the daily and seasonal work of agrarian settlements, and is rapidly responding to industrialization and

* An earlier version of this article was presented in November 1979 at the Conference on China's New Development Strategy, sponsored by the Institute of Development Studies of the University of Sussex, England. We thank Gordon White and Jack Gray, the conference organizers, for inviting us to present our work there and together with the numerous conference participants, for providing three of the most stimulating days we can remember. A different version of this article will be published in the volume from that conference: Gordon White and Jack Gray, eds., *China's New Development Strategy* (London: Academic Press). Our thanks to Academic Press for permission to publish the article here.

other modernizing forces—all within a conflictual socialist framework—is a difficult task. There are no historic formulae, no simple solutions straddling the consideration of economic efficiency, social equality and popular power. The work of Mark Selden (1971) on the "mass line" in the administration of border region government and economy in the Yan'an period has been helpful, as has the pathbreaking political analysis by Franz Schurmann (1968) of the social implications of inner-party conflict in the 1950s and 60s.[3] In particular, Schurmann's work on alternative forms of decentralization of political and economic administration may shed light on the social implications of current shifts. We will consider major outlines of Schurmann's analysis, ascribing class implications to the decentralization debates of 1957, in more detail later. However, the earlier lines of class analysis may not be so useful for changes originating in today's political economy. We shall argue that the 1975 Xiyang-Dazhai program, at least in its ideal design, pushed certain class issues, particularly those involving inequality of collective units and the loci of political power, quite far. In the China of the 1970s and 1980s such policies may not have been practicable and rested perhaps on unworkable or outdated conceptions of class relations and class conflict.

The Structural Significance of the County

Several major questions arose when the Chinese revolution achieved state power: problems of social relations and economic development posed questions for the form of organization of the nascent Communist governmental and administrative system. The nature of the state and its involvement in social-economic management and development issues of urban-rural and industrial-agricultural institutions, including the degree and speed with which collective forms would take precedence over private ownership, were intertwined with and had obvious implications for changing social relations. Issues of relations among old and new rural strata (and also among the latter themselves) emerged from land reform, from ensuing rural-urban stratification, and eventually, from divisions among richer and poorer collective communities.

In the summer of 1955, Mao Zedong successfully pushed through a policy of full-scale agricultural collectivization. But given the rapid pace of that change, tensions having to do with size and management of the collective unit, productive relations within the collective economy, and the relation of the collectives to surviving private endeavors remained. These fundamental tensions in development policy and socio-economic structure continued to pose problems for evolving units of state administration such as the county.

Historical Background

The county has been an important unit of basic territorial government since Imperial times, and throughout the Nationalist and Communist periods. In the past, longevity may have been the county's greatest attribute, but in the 1970s as a focal point of development efforts, the county acquired new functions and renewed significance.[4]

County government is a structured meeting between state and society. In the Imperial period, the county was the lowest level of direct governance and the primary point of contact with rural society. The county magistrate supervised the collection of taxes, adjudicated local civil and criminal cases, and maintained public order and welfare. Effectiveness of county administration, however, did not rest simply on its own operations. The powers of the magistrate, a civil official assigned from outside, were reinforced by a system of local social and economic power in which local land-holding gentry sought to secure their interests.

The orbit of the gentry reached to the county capital, but tended in the main to connect through a series of social pathways that ran to the basic "standard marketing towns" (later urban centers of the enlarged townships or *da xiang* in the 1950s). The local market towns were common crossroads for members of all rural strata and special meeting places for the gentry.[5] The gentry helped to arrange large-scale water control projects, public (and private) defense and relief; and local elites generally held the reins (with regional variations) of clan-based social networks that cut vertically through class divisions. By these civic and social webs of affiliation and control, the labor and loyalty of ordinary peasant-producers were harnessed by rural elites.

Peasant village communities were not autonomous, nor were poor peasants easily unified. There were no significant common village landholdings or other public goods, for example, and as private small-holders or tenants, peasants could not easily affiliate on a class basis. To be successful, then, peasant movements needed the adherence of portions of the local gentry and other mobile or lumpen classes, the suspension of local authority structures, or the protection of an outside armed force. It was the structural position of the peasantry in rural society which Mao (1927) was trying to describe when, on the basis of his investigations in Hunan province in 1926–27, he wrote:

> *A man in China is usually subjected to the domination of three systems of authority: (1) the state system (political authority), ranging from the national, provincial and county government down to that of the township; (2) the clan system (clan authority), ranging from the central ancestral temple and its branch temples down to the head of the household; and (3) the supernatural system (religious authority), ranging from the King of Hell down to the town and village gods belonging to the nether world, and from the Emperor of Heaven down to all the various gods and spirits belonging to the celestial world. As for women, in addition to being dominated by these three systems of authority, they are also dominated by the men (the authority of the husband). These four authorities—political, clan, religious and masculine—are the embodiment of the whole feudal-patriarchal system and ideology, and are the four thick ropes binding the Chinese people, particularly the peasants.*

Attacking these hegemonic networks during the protracted rural revolutionary struggle, the Communist Party managed to replace customary rural authorities at the county level and below with its own offices and armed power. This provided the basis for fundamental restructuring of rural society and economy through the destruction of the landed gentry and a more egalitarian division of landed property and other agricultural assets. After land reform, a series of collectivization measures led within a decade to the formation of a large, integrating unit of rural collective economy and government, the people's commune.

The County After Collectivization

During the Chinese Revolution, both before and after 1949, the county continued to be a major unit of political and administrative control in Chinese rural society. The Communist Party supervised land reform from the county and its subunits. County government became thoroughly bound up in rapid successions of economic development strategies linked to societal transformation. The relation of specific institutional arrangements and development programs has been a subject of great interest.[6]

After much experimentation with the composition of units of rural government and collective ownership, the people's commune settled down by 1961 to about the size of the former enlarged township, and the county remaining entirely a unit of the state.[7] The commune, which incorporated the former township government, remains *partly* a unit of state administration. Its highest ranking (i.e., commune-*level*) officials are civil servants appointed, ranked, and paid by the *state*. But the commune-level administration is at the same time the highest of a three-tiered system of *collective* rural ownership. Thus, though commune-level administration carries out many normal governmental functions such as financial administrations, local marketing, management of schools and medical facilities, and local militia defense, its economic base is juridically and practically rooted in local society. The brigades and teams which comprise the commune as a whole are hamlet- or village-level collectives, and even industrial and sideline enterprises operated by the commune-level are treated as collective rather than state-run units of management and finance (although, for reasons which remain mysterious to us, for *statistical* purposes they are grouped with state-sector enterprises of all types at the county level and above). In the socialist vocabulary, the persistence of the commune system signifies the continued existence of collective ownership rather than, as in the case of industry, a higher stage in the march toward communist society of "owership by the whole people." Thus, the great bulk of the rural economy is organized within tiered units of collective ownership, whose workers—the Chinese peasants—are, significantly, called "members" (*sheyuan*) and are, more like coequal shareholders than employees, especially at the team level. The "wage" (i.e., the work-day value) of the members of a rural collective, unlike that of workers in state enterprises owned by the "whole people," varies much more directly with the rise or fall of collective profits.

If the commune, despite its partial state character and many governmental functions is in economic terms essentially an aggregation of local village collectives, the county, though small enough to have regular, immediate communications with basic levels, has always been entirely a unit of the state. The county contains both government and Party offices, but for practical purposes these have been combined under the principle of "unified leadership by the Communist Party" (though this may become subject to change). This means that the Party organization has been dominant in all decision-making at county level.

Because the county leadership is expected by higher level policy-makers to show results in program implementation that depend on its direct leadership within the area, the county has the burden of establishing an effective connection between itself and the collective, local institutions. Higher-level bodies like the province and the prefecture do not have to make such a connection. Thus, as with the county of Imperial China, the contemporary problem for the county's role in development administration is set by its location at the most sharply defined structural meeting point between institutions of state and society.[8]

The county is the major political center at the basic levels of rural society. As the heart of the Communist Party organization in the countryside, the county has been responsible for leading reforms, for medium-scale planning and project management, and for supervising routine agricultural activities carried out by the collectives. The county Party committee is in charge of overseeing the careers, education and activities of Party members and cadres at the grassroots who, though local farmers, villagers and neighbors, must observe central party discipline and view the revolution as a whole. The pre-eminence of the Party in all spheres of rural governance and of the county within the rural local Party organization has distinguished the county as the locus of political power in the countryside. This has dismayed some analysts (including many in China) who regard a super-ordinate political orientation as an irrational displacement of more useful administrative or technical matters and market forces.[9]

The county as a unit of state government has a series of administrative/technical bureaus (*jü*) and sub-bureaus (*Ke*, or "sections") for dealing with subject matter ranging from agrarian science and technology to finance and trade, and important technical staff offices within the county executive itself. The counties are in charge of making available to lower-level units resources allocated from the greater economy [10]

Students of Chinese development administration have wondered about the degree to which the county enjoys autonomy within its sphere of operations. Of course county cadres are subject to supervision from higher authorities both in policy matters and in career terms. Top county officials apparently are ranked in the State civil service according to the size and economic strength of the county.[11] Falkenheim argues that province-level authorities make decisions and county leaders carry them out: the county cannot on the whole be understood as a unit expressing local interest. The degree of autonomy of the county may depend on the issue. Major campaigns based on central policy decisions or special economic efforts such as agricultural mechanization depend considerably on orders and inputs from above.[12] For example, according to one former county official,

> *In 1971 [our] county set up electrical industries, producing motors and transformers, as well as radio components. The county didn't really push this, but the province had called on every county to get into production of electrical items, so we did a little. So no, it wasn't the county's idea to go into production of electrical items; but given that the province called on them to do so, it was their idea to produce the transformers, of which we couldn't get enough through unified distribution.*[13]

In this case the county followed a production decision from above, at the same time serving its own need for materials that could not be acquired from outside.

The activities of the county in local development reflect the degree to which county leaders act as administrators of central policies to the broad society. In his very useful treatment of pre-Cultural Revolution politics, B. Y. Ahn discusses Chinese criticism of the county for functioning mainly as a "conveying center" of tasks set at higher levels. In turn, the county leaders spent much time reporting to provincial/prefectural supervisors on the implementation of their orders. According to one report, leading cadres of YingKou County in Liaoning Province spent two-thirds of their time conferring at the provincial or prefectural levels.[14]

One particularly explicit self-criticism published in the *People's Daily* in 1965 states:

> *The [county] committee also discussed the problems of what were called 'hard' and 'soft' tasks. A 'hard' task refers to a task which is required to attain certain targets as set by the leading organ at a higher level, while a 'soft' task refers to the task originating from the demand of the peasant masses . . . . Formerly, two different attitudes were adopted toward these two tasks. The 'hard' task was firmly fulfilled, while the 'soft' task might be fulfilled or left unfulfilled.*[15]

In contrast, the strongest case made for county autonomy, rooted in what she sees as a growing material base or near autarky, was made by Audrey Donnithorne, describing the possibility of a "cellular economy" at county level.[16]

There is no question but that the complexity of county government, the size of the rural economy partly under its purview (by virtue of the dramatic growth of rural industry), and the possible opportunities for intervention into the collective sector available to it, all give the county a significant position in Chinese rural development today. Yet, even this statement must be qualified in light of current adjustments. For example, one may point to the overall growth of both state-owned industry located in or directly managed by the county, as well as commune and brigade-run industry within the collective sector, and under the supervision of a branch of the county government as evidence of the growing weight of a diversified county-level economic establishment.[17] But recent changes in state policy also suggest that from the county's point of view some of the more autonomous industrial developments at and below the county level may be disappearing. For example, in Shulu County, various forms of collective or "county-run collective enterprises" (not speaking of those strictly within the people's commune sector) had at least until 1979 contributed some of their profits to the use of vertically organized bureaus (such as the Second Light Industry Bureau) or to an "extra-budgetary fund" outside the purview of the higher-level state fiscal and planning authorities. Such income had been invested by county government authorities in industry or agricultural support projects. A major water-control project affecting the land of ten communes was thus undertaken in 1977–78 using several million yuan from an "extra-budgetary fund." Such unattached monies had been important because many prosperous counties (and apparently at least the better-off ones) tend to contribute to the provincial (or higher) levels a larger sum in industrial and other income from taxes and profits than they get back for expenditures. But in interviews in 1979, Shijiazhuang prefecture officials outlined new reforms which would have the effect of bringing these untied monies under prefectural control. There is a tendency to leave more profits in the hands of local level enterprises, a decentralizing move that may also take away from the power of county officials. This shift was started experimentally in Sichuan under the current Prime Minister, Zhao Ziyang, and is now being generalized. But in this change, though enterprise autonomy in the locality may benefit considerably, the powers granted to factories are essentially opposed to those that might otherwise be enjoyed by local *state* authorities at the county level. In other words, the shift of control may be up to higher levels or down to the enterprise, the latter a structural move resembling what Schurmann called Decentralization I.

Also, current attempts within the industrial sector to rationalize and standardize the production of machinery—including, importantly, agricultural machinery—also suggest that production initiatives undertaken at county level in a blaze of publicity in the 1970s are being centralized. The recent attack on Xiyang County for the economic failure and continuing "coverup" of the problems at its hand tractor factory may in part be related to political attacks against the post-Cultural Revolution leadership of the model county and Jinzhong prefecture. But we found examples of similar critiques and moves toward specialization, rationalization, and centralization in farm machinery manufacture in both Hebei and Jiangsu provinces.[18] In some cases, commune and brigade enterprises were being integrated into county machinery enterprises as parts subcontractors; in others, independent manufacturing efforts (of tractors, for example) were being closed down, closely supervised for specifications, or integrated as specialized subsidiaries to enterprises which design and supply farm machinery to a wider region.

Moreover, in terms of budgetary and other financial relations with the province and the center, the county is scarcely autonomous. The county government collects revenues according to quotas set by the higher levels of the state and makes expenditures only in categories and amounts fixed and allocated by those same higher levels. It undercollects or overspends only at the peril of incurring financial penalties.[19] As mentioned above, untied sources of funds seem to be disappearing under current policies. In addition, though the industrial base at the county level has grown considerably, the profits on the whole have flowed upward into higher level state coffers. The third session of the Fifth National People's Congress has announced its intention, unclear in precise form as yet, to reform this system by requiring state-run enterprises to remit only taxes, but not profits, to the higher levels of the state. On the other hand, the very recent (March 1981) and still sketchily described attempt by the state to get central control over excess funds through a bond issue and a requirement that state-sector (and perhaps even rural collective-sector) units purchase a certain quota of them suggests that at least some influential state leaders and economic planners are unwilling to give up central control over locally- (in many cases, county-) generated surpluses.

The quality of county administration may be important in helping along an ever more important county and commune industrial base, but such responsibility does not necessarily constitute a case for growing autonomy; as we have suggested, the apparent direction at present seems to be toward enveloping the county in an increasingly interdependent set of relationships rooted in a more complex, widely integrated structure of industrial planning and production.

The County as Focal Point of Development

All issues surrounding the relation of county to society and to upper levels of the State appeared weightier in the fall of 1975 when a month-long conference, convened first in Xiyang County, Shanxi Province and then in Beijing, attempted to focus future Chinese agricultural development around a specific county model. The major thrust of this conference was to focus the endeavors of lower-level collective units in an increasingly county-centered development effort and to link that effort with a comprehensive national drive to increase rural mechanization. The movement to build so-called "Dazhai-type counties," based on the phenomenal growth of Xiyang county, the home of the national model Dazhai brigade and the first county dubbed "Dazhai-type," dated on a national level from the North China Agricultural Conference of 1970. But never before had the specific criteria of the model been grouped together and made so explicit.

It should be noted that Chairman Hua Guofeng's speech at the 1975 conference placed a concurrent emphasis on the "great task of mechanizing agriculture"—to be accomplished in the main by national (and provincial) authorities. But agricultural mechanization was to be related both to the further stimulation of local industrialization and to the growth of brigade and commune-run enterprises, while also being furthered by increased investments from within the collectives of labor and other resources in farmland capital construction and infrastructural development.[20]

In his address, Hua projected that by 1980, at least one-third of all counties in China should be "Dazhai-type." What was a Dazhai-type county? Hua listed six criteria:

- 1. A county Party committee leadership core that firmly grasps the Party's line and policy and is united in struggle.
- 2. Established the dominant class power of the poor and lower-middle peasants, able to struggle resolutely against bourgeois activities and to exercise effective supervision and reform measures over class enemies.
- 3. Cadres at the three levels of county, commune, and brigade who like Xiyang cadres persevere in participating in collective production labor.
- 4. Rapid development and sizeable results in basic farm field construction, agricultural mechanization, and scientific cultivation.
- 5. Collective economies expanding uninterruptedly, with production and income of poor communes and brigades attaining or surpassing those of middle-level communes and brigades in the locality.
- 6. An all-around development of agriculture, forestry, animal husbandry, sideline industries, and fisheries, a great increase in productive output insuring a big contribution to the State and for commune members, a step-by-step improvement in standard of living.

Xiyang County, in Shanxi Province's mountainous Taihang region, suffered from a short growing season, water conservancy problems and a shortage of arable land. From the fall of 1970, the Xiyang success story was promoted in China as an inspiration to rural development in all areas of the country, rich or poor. The message appeared in another wave of media publicity in the spring of 1973, and there is reason to believe that the elements identified with the Dazhai-Xiyang experience, especially since 1967, were given very high priority in development policy throughout these years, in central pronouncements at least, and in varying degrees in various localities.[21a]

Of Hua's six criteria, two concern the role of leadership, perhaps as a way of emulating Dazhai Brigade's own experience of a long-tenured, vigorous leadership "core" (i.e., Party branch committee) dedicated to unity and continuity.[21b] In a late 1973 report to a meeting held jointly by the Ministry of Agriculture and Forestry and the CCP Beijing Municipal Committee, Chen Yonggui stressed the importance of local leadership most strongly, arguing that there is a link between active leadership and maintaining the "relative stability of the work force"—the latter a key substantive goal of the 1975 program.[22]

Although in 1980 the Dazhai-Xiyang program would begin to be linked with "ultra-left" political and economic policies, the actual criteria enunciated by Hua and other leaders suggest a critique or at least a modification of some such elements. For example, emphasis on the unity of the county Party committee leadership core (i.e., its standing committee) suggests the need to promote strong political direction while guarding against factionalism, a negative legacy of Cultural Revolution politics. In addition, the growing scope of county functions, in particular responsibility for rural industrialization, suggests a concern for insuring effective executive power in the county.[23]

A second leadership criterion (third on Hua's list) calling for heavy participation in collective productive labor by county, commune and brigade cadres seemed to strike at bureaucratic elitism and the separation of the local cadres from the everyday toil of the peasants. The model Xiyang leadership had in 1967 established guidelines for such participation: 100 days per year for county cadres, 200 for commune cadres, and 300 for brigade cadres.[24] As Hua emphasized, the experience might help county leaders to deal with their inadequacies. Some county Party committee leaderships suffer from "softness," "lack of concentration," and "laziness" (*"ruan," "san,"* and *"lan"*), said Hua. In his address Hua also stated that new blood should be recruited into county Party leaderships from among basic-level activists distinguished in the movement to learn from Dazhai. These would most likely be brigade cadres who head the most dynamic unit within the commune structure. For example, Li Xishen, the county vice-secretary and *de facto* leader of Xiyang County until his dismissal in 1980, was recruited from a local brigade (Wujiaping); and Li Suoshou, the first secretary of neighboring Pingding County, was formerly Party branch secretary of Nannao Brigade in Dazhai Commune. In general, however, other evidence, both from interviews with emigres and with Chinese officials in 1979, does not suggest widespread existence of this recruitment/promotion pattern in the years that followed. It is now regarded, in fact, as a version of the Cultural Revolution practice of officials rising too precipitously—in the Chinese metaphor, like helicopters.[25]

Hua's second criterion argues for the "dominant class power of the poor and lower-middle peasants, able to struggle resolutely against bourgeois activities and to exercise effective supervision over class enemies." This points to insuring support for the growth of collective economic institutions and adherence to them as a main source of accumulation and income distribution. With an economy that still relies on manual labor, and with major investments to be made in land improvement and water conservancy (to provide a field for efficient introduction of machinery and modern inputs), the most crucial of all goals was to maintain full commitment to a stable, collectively-organized agricultural work force. Hua stated:

> *For example, we must pull back labor power who have left the area to engage in individual endeavors, organize dispersed individual craft workers, return to the collective wasteland or private plots cultivated in excess of amounts stipulated by government policy, and straighten out tendencies to neglect accumulation by distributing all and consuming all.*

But why the strong class-oriented guideline? Here the program veers to the left and suggests a very questionable analysis.

The recall or control of labor outflow is obviously not a cure-all in every type of rural environment in China, although it is held to have been crucial in the experiences of Dazhai and Xiyang themselves.[26] For example, it was argued by one former county-level official interviewed in Hong Kong that in parts of Guangdong which had better conditions and/or higher labor density, recalling labor from extra-agricultural pursuits really did not bring much improvement in agriculture—in fact, it could lead to serious losses in both private *and* collective income.[27] Nonetheless, in that region, the recall of labor power was emphasized by county leadership, apparently in an overly rigid way. Particularly in areas where peasant culture remains strongly wedded to private as opposed to collective sources of income, an unbending insistence on carrying out such restrictive measures could have a negative effect.

Hua also stressed the need for major improvement in the productive base to provide a material basis for the social/political goals of the model. Obviously material and technical capacity and not just inspired leadership were needed.[28] He specifically called for diversification in agricultural production and enterprises, and linked this with both public accumulation and improvement in the standard of living for individual peasants—points strongly emphasized in present policies as well. It is notable that this document does not, at least on its face, signify the ''grain-first'' policy that is now so vigorously criticized. Improvement in the agrarian base, technology, and diversity of production should be associated with increasing economic equality among lower-level collective units. This may appear to be a leftist goal, but as Nicholas Lardy (1980) has recently suggested, the present policies encouraging specialization also embody an economic logic leading to increased equality among units, localities or regions. Places which suffered economic losses because of policies emphasizing grain production can now realize greater prosperity through production of higher priced commodities to which their natural and human conditions are more suited.

Farmland capital construction and water conservancy projects are immense enterprises in China. They are seen as bases for securing stable yields and for making it possible efficiently to apply mechanical means to agricultural production. Farmland capital construction, costly as it is to collective budgets and the private endeavors or leisure-time of peasants, can have long-term benefits at any level of collective organization. Its most successful development seems to come when county leadership, on the one hand, can mobilize the basic-level units to contribute labor to individual projects, and on the other, organize special county-sponsored teams and equipment to implement major projects. Depending on how they are financed, such county-centered capital construction projects may have a redistributive effect among as well as within the local collective units—both because the benefits of county-sponsored projects may go to poorer units or because the county may hire and pay well extra workers from poorer units. Certainly the optimal effort in long-term capital improvement to the agrarian economy is a major part of present agricultural development programs, and no unit below (or above) the county level really has the ability that the county has to mobilize, direct, and finance such work.[29]

The criterion that calls for the equalization of production and income of poor collectives within the county points to an enormous problem and helps to understand better the strategic emphasis placed on the county in 1975 (as well as some of the great difficulties in this strategy). If collectivization enables China to narrow individual income gaps *within* collectives, there is no guarantee against polarization *among* collective units. The persistence or increase of inequality among collectives militates against enlargement of the collective unit and may be a source of discontent and setbacks to socialist goals. Why was the county chosen to solve the problem of inequality among collective units?

First, the county is a source of funds and other inputs that can be used to help promote equality among units, less through direct subsidy than by promoting a capacity for growth in selected units. Pairault points to evidence of significant use of county funds to improve the productive capabilities of poorer units in Xiyang County.[30] In Xiyang 80 percent of the county budget was allocated to agricultural investment in 1976, and the county secured some 17 percent of the total cost of basic farmland construction and water conservancy from the state.[31] The example of a large water conservancy project in Shulu County has already been mentioned. Communes do use funds accumulated at the commune level for internal redistribution in the form of projects or assistance to strengthen the economic performance of poorer brigades and teams.[32] But without strong county leadership they are not likely to contribute in any way outside their own jurisdictions.

Second, as Communist Party center, the county is best able to translate into practice overall policy. At the basic levels the brigade Party branch is an equivalently strong Party organization, and it is arguable that dynamic brigade party leaders, in conjunction with the county Party committee, are most likely to implement equalization programs.[33] The brigade is most suited to organize its economic and human resources to make maximum use of new opportunities, and the county is best able to maximize and direct new resources to where they can be best used.

Here the commune is in a more difficult position than the county because it is rooted partly in local society, and because it is a collective unit responsible solely for its own affairs rather than the interests of the state. The commune is more subject to conservative or cautious local impulses in the face of risky programs—yet it lacks the direct economic power and opportunities for long-term, face-to-face relations with the peasants and their grassroots leaders in the production teams that brigade leaders can have. The commune is ''tainted'' with the identity of the State among those members of rural society suspicious of statist designs, yet it lacks the concentrated political organization and awesomeness of the county not to mention its access to valuable material and technical resources.[34]

Strategic Factors and Implicit Political Program

In summary, we would like to specify three important factors in the prominent role of the county in Chinese rural development programs. The first is the structural characteristics of the county located just above the junction of state and society. An entirely state unit, the county can be knowledgeable about and in direct contact with daily affairs at the production levels of society. Cadres' participation in labor and supervision of all Party members in rural society provide avenues of contact. Low enough to have direct contact with leading grassroots cadres of local communities, county officials at the same time have bureaucratic ties and obligations to higher levels of the state, and there the factor of direct, face-to-face contact exists as well. Commune cadres do not have those contacts, whereas leading county cadres frequently attend enlarged national-level Party/government meetings.

A second major factor is that counties have increasingly become industrial entrepreneurs or managers. Industry is both intended as a direct producer for agricultural needs and a consumer of agricultural raw materials. At the same time, it produces county revenue and employs peasants. Aside from making the county government larger and more complex and bringing the county into closer relation with the urban/industrial sector, the development of rural small-scale industry gives the county increased resources with which to affect the economic lives of rural residents—*cum*—members of the people's communes. The development of rural small-scale industry increases the ability of the county to play a redistributive role in relation to the production and incomes of lower-level collective units. It is likely that more balanced demand for the products of county industry will increase the ability to plan for more uniform production and distribution of certain products.

Along with rural industrialization at the county level, major aspects of farmland capital construction, water conservancy, and other infrastructural developments as well as scientific and technological research and extension can only be carried out with county leadership and sponsorship. The enlargement and *planned* development of these programs which, with agricultural mechanization, will provide the effective material basis of rural modernization, should make possible much more balanced and efficient application of labor in the rural sector. Making best use of labor in the rural setting, coordinating labor-saving improvements and seasonal labor surpluses with new labor-utilizing projects will be of major value in Chinese economic development.[35]

The position of the county in a state-society nexus, and the increasing resources and complexity of the county economy due to rural industrialization and other large-scale projects are linked to the third and final factor: the quality and political character of leadership capacities vested at the county level. County leadership is placed and equipped to promote far-reaching, collectively-based, and redistributive economic development projects. Pairault notes that the movement to learn from Dazhai (the "self-reliant" brigade) became in the Dazhai-type county movement in actuality an "interventionist politics" designed to offer active assistance to backward units.[36] The characterization is apt, but as Pairault himself suggests, it would not be a politics of charity, but a program intended to supply aid that will be of utmost utility precisely because it goes to those who, by receiving it, are most able to help themselves. Such a process was demonstrated in Xiyang County. Maximum efforts by its constituent collectives was stimulated by means of leadership, labor and financial investment provided by the county. Whether or not such county aid was possible partly because of large outside investments of state aid in the 1970s, as is now alleged by Xiyang's critics in China and out, remains to be investigated further. But it does appear that county leadership was especially valuable in carrying out massive land reconstruction and water conservancy projects. It also intervened at times to provide support to get communities through hard times and to bolster *collective* morale. Such policies in turn made it more possible to carry out the overall goal of stabilizing the collective agricultural work force at the highest possible level.[37]

The promise of a county-focused development plan was to link the potential energies and initiatives of collective units to supplies of local or external resources that could boost them to a level where collective efforts begin to pay off. On a broad and flexible scale within a county, especially in line with a growing county industrial system, such a strategy would be likely to pay off in balanced and resilient patterns of growth.

What the Dazhai-type county development program offered, then, was the extension through the county of political and material incentives to local cadres, especially those at the brigade level, to assess local problems and potentials and to formulate plans by which to achieve significant growth. In essence, the Dazhai-type county program called for entrepreneurial linkages between the collectives (that is, the communes and brigades) and the primary agent of the state (county)—linkages oriented toward both growth and redistribution of development capabilities. In this program, both county and collectives committed themselves to a collectivist pattern of development that relied on activist political leadership within given institutional forms to provide the major dynamic force for incorporating increasingly available material inputs in a successful pattern of economic growth.

As Marianne Bastid has written:

> *Since the Cultural Revolution, the authority and responsibilities of the county level are going through a revival which reminds one of the administrative pattern in imperial times, though its basis is different.*[38]

The net effect of the approach to rural development enunciated in the 1975 National Conference on Learning from Dazhai in Agriculture was to place a very great stress on political leadership and political considerations in economic life. This was because of the redistributive character of the overall criteria for economic success and because of the relative inclination toward self-reliance. Given the continuous growth of a diversified local rural economy, especially its industrial sector, it is hard to imagine any Chinese rural development policy that would not give a place of some importance to the role of functional leadership by county agencies. But a redistributive growth policy based on integrated planning for the county as a whole and requiring mutual, perhaps sacrificial, contributions by collective units is one that requires political and ideological commitment, especially if grandiose, labor-intensive projects are tried. That is all the more true if the starting point of the various collectives is relatively unequal, and if the level of outside aid available (and of farm commodity prices) is not high. Competitiveness among collectives could intensify to the extent that recognition as a successful unit eligible for aid comes about as a result of political wheeling and dealing, favoritism, factionalism, etc. Undoubtedly, the 1975 policy strengthened political authorities and factors—the county Party committee, its allies within the collective leaderships and supporters at the prefecture and province, and the fighting slogans associated with class struggle that gave such leadership its putative legitimacy. The effect of these factors would be particularly strong because of the structure of the Chinese state at the time, the unified leadership exercised by the Party over government affairs, and the power of Party bureaucrats in relation to the individual lives and careers of Party members at the grassroots. We believe that it is partly this highly demanding, if not loaded, *political* character of the Dazhai-type county program, as well as possible economic insufficiencies it entailed, that contributed to its dismantling at the end of the decade.

Recent Policy Shifts

The passage from Bastid, recalling the role of the county in imperial administration, suggests that this is where we came in and will exit. But Chinese politics refuses to allow research and pronouncements to end. For some time after the changes of leadership following the death of Mao Zedong, it appeared that agrarian policies associated with Hua Guofeng's 1975 Dazhai Conference address would remain effective. But by the turn of the 1980s, a qualitative shift of major dimensions was underway. We now perceive within the past few years two types of directions available for rural development.

For several decades, growth in Chinese agriculture has been seriously deficient, a fact (and criticism) that has prompted a series of policy changes. Most dramatically the salience of political leadership and political desiderata in rural economy has been diminished. Emphasis has been placed on the role of economic forces worked out through market relations and strengthened by the economic institutions that make such relations possible. Specifically, the current Chinese leaders have weakened the direct decision-making powers of party and government officials and instead granted more leeway to directors of production units, letting them shift for themselves in a world of profits, prices, competitive contracts, etc. In addition, more straightforwardly economic, individuated incentives are used for employees, while market and internal trade systems are elaborated and legitimated for enterprise and even private exchange.[39] The rehabilitation of the long-silenced "revisionist" economist, Sun Yefang, the publication of his economic writings, and the prominent role of Xue Muqiao are very important indicators of this change.The basic tenor of present policy critiques is to insist that the best indication of good leadership is the extent to which leaders are able to grasp and follow "economic laws"; this is the philosophical core of contemporary Chinese pragmatism.

Severe criticism has been levelled at all practices that use administrative methods ("handing down orders") as a substitute for indigenous motivation calculated according to economic advantage. In institutional terms, the autonomy of the team has been guaranteed protection as never before—this, obviously, in contradistinction to the ambitions of brigade leaders to "level-up." The team is to have maximum control of its production plan without interference from upper levels, and it is to have the right to seek income from a variety of sources. The leadership now warns against overemphasizing grain production as a key to capital accumulation in collectives. In some instances, perhaps even in terms of broad regional specialization, cash-crop production (e.g., fruits and nuts, timber, animal husbandry) and sideline industry may legitimately serve as the principal sources of collective income. Simply put, teams *and* individual households are encouraged to get rich. Editorials characterize earlier programs as having started from the premise that to be poor is good. A variety of privately-oriented practices such as household sidelines, private plot production, and petty-trading on rural free markets are at minimum to be protected, and in effect encouraged. In a revival of some institutional forms of local productive organization that appeared in the wake of the Great Leap Forward and were subsequently criticized during the Cultural Revolution as signposts on the "capitalist road," subcontracting to small work groups and even to households has now reappeared with official imprimatur.[40] Finally, several recent articles indicating direct criticism of Xiyang county "ultraleft practices," their leadership and institutions, add to the urgency and political weight of the policy shifts.[41]

Another change makes clearcut planning distinctions between policies for different areas: some will be handled as "commodity grain bases"; others as "industrial crop bases." The actual administrative content of this program remains elusive even in discussions with Chinese planners[42] and the policy itself may be formative, subject to change, or even fleeting in existence. It appears, however, that these base areas will receive special allocations of modern producer inputs. While it is generally felt among Western observers that such regions will be selected on the basis of an established record of high production and prosperity, Nicholas Lardy reminds us that some of these grain base regions "lack adequate water resources and consequently now achieve relatively low per unit grain yields." Be that as it may, a recent editorial states explicitly that the benefits of agricultural mechanization cannot, as was suggested in the 1975 program, be achieved for all units across the board. Certain regions, localities and units will be targeted for maximum available supplies of agricultural machinery or subsidized investments for their production, while in others semi-mechanization or manual labor will continue to be the main basis for agricultural production for some time to come. And these areas may have to depend for their advancement on a much more completely self-reliant policy in capital accumulation.[43]

Related to this, it is likely that in poor areas in general there will be less emphasis on farm capital construction and grain production and more on the development of subsidiary sidelines, special industries, and other income producing measures. There may even be an increasing willingness to tolerate the outflow of labor as an income maintenance measure for poorer households or units.[44] Criticisms of past policy—that it was contrary to the economic demands and motives of the pesantry, overly redistributive in nature, and that it ignored "economic laws"—suggest that market relations organized on a freer basis will become much more important in rural economy. Obviously, the Chinese leadership at present argues that, despite some success stories of full-blown collective commitment to "common prosperity" (rising together), by and large peasants have been demoralized by overemphasis on collective accumulation and need to be released to follow their economic noses. This will be in harmony with policies that no longer stress self-sufficiency in grain production, that allow for local and regional specialization, and, by implication, that call for an expansion of exchange among areas to make up for local deficiencies.[45]

What will happen to the county as focal point for development? All evidence points to a lowering of its sights and a reduction of its power, especially to combine economic growth policies with specific socio-economic and political goals. In development, the stress on free play of economic forces as opposed to political leadership is a key indication of this. The current criticism of redistributive measures which is that they dangerously blunted the "socialist enthusiasm" of the peasants is likely to result in a weakening of the relationship in the Xiyang strategy between county political centers and activist commune and brigade leaderships. In all likelihood, state functional bureaucracies and planning agencies on the one hand and individual households on the other will also become more prominent in economic decision-making, in technical innovation, greater flexibility in cropping, and in other fiscal changes wrought by the third session of the Fifth N.P.C. For example, in a 1978 comment on the relation between present agricultural development plans and the 1975 Dazhai-type county "package of policies," Dernberger and Fasenfest argue that, while some of the more radical political-institutional elements of the program (e.g., brigade decision-making) were removed, rural material investment aspects of the program were not. They mention specifically farmland capital construction, water conservancy, changes in cropping patterns, rural small-scale industries, increasing application of technical innovations, and various forms of agricultural mechanization (including wider electrification) all of which are to remain.[46] It would seem that, given the dimensions of these projects and the already significant accumulation of industrial investment at county levels, a major role for county government will remain in any event.

Of all the questions raised by the appearance in rapid succession of two contrasting rural development strategies in the past five years, the most provocative concerns the interests of the societal groups potentially served by each. Since this question suggests consideration of the interrelationship of societal interests and state structures, we turn for inspiration to Franz Schurmann's insightful work (1968) on the Chinese policy debates of the 1956–57 period over alternative plans for decentralization. In his analysis, Schurmann explicitly connected disputes about the organization of political and administrative leadership over economic activity with the impact of alternative policy outcomes on differentiated societal interests.

In that debate, Schurmann argued, two identifiable sets of advocates within the Communist Party promoted two varying strategies for decentralization of economic leadership. Schurmann tied "Decentralization I" to Chen Yun, a long-time Communist Party leader active in economic policy-making and a "conservative" who advocated less mobilization, less heavy industry, and more reliance on market forces, material incentives, and smaller collectives. "Decentralization I" called for a maximum degree of decision-making power to be vested in the hands of producing units. Schurmann argued (p. 198) that "putting decision-making power into the hands of producing units also meant creating external conditions for the autonomous exercise of such power, namely some form of market conditions." The emphasis on markets and more direct material incentives is, in Schurmann's view, associated with a more liberal class policy and "the growth of free-market tendencies [which] would have reduced the power of regional administration to direct the economy in the area of their jurisdiction."

The alternative, "Decentralization II," and the form adopted at the end of the debate, Schurmann associates (p. 196) with Mao, Liu Shaoqi and Deng Xiaoping. This called for placing greater power in the "hands of lower-echelon administrative units," i.e., the provinces, prefectures, and counties. Decentralization II is based on the principle of social mobilization, coordinative rather than vertical forms of administration and control (emphasizing strongly the role of the Communist Party organization at the several regional jurisdictional levels), and, we would add, the prominence of political leadership and class-oriented collective institutions over market arrangements.

In a brief observation of relevance to the present policy shifts, Schurmann notes that one reason behind the preference of the majority at that time for the second model of decentralization was

> . . . *the fact that the Agricultural Producers Cooperatives in 1957 were apparently again coming under the control of what was euphemistically called 'prosperous middle peasants.' Tolerance toward 'prosperous' peasants in Communist China has generally gone together with economic relaxation and permissiveness toward the market. Since the 'prosperous' peasants were less amenable to Party control, greater freedom for them inevitably meant less control by Party-dominated regional government over the peasantry. Social mobilization, of course,was intended to have the opposite effect. Thus both the* economic *consequences of Decentralization I and the* social *consequences of cooperatives dominated by 'prosperous' peasants would have had significant* political *consequences*.

Looking at the tentative outcome of major policy shifts more than two decades later, there appears at first glance a suggestion of parallel occurrences and parallel implications. The present policy that looks very much like a (belated!) victory for Decentralization I may have been achieved by the shift or absorption of the advocacy of Deng Xiaoping and like-minded colleagues from the decentralized compromise of the centralists (i.e., Decentralization II) with its heavy statist component to what for convenience sake may be called the Chen Yun or "economists" position.[47] Preliminary reports of the deliberations of the August-September 1980 National People's Congress present evidence of decentralization, especially the placing of much more authority (and autonomous control of vital funds) in the hands of the managers of economic producing units.

Given this ultimate shift, what is to be made today of Schurmann's suggestion that the effect of Decentralization I in the rural areas would have amounted in 1957 to a change in relative class positions, favoring former advantaged rural classes or individual class members who survived land reform and early collectivization? Are there implications for the class structure of rural society in the present policy of development? To the extent that Decentralization I depends on a freeing up of private economic activities and market-oriented production planning, even today it may be argued that the prestige and relative importance of former middle peasants, prosperous "new" middle peasants who emerged right after land reform, and rich peasants and their children and allies in the villages (including some cadres) would be enhanced. Although individuals from all rural strata have in the past taken part in activities that in radical phases are labeled "spontaneous capitalist tendencies," such persons in the early 1960s and in some places even in the mid-1970s come from among the formerly more economically advanced or entrepreneurial strata of rural society.[48] The group that might lose out from this new policy mix will be those commune members whose income potential for one reason or another had been lower and had benefitted from county-localized redistributive growth. Similarly, poorer units, or even counties or regions, are not likely to have the same range of material and capital investment funds extended to them under the new policy as in the past Dazhai-type county approach. It remains an open question whether or not greater opportunity given such units to participate in self-enriching sideline activities and specialized agricultural production will make up the difference.

In addition, the recent alteration of the class line in the countryside, and in most cases the dissolution of land reform-era categories speaks to an even stronger analogy between Schurmann's interpretation of the class implication of Decentralization I and our view of the possible social significance of the eclipse of the county-centered, class conflict oriented program of the Dazhai-type county strategy. In a momentous historical judgment, the Communist Party decided in early 1979 to lift the last sanctions against former landlords and rich peasants who since land reform have been stigmatized as class enemies, targeted in frequent political campaigns in the countryside, and subjected to economic discrimination as well as to limitations on their civil and political rights. The new policy has stated that the children of such people are to be treated from the outset as ordinary peasants and not saddled with their parents' class labels.

However, such similarities may be more apparent than real, or appropriate only in a partial or marginal way. In 1957, Deng Xiaoping endorsed Decentralization II and the policies of rapid mobilization and large collectives which were later embodied in the Great Leap Forward. His transparent use of a metaphor of conflicting cats and rats to depict solutions to economic problems—conflicts and solutions hitherto understood as embodying class struggles—signified a renunciation of that earlier policy and an abandonment by some veteran revolutionaries of the use of 1940s class labels to analyze contemporary economic relationships. It is true that in the present day we do see, even in economic terms, unevenness in the distribution of income and opportunity. But these seem related more fundamentally to differences among localities in the level of development of the productive and material base and of the specific branch of the economy than they do to class status as fixed in the land reform.

While some descendents of former elite classes may, if given greater freedom, still be the most powerful and energetic seekers of individual advancement, so there are manifold other sources of differentiation emerging with the growth of a modern Chinese economy: differences between urban and rural residence, industrial and agricultural employment, official or non-official position, household size and "hand-mouth ratio," as well as the significant material differences among collective units, areas, and regions. Of these, the original type of class differentiation in the old rural society may be the least important factor. Thus, the recent decision to remove class discrimination against the remnants of old village elites may be more a recognition of reality and the need for ending an atavistic form of discrimination than a pandering to the interests of a group ready to seize the reins of economic ambition and leadership. It may also be an attempt to harness the economic skills and energies of some of the old economic elites and their children within a basically collective economic framework.

Conclusion

We may now make several points about the analytical basis of the Dazhai-Xiyang county emulation program for rural development. First of all, the program attempted to overcome inequalities arising from the new collective institutions and productive relations in socialist China. The most important and original parts of the program were 1) the desire to find ways of resolving inequalities among communes and units within them and, 2) by means of the political and economic leadership of county authorities, making maximum use of local resources and competing with other counties for additional financial aids from higher levels of the state. At the same time, however,the political analysis and basis of legitimation of political power used to undergird this objective was one that invoked the old language of rural class and class conflict, "poor and lower-middle peasants," etc. each having organizational surrogates in the county and collective Party committees. Although the 1975 program was *not* a creature of what has now become known as the ultraleft of the 1970s, its use by a variety of political leaders at the sub-provincial and county level may well have tended to promote radical policies on a wholesale and militantly politicized basis, as is now charged. The complex sources of inequality in contemporary China, especially inter-unit and inter-regional inequality within the form of socialist collective ownership, may well mean that any effort to base a comprehensive program on a class analysis that harkens back to the old days of the Civil War and Land Reform will, as Mao once warned, fail to distinguish properly between enemies and friends.

What we may see, then, in the flight from "politics" to "pragmatism" is the continuing inability to find a socio-economic or class analysis that is appropriate to the present Chinese situation while at the same time adequate for economic development programs and socialist political leadership. The goal of redistribution has not been abandoned;[48] rather, with the policy favoring local politics and the decentralization of leadership, it has been reoriented in a very important structural way.

To illustrate this point by comparison, the kind of redistribution envisaged in the "Dazhai-type county" strategy called for a high degree of redistributive growth *within* the local county milieu, relying in the first instance on the maximum generation of local resources, based on the mobilization of labor power and other capacities, and supplemented by external funding to activist county leaderships and their subordinate units.[49] Today we see *another type* of redistributive policy being attempted, one that is more macro-economic in scope and that deals with different societal inequalities. Current criticisms, including those of the degree of state aid given to Xiyang County itself, suggest that self-reliance by the poor and continued growth by the better-off—as parallel means toward growth with increased equality—may both be illusory strategies in present-day China. Instead, policy-makers are pursuing a program that involves—at least for the immediate years—a large-scale redistribution of income mainly between urban and rural society and between industry and agriculture via across-the-board, massive rises in prices for agricultural commodities, especially for above-quota sales. This would certainly benefit all agricultural producers, but because of the 50 percent bonus for above-quota sales of grain, the very biggest and most efficient producers would do the best. The poorer and less well endowed units or areas, therefore, would be left with the other options of the policy: *viz.*, the encouragement to engage in specialized production of cash-crops or sidelines, to go on the market individually or collectively, and the like. This set of approaches would seem to portend a reduced role for the county in economic redistribution.

Despite the present view that political leadership, collective incentives, and redistributive policies have acted as brakes on peasant enthusiasm, and therefore hindered the growth of productive forces and output in rural China, it may turn out that the rural population, and crucial members of rural society (such as many brigade cadres) are divided on this point. It could be that we are in for a period of conflict, compromise or combination of elements from the two approaches. But it is also possible that relative movement from one to another approach will engender a new round of political conflict, with a different set of aggrieved rural actors. Whether county "leading cores" will slip back into a more relaxed administrative posture and tend to their tractor factories or take a more activist and "radical" (if the word still means anything) posture may depend both on the strength of inheritance of their "Dazhai spirit" and the relative economic capacities of their units. Because of the scope and size of the economic base and functions of the county in 1979 as compared to 1956 or 1957, it may be less easy—or even less intended—then it would have been in 1956 to dismiss the political weight of the county government. If the present policies suggest that "Decentralization I" is in the works today, it will run up at least against the accumulated economic endowments and increased functional responsibility of county government.

One final point remains to be made. The extreme and sustained upheavals of the Cultural Revolution, continuing factional conflicts in Party and non-Party units, and uncertainties, setbacks, or uneven successes in economic development have led to some degree of crisis of political legitimacy of the Chinese revolutionary state. Many of the steps taken by Chinese leaders since 1976 seem designed to deal with this crisis—tightening Party organization, placing impediments in the path of more unregulated forms of dissent (such as the "four big freedoms"), and seeking ways to involve members of the public and of various institutions of the social economy in regular, orderly procedures of representation, participation, and conflict resolution. Hence, for example, we may understand attempts to explore patterns of political participation by workers and staff members in industrial units as part of the search for an orderly democratic element in Chinese institutional practice. Similarly, despite the apparent downgrading of the political pre-eminence of county Party leaderships in overall economic decision-making, we note with interest the initiation of constitutional changes that call for popular elections to county legislative bodies.[50] Such activity may well have the cumulative effect of restoring and strengthening the popular legitimacy of county leadership institutions—therefore making it easier for the county to resume a more extensive role in integrating rural economic and social development policies. The structural preconditions are already in place.

Notes

1. The decline of the Dazhai-Xiyang model and the attacks upon Dazhai and Xiyang themselves are discussed at length in: Tang Tsou, Marc Blecher and Mitch Meisner, "Policy Change at the National Summit and Institutional Transformation at the Local Level: The Case of Tachai and Hsiyuang County in the Post-Mao Era," *Proceedings of the Center for Far Eastern Studies*, University of Chicago Center for Far Eastern Studies (Chicago: 1981), pp. 241–391.

2. For a full discussion of the theme of the decline of political factors in economic, cultural and social life in post-Mao China, see Tang Tsou, "Back From the Brink of Revolutionary-'Feudal' Totalitarianism: Some Preliminary Reflections," paper presented at the Luce Seminar, University of Chicago, May 30, 1980.

3. Mark Selden, *The Yenan Way in Revolutionary China* (Cambridge, MA: Harvard Univ. Press, 1971). Franz Schurmann, *Ideology and Organization in Communist China* (Berkeley, CA: Univ. of California Press, 1968).

4. There were about 2,200 counties in China in 1971. Whitaker and Rinn-Sup Shinn, *Area Handbook for the People's Republic of China*, (Washington D.C.: Department of the Army, U.S. GPO, 1971) p. 25. In 1967, Barnett estimated the average county population to be 300,000 and number of counties per province between 60–100, although both saw wide variations. Today the average county population is undoubtedly at least 400,000.

5. In this section we are indebted to the comparative study of Theda Skocpol who examines the relationship between social structure and political power. "France, Russia, and China: A Structural Analysis of Social Revolutions" in *Comparative Studies in Society and History*, 18 (April 1976): pp. 175–210, esp. 198–201. Skocpol believes that the extent and complexity of social control wielded in local areas by the landlord-gentry made autonomous, effective political activity by small peasants very difficult and posed the key problem for Communist revolutionaries operating in the countryside. Also see Ben Stavis, *People's Communes and Rural Development in China* (Ithaca, NY: Cornell Univ., Center for International Studies, 1974).

6. For a recent example of such analysis, see Tsou, Blecher and Meisner (1979). The subject of study is the sub-commune unit, the production brigade.

7. Jack Gray has reminded us of one outlandish idea, current around 1958 in some parts of China, for a "county-wide commune." Personal communication. See also G. William Skinner's articles in the *Journal of Asian Studies*, Vol. 24 (1964–65).

8. We are aware that there is always some ambiguity to this formulation because of the mixed character of the people's commune as well as the significant institution of Communist Party (hence, "state") power at the brigade level. This paper does not explore the commune as such, but evidence suggests that, though the commune may at times play the role of purely implementing state-sponsored programs to lower levels of local society, its collective economic character imparts a strong societal component as well and subjects it to strong influences from basic-level interest.

An interesting example of the "mixed" character of the commune level in relation to State policies comes from an interview with a former county (technical cadre in Guangdong province. Commenting on the role of county agencies in carrying out policies to cut off "labor outflow" from the agricultural economy to other areas of employment, he states that:

> *. . . the communes also took a part in controlling this. You need papers from the communeto get outside work, and these have to be renewed every month by the commune at the time when you remit part of your salary to your team. At these times of control of labor outflow, the communes would refuse to reissue papers to these people. But after a short time, the communes—particularly the poorer ones with excess labor power and population, where the outflow problem was most serious—would permit them to go again, since the outflow has advantages for the communes, which receive their sideline fee.*

When individual peasants contracted to work outside the collective, they were required to remit a set amount of money from their earnings to the production team they belonged to. The team in turn sent a percentage (10–15 percent each) to the brigade and the commune as a so-called "management fee." (Marc Blecher: Interviews conducted at the Universities' Service Centre, Hong Kong, 1978).

9. A. Doak Barnett, *Cadres, Bureaucracy and Political Power in China* (New York: Columbia Univ. Press, 1967).

10. In his analysis of the county as a strategic unit for administering agricultural modernization, Butler sees one of the two key functions of the county as being a distribution point for sophisticated inputs produced elsewhere. S. Butler, "Agricultural Mechanization in China," East Asian Institute, Columbia University, 1978, p. 43.

11. Blecher, 1978.

12. Victor Falkenheim, in *China Quarterly*, 59 (1974), pp. 518–543. Our major informant on recent county governance informs us that "Of course, one factor motivating the expansion of agricultural mechanization was the needs of the county itself. But more important was the demands of the higher levels. But the higher levels also supported this county-level undertaking, with bank loans and materials distributed." Also, "If other kinds of machinery production lost money, they [the county] got criticized; but not agricultural machinery factories. Yes, I think this has to do with the movement to learn from Dazhai." Blecher, 1978.

13. Blecher, 1978.

14. B.Y. Ahn, *Chinese Politics and the Cultural Revolution* (Seattle, WA: Univ. of Washington Press, 1976).

15. "Forum on Building a Socialist New Countryside Through Revolutionizing the Leadership of CCP Hsien Committees," *People's Daily* (beginning October 12, 1965), in *Current Background*, no. 779 (January 17, 1966), p. 28.

16. Audrey Donnithorne in *China Quarterly* No. 52 (1972) pp. 605–619.

17. The Second Light Industry Bureau in Hebei's Shulu County which we have studied in depth. Interviews, Shulu County, 1979.

18. Interviews, Shulu County and Changzhou City, 1979.

19. Interviews, Shulu County, 1979.

20. Hua Guofeng in the *People's Daily*, (31 October, 1975).

21a. For a short description of this period, based on accounts in the Chinese press and related documents, see Mitch Meisner, "In Agriculture Learn from Dazhai: Theory and Practice in Chinese Rural Development" dissertation, University of Chicago, 1977, pp. 384–412. Pp. 353–373 discuss the pattern of change in Xiyang county itself after the Cultural Revolution shifted the county leadership. Insitutional and political-economic aspects of the development in Xiyang county, especially around the theme of the relationship of growth and equality, are dealt with in considerable analytic detail by Tsou, Blecher, and Meisner, *Modern China* No. 5 (1979), pp. 3–39, 139–185. Thierry Pairault, in *Dazhai recupéré*: La politique économique rurale au début des années 1970, takes a close, hardheaded economist's political-economic look at the implications of the directions for agriculture posed at the beginning of the 1970s. He also includes a direct analysis of a number of the important texts of this period, and reproduces them in Chinese, including the lead article in *People's Daily*, "In Agriculture Learn from Dazhai," September 23, 1970, which really started the major media publicity that fall. (Publications Orientalists de France, Paris: 1977). Another important article by Pairault, on the 1975 Conference itself also should be cited here because we shall have occasion to refer to it: "Étude de Tachai et développement économique en Chine: La conférence nationale de l'automne 1975," *Mondes Asiatiques*, No. 8 (Winter 1976–1977) pp. 467–498. Also, Neville Maxwell, "The Fourth Mobilization: New Phase of the Tachai Movement," *World Development* No. 6 (1978) pp. 499–518.

In Guangdong province by late 1970, the province, prefectures, and counties had ostensibly all set up special offices and programs to implement the "Dazhai-type county" program. The province and prefecture circulated periodicals specially directed to assist the movement, and the Yunfu county "Learn from Dazhai Small Group" of the county Party committee also circulated a bulletin on the subject twice a month. Blecher, 1978.

Interviews and research carried out in 1979 in Wuxi County, Jiangsu, provide eloquent testimony to the high level of variability in substantive content which the Dazhai-Xiyang Program could have in localities very different from the originals. Wuxi closely identified with the movement to emulate Dazhai and Xiyang, starting in 1970 at the time of the North China Conference on Agriculture; and officials there stated with considerable pride that Wuxi became a "Dazhai-type county" in 1975. Yet in looking at the substance of its program, one sees that it identified its emulation efforts (and successes) primarily with point 4—undertaking a massive program of farmland capital construction financed primarily with local sources of accumulation.

21b. For a discussion of Dazhai's leadership, see Meisner, 1977.

22. "Comrade Ch'en Yung-kuei's [Chen Yonggui's] Report at the Reporting Meeting held Jointly by the Ministry of Agriculture and Forestry and the Chinese Communist Party Peking Municipal Committee," Union Research Service 74, nos. 14 and 15 (February 15 and 19, 1974): pp. 187–188. In his talk, Chen spoke of one brigade that had changed its leaders every month for a year. Dazhai's neighboring Wujiaping brigade, whose Party secretary Li Xishen was a close ally of Chen's and is now Vice Secretary of the Xiyang County Party Committee, is reported to have had eight brigade leaderships and 24 production team leaderships between 1958 and 1965. (Wilfred Burchett with Rewi Alley, *China: The Quality of Life*, (London: Penguin Books, 1976), p. 128. In Guangdong around the time of the Cultural Revolution, a lot of county secretaries were transferred from one county to the next to help shield them from more criticism, "since in the new county their background would not be known so well." Blecher, 1978.

23. Pairault makes the point particularly strongly when he connects emphasis on revolutionization of county cadres to the program of the linking of Dazhai-type agricultural development to the establishment of an industrial base at the county level. This was an outcome, in his opinion, of a period of relative separation in agricultural and industrial development since the early 1960s in which each sector was to pursue its own "egocentric" development. (1976–77, pp. 489–491).

24. Guo Fenglian, "Jianchi da pi zibenzhuyi, jianchi da gan shehuizhuyi," *People's Daily*, September 25, 1975. Guo is the present secretary of the Dazhai brigade Party branch. She was a protege of Chen's and succeeded him. Today we see considerable criticism of the program of cadre participation in labor on a number of points: that they need time to attend to their official duties; that they ought to be able to undertake them free of the concern that if they fail to participate in manual labor their families may go hungry; and that such labor participation makes only a marginal contribution to productive work while actually hurting administration.

25. Interview, Hebei Province (Shijiazhuang), 1979. The high Hebei Province official with whom we were discussing this matter used the analogy of "going up by airplane" (*zuo feiji shangqu*) as well as the more familiar "helicopter" analogy!

26. Tang Tsou, M. Blecher, and M. Meisner in *Modern China* No. 5 (1979) pp. 3–39, 139–185.

27. Blecher, interviews, 1974–75.

28. Pairault believes (and with good sense, we think) that the kind of leader desired in the development strategy implied by the Dazhai-county program is not above all a technician, but rather, "a leader of men, a guide . . . read more than expert, more a Schumpeterian entrepreneur than a Burnhamian manager."

29. See Pairault, 1976–77, pp. 495–498 for a good statement analyzing the primacy of farm capital (or infrastructural) construction for rural development. Also, see Chin Chi-chu, "All-Out Effort to Develop Agriculture," *Peking Review*, No. 26 (June 30, 1978). This article on Pingding county in Shanxi province has a good description of extensive projects, including a major water conservancy endeavor, of the "Xiyang-type" sponsored or supervised by the county.

30. T. Pairault, *Mondes Asiatiques*, No. 8 (1976–77), pp. 467–498.

31. Tsou, Blecher, Meisner (1979) op. cit.

32. Interview, Chinese Academy of Social Sciences, June 1979.

33. For example, in Xitang Brigade, Qianzhou Commune, Wuxi County, visited in 1979, complex measures have been taken under brigade supervision to amalgamate the economies of the production teams into several sub-brigade units to provide a transitional form to facilitate a move underway toward brigade-level accounting. It is clear that the brigade Party leadership played an unusually creative and active role in devising a system to smooth over likely conflicts during this transition.

34. Neville Maxwell has the following to say about the attitudes, relatively speaking, of county and commune cadres about taking measures (here a relatively radical one) to promote equalization:

> *The writer's discussions with cadres of the Chinese administration have shown a divergence of attitude . . . . at county level, for example, cadres are more likely to stress the raising of the unit of account to brigade level as a necessary consequence of the Tachai campaign; while down at commune level cadres are much more cautious and tentative about the prospects for widespread raising of the level of account. Seeing this as basically a matter of peasant attitudes, they emphasize that decisions on the timing of such changes must come 'from the masses,' they know from their own experience that reforms imposed from above are likely to be abortive.*

World Development No. 6 (1978) p.513. In Yunfu County, "In the peasants' eyes, the commune and county represent the state, and the team and brigade represent them" Blecher, 1978.

35. For comments on this point see: *Rural Small-Scale Industry Delegation* (Berkeley: Univ. of California Press, 1977), p. 152; also Pairault, pp.482–494.

36. Pairault, op. cit.

37. For example, Chen Yonggui reported in 1973 that when the past year's drought conditions had caused what appeared to be a likely failure of the harvest in six communes, there was considerable unrest, and "bad elements" complained that, "without grain, without money, what are we supposed to do?" These people, "incited the labor powers to leave the locality. They abandoned the water conservancy projects and disbanded the specialized work teams."

The response of the county Party committee to the precarious situation was to announce that they would guarantee the receipt of 460 *jin* (506 pounds) of grain whatever the outcome of the harvest. "Comrade Ch'en Yung-Kuei's Report," *Union Research Service* No. 74, p. 185.

38. M. Bastid in S. Schram (ed.) *Authority, Participation and Cultural Change* (Cambridge, MA: Univ. Press, 1973).

39. In this shift, undoubtedly, real power has passed into different sets of hands in a structural sense and probably in relation to ideological viewpoint. The application of class criteria to this shift is a difficult problem, one we discuss to some extent in the body of this analysis. But we do however recognize that in a "real" sense, the notion of such an economic/political separation is a fictitious idea. In 1980s China, economic relations among individuals or organized groups involving questions of domination or association, inequality or equality still go on, and legitimate interactions are organized and protected by agencies established in terms of the particular structures and ideology of Chinese state power.

40. For a detailed discussion of the new "responsibility systems," see Tsou, Blecher and Meisner, *Proceedings of the Center for Far Eastern Studies*, (Chicago: Univ. of Chicago, Center for Far Eastern Studies, 1981).

41. See for example, "Ba Dazhai di jüti jingyan dangzuo falü jiushi buminzhu," ["Treating the Concrete Experience of Dazhai as a Law is Undemocratic"), *Nanfang Ribao*, March 14, 1979, p. 2, "Bixü zhaidiao 'fan Dazhai' di jinguzhou," ("It Is Necessary to Take Off the 'Anti-Dazhai' Evil Spell"), *Jiefang Ribao*, March 7, 1979, p. 3, "Li Xishen tongzhi zai Xiyang xianwei changwei kuoda huiyi he xianwei kuoda huiyi shang daibiao Xiyang xianwei jiancha qi fanmian wenti," ("At Enlarged Meetings of the Xiyang County Party Committee and Party Standing Committee, Comrade Xishen, on behalf of the

County Party Committee, Examined Seven Problem-areas'') *Wenhui Bao*, March 8, 1979.

42. Interview, Jiangsu Province (Nanjing), 1979.

43. ''Jia Juai nongye jixiehua de zhengque fangzhen,'' (''The Correct Direction for Hastening Agricultural Mechanization''), *People's Daily*, February 6, 1979.

44. An interesting question arises here: Will this compete or conflict with measures taken to decrease urban unemployment, especially among youth?

45. Our thanks to Ben Stavis for this point.

46. Robert F. Dernberger and David Fasenfest, ''China's Post-Mao Economic Future,'' in *Chinese Economy Post-Mao, Volume I, Policy and Performance*, (Washington, D.C.: U.S. Congress Joint Economic Committee, 1978), pp. 24–26. The authors argue that the efficient use in boosting productive output in agriculture by even the technical-capital improvement package alone may be limited effectively to better endowed regions with more access to water, transport, urban markets, and good communications. While this may seem in contradiction with the Xiyang county experience which took place in a backward, poorly endowed region, the argument may be made that the Chinese leadership has decided that they simply cannot supply the material inputs necessary for such growth in poor regions across the board, even if they can increase the availability of agricultural producer goods and financial subsidies to the better off areas so that they may continue to get a reasonable return in increased production. This may help to explain the recent policy shift to more of a ''dual strategy'' in promoting mechanization of agriculture.

47. See Deng's interview with Oriana Fallacci, *Washington Post*, August 31, 1980.

48. During a year-long interview project in Hong Kong in 1974–75, Blecher was surprised to find repeatedly that old class distinctions fixed at that time 25 years or more in the past still seemed to be discernibly related to the distribution of entrepreneurial skills and economic acumen (but not wealth or income). Specifically, while these traits were hardly monopolized by former landlords and rich peasants, the former economic elites tended more than members of other classes to be likely to have such traits. In one village, for example, basic-level cadres made use of the continuing network of personal contacts of a former landlord in establishing an unofficial electric motor factory. In another, former landlords and rich peasants monopolized profitable carpentry and construction skills. There, the son of a mason who was a former landlord was apprenticed to him. In another village, ''the educated people are mostly landlords and rich peasants.'' Blecher, Interviews, Universities' Service Centre, Hong Kong, 1974–75.

49. Tsou, Blecher and Meisner, op. cit.

50. We are grateful to Jack Gray for suggesting this point.

The People's Communes and China's New Development Strategy

by Victor Lippit

Since the overthrow of the Gang of Four in 1976, China has sharply shifted its development strategy. Many of the policies associated with the Cultural Revolution and its aftermath have been eliminated. Since those policies were associated with a unique strategy for rural development with the people's communes at its core, it is appropriate to reconsider the future prospects for the communes under the new policies. It is this question that I would like to address here. Beginning with a review of the principal characteristics of the communes and turning next to an examination of agricultural policy and performance in the 1957–1977 period, I will continue with a review of the new overall development strategy and conclude with an analysis of its implications for the agricultural sector and for the commune as an institution in particular. I hope to show that despite a number of significant changes, the successful development of the communes remains an intrinsic part of the new development strategy, which appears likely to strengthen them in a number of critical respects.

Commune Characteristics

In China, unlike most third world countries, rural development has been a central component of the overall development strategy. The key institution making this possible is the people's commune, which combines agriculture, capital construction and local industry with health, welfare, education and cultural activities. The commune is a unique institution which, by combining farming and other productive activities with the activities of local government, integrates the social, political and economic life of the countryside within a single unit.

China's overall population is now approaching one billion people; at the end of 1980 it was 982.6 million, excluding Taiwan, and growing at 1.2% per year.[1] Approximately 80 percent of the population or 800 million people live on communes, which now number 50,000. The communes average about 16,000 persons or 3,800 households each; individual commune sizes vary widely from the average, with communes in mountainous regions typically much smaller than the average while those in flat, densely-populated plains areas not uncommonly reaching 60-70,000 members. When the entire countryside was first organized into communes in 1958, 26,000 communes were established. These proved to be too large for efficient administration and the number was increased to a peak of 78,000 in the early 1960s before a new round of consolidation brought the total down to the present number around the end of the decade.

The communes are divided into four levels, each of which has its own sources of income and each of which has its own sphere of decision-making autonomy. The four levels are the commune, the brigade, the team and the household. The commune level is typically responsible for providing secondary school education, maintaining a hospital, organizing cultural activities and carrying out the functions of local government. At the same time, it carries out larger-scale industrial activities, capital construction and some farming activities. At the Changjun (Long March) People's Commune near Shanghai, for example, the commune level has six small factories and four service enterprises in addition to an animal-breeding and seed farm.[2] The factories make agricultural machinery, agricultural tools, chemical fertilizer, chemical dies, rubber and fence-wire; the products are sold both outside and inside the commune. The four service enterprises include a tractor station, a construction team, a (boat) transportation team and a packaging team. The eleven enterprises employ 1,900 workers out of the commune's labor force of 19,500. In China as a whole, commune and brigade enterprises together employ 28 million rural workers out of a total commune labor force of 300 million.

Brigades

An average commune has 15 brigades, which in turn average about 253 households or 1,067 people. The brigades operate enterprises that are smaller in scale than those of the commune and sometimes receive income as well from assessments levied on teams which are members. The brigades, which are typically organized around natural villages, carry out smaller-scale capital construction projects and provide smaller-scale educational and health facilities; elementary schools and clinics, for example, are normally operated at the brigade level. At the Malienhua Brigade of the Sino-Japanese Friendship People's Commune near Beijing, for example, there are 180 households divided into 3 production teams (the average brigade in China has 6.7 teams and the average commune 100). Of the brigade's 820-member labor force, over 80 work in the brigade-level enterprises, which are engaged in polishing magnifying glasses, making tiles for house construction, operating a fish pond,

Brigade leader of the Malienhua Brigade, Sino-Japanese People's Friendship Commune, suburban Beijing. Translator-interpreter at left. (photo by V. Lippit)

making glass display cases and making paper bags for herbal medicine. The brigade receives 80 percent of its income from its enterprises, 20 percent from its member teams.

Teams

The teams are the basic units for agricultural production and, with the exception of a limited number of instances in which brigade-level accounting is practiced, of income-distribution as well. The average team in China has about 38 households or 160 people. At the No. 2 team of the Malienhua Brigade, however, there are over 90 households. In 1979, the gross income of the team was 450,000 *yuan* (one *yuan* is about U.S. $0.65), of which 170,000 *yuan* (38%) represented costs of production. For China as a whole, the cost of production is typically some 30 percent of gross agricultural income, but the figure may range over 40 percent in highly mechanized communes. At the No. 2 team, further deductions for taxes (which nationally average 3% of gross agricultural income), the accumulation fund (for expanding investment), the welfare fund (for which most teams use about 2% of gross income), and dues paid to the brigade, which in 1979 provided electric meters and piped running water to each household among its other activities, left 153,200 *yuan* to be distributed to team members as collective income. For the Sino-Japanese Friendship Commune as a whole, cash income from the collective economy was 493 *yuan* per member of the labor force in 1979, or 243 *yuan* per capita. As the discussion (below) of the agricultural sector as a whole will show, these income figures are exceptionally high, reflecting in large measure the commune's suburban Beijing location.

Households

In addition to their collective activity, commune members have a right to maintain private plots, which typically amount in the aggregate to some 5 percent of the collective lands. At the Sino-Japanese Friendship Commune, each family has about 66 square meters of land, yielding an estimated cash income of about 150 *yuan* per family. In China as a whole, the per capita income from collective labor in agriculture was 83.4 *yuan* in 1979,[3] roughly half in kind and half in cash, and the Ministry of Agriculture estimates that family sideline activities and private plots added about 30 to 40 *yuan* more to this figure.[4] Peasants can use the plots to grow food for their own consumption or for sale to the state or, except for grain and cooking oil, at local free markets, where somewhat higher prices prevail. Many urban consumers buy agricultural produce both at state stores, where prices are lower, and at free markets, where the food is fresher.

Reflecting 1980's 4.2 percent decrease in grain output to 318.2 million tons[5]—a consequence of bad weather—the per-capita income from collective labor rose by only 2.5 *yuan* in 1980. (Higher purchasing prices and non-grain products accounted for the gain.[6]) Although precise figures are lacking, income from sideline activities and private plots appears to have risen by a substantially greater amount. This is reflected in the fact that retail sales for China as a whole rose by 12.2 percent in real terms in 1980,[7] and the increase in rural areas was greater than that in urban ones.

It is common to find team and brigade leaders elected by their members, but commune-level cadres are typically appointed by the state; their charge is to see that the commune as a whole operates in accordance with public policy and party principles. Thus the commune blends in a unique way not only different aspects of social life but also grass-roots self-determination with state power.

In order to grasp the organization of agricultural activity in China, it is important to note that the commune level is merely one level in a structured hierarchy of authority and initiative. This hierarchy appears in somewhat simplified form as follows:

State Council

Ministry of Agriculture | **State Planning Commission**

province
prefecture
county
commune
brigade
team
family

Other government agencies also play a role, but the point here is to emphasize the character of the vertical linkages. Thus the county, for example, stands in relation to the commune much as the commune does to the brigade; communes are not isolated, discrete units. Important targets like those for grain will be determined by the State Council in consultation with the State Planning Commission, Ministry of Agriculture and other competent bodies. These will be disaggregated at the levels of province, prefecture and county. The counties disaggregate their targets among the communes, which do likewise among their brigades; the brigades assign the team targets. Each level is supposed to be intimately acquainted with the local conditions within its own region and to consult extensively before reaching final plans for the localities or production units within it. Innovation-initiative in the technical transformation of agriculture can come at any level and spread rapidly via the vertical linkages indicated.

Agricultural Policy and Performance, 1957–1977

The communes were first formed in 1958, and by September of that year, 98.2 percent of China's rural households were commune members. The main drive for the formation of communes came during the summer, by which time favorable weather conditions seemed to assure a bumper crop. This materialized as expected in 1958, but in the succeeding three years output fell sharply, creating near-crisis conditions in the agricultural sector and forcing a sharp shift in national policy toward agriculture. Whereas the development of heavy industry had been stressed in the 1950s, from 1960 agriculture was supposed to have been accorded priority. The terms of trade between industry and agriculture shifted gradually in favor of agriculture and the development of industries which provided inputs for agriculture (chemical fertilizer, farm machinery, etc.) was accorded priority. At the same time, reorganization of the communes emphasized making the production team, rather than the commune, the basic unit of accounting and distribution, thus linking income more closely to productive effort.

Changes at the macro-level appeared to be reinforced by the shift in ideological orientation ushered in with the Cultural Revolution, whose active phase was from 1966 to 1969. Since the Cultural Revolution policies were maintained, on the whole, until the fall of the Gang of Four in 1976, however, we may consider the entire 1966–76 period as the Cultural Revolution period. Between 1960 and 1965, the changes in agricultural policy had primarily been pragmatic, but these were reinforced from 1966 by the broader vision of social change which the Cultural Revolution incorporated. Self-reliance, the development of local industry and elimination of the three great differences (between town and country, agriculture and industry, and mental and manual labor) gave a distinctive cast to rural development in China.

The common pattern in capitalist countries and in the Soviet Union has been to focus on urban-industrial development, usually at the expense of the countryside, which provides resources and cheap labor but begins to draw some benefits from the development process only when it is relatively far advanced. China, by contrast, has been trying to make the development of the countryside one of the central pillars of the overall development effort. Peasants are not free to migrate to the cities; improvement in their lives must come through the transformation of their own environments. The development of industry at the brigade and commune levels is a part of this process. These local industries provide cash income for the collectives (which can use this to purchase agricultural machinery), employment opportunities for the commune members, important agricultural inputs and everyday consumption necessities. The state will provide technical guidance in the establishment of these local industries and sometimes help with the financing, but they rely on a combination of state and local initiative to get under way. The spread of health services to the countryside, a hallmark of the Cultural Revolution period especially, the spread of rural

Peasant member of the No. 2 Team of the Malienhua Brigade.

education (which took place from the 1950s), and innovation in educational and cultural services have also been important components of rural development.

Until recently, in the absence of direct data on changes in per-capita income in the countryside, indirect or partial indicators were used in the West to assess changes in living standards. These have proved in the light of recent evidence, however, to have been highly misleading. Increases in grain production and the gross value of agricultural output, combined with improving terms of trade for the agricultural sector, gave the appearance of firmly rising living standards in the countryside, and the model units open to foreign inspection tended to confirm this. In fact, however, evidence available only recently has made it clear that gains in income over the entire 1957–77 period were marginal.

Even if output is increasing and the terms of trade improving, incomes do not necessarily rise. If the costs of production rise sharply or an increasing share of net income is used for re-investment, then the income available for distribution to commune members may fall. During the Cultural Revolution period especially, at least the former factor—and possibly the latter as well—either limited gains in peasant incomes or led to actual declines. How this can happen is shown clearly by the case of the Nanshunchun Production Brigade in Nanyang People's Commune, Baixiang County, Hebei Province.[8]

The average cash income per production worker in the Nanshunchun Brigade was in excess of 100 *yuan* in 1969, when average grain yields were 500-510 *jin/mou*.* Three years later, in 1972, the average yield passed 700 *jin/mou*, a gain of some 40%, but only 10% of the production workers received more than 100 *yuan* for the year. There was a drought in 1972. The commune administration required each team to buy for irrigation purposes at least four diesel pumps costing 5,500 *yuan* each and four electric motors costing in excess of 300 *yuan* each. The electric motors were used for pumping, but power failures were

* 1 *jin* = 1 *catty* or 1.1 lb. 1 *mou* = 1/6th of an acre.

frequent so the diesel pumps were necessary as well. The state stood ready to make partial loans—or complete ones for the poorest teams—but these had to be paid back. The great increase in production cost led to a sharp decline in members' incomes; in 1972 some families received *negative* cash income—the net earnings for their collective work at the end of the year were insufficient to cover the cost of the food they had been advanced during the year.

This case is of particular interest because it reveals the importance of perspective in assessing agricultural performance. During the 1966–76 Cultural Revolution period, the Chinese press was filled with accounts of successful struggle against droughts and other natural disasters. The record of the Nanshunchun Brigade in raising output markedly despite the drought provides an example of the kind of "success story" frequently cited by the press at that time. And if maintaining or increasing output in the face of natural adversity is the criterion of success, there can be no doubt that this was indeed a success story. At the same time, however, information on changes in real income tended to be suppressed systematically during the Cultural Revolution period. And if changes in real income are considered part of the success criteria, then the record of the Nanshunchun Brigade and indeed of Chinese agriculture as a whole is much more ambiguous.

Although the evidence is impressionistic, former employees in the provincial governments of Hebei and Heilongjiang indicate that they believe that with the exception of brigades with successful enterprises, peasant living standards in those provinces declined during the Cultural Revolution period.[9] During this period, rural cadres were judged and promoted largely according to their success in increasing grain output. Taking "grain as the key link" received so much emphasis, and the "Dazhai model" emphasizing grain output rather than cost of production or net output was so popularized, that peasant living standards were relatively neglected.

The data for the period immediately prior to the Cultural Revolution are lacking, but data on peasant incomes between 1957 and 1977 confirm the extent to which China's development strategy neglected the peasants' livelihood. In 1957, per-capita income from collective labor in the countryside was 57 *yuan,* half in cash and half in kind.[10] In 1977 it was 65 *yuan.* Thus in a twenty-year period, cash income rose by 4 *yuan* or about U.S. $2.60. Now the cost of living in the Chinese countryside is not high and medical and other services are subsidized, but people remain quite poor despite working extremely hard, and a $2.60 gain over 20 years can scarcely be considered adequate. Further, it should be noted that the average is pulled up by the highly successful suburban communes, which means incomes are often much below the average in less-favored locales. Thus the case of a father and son on a Shandong commune, aged 55 and 25, both strong workers and in good health, earning together a total cash income of 20 *yuan* in 1979 for an entire year's collective labor is somewhat unusual but by no means extraordinary.[11]

Living standards depend on both personal income and public services. In China's countryside, the provision of public services still accounts for a very small portion of real income, so even a substantial improvement in public services would have a limited impact on living standards. In fact there was a substantial improvement only in medical care and not in public services as a whole during the Cultural Revolution period, so the stagnation in personal income was not offset to any material extent by an improvement in such services.

The stagnation in rural incomes had its counterpart in urban-worker incomes, as I will show below. Both phenomena, far from being coincidental, were natural outgrowths of the development strategy China had adopted after the First Five Year Plan ended in 1957, a strategy which reached its zenith during the Cultural Revolution period. The strategy relied upon stepping up the pace of capital formation to sustain economic growth, thus limiting the resources available for consumption. It involved holding down price increases for agricultural products, leaving the terms of trade with the industrial sector unfavorable to agriculture, despite the gradual improvement from the extremely unfavorable terms established in 1950; higher payments to peasants would have required diverting industrial production from producer to consumer goods.

The development strategy also downplayed material incentives, hoping in effect that the growth of consciousness could replace such incentives as a motivational force. in resource allocation, the strategy emphasized administrative decision-making rather than a significant role for the market. The cost of the doctrinaire rejection of the market was a high level of inefficiency. Firms, for example, that were unable to go out and buy needed parts, tended to stockpile them or even develop facilities to produce them, thus leading to exceptionally high investments in inventories or in uneconomically small, duplicative production facilities. Growing inefficiencies of this sort underlay the need to raise investment levels to sustain economic growth, thus limiting the resources that could be channeled into the production of consumer goods. Thus, whereas 24.2 percent of China's material output went into investment during the First Five Year Plan period (1953–57), the figure averaged 33 percent between 1970 and 1978.[12] By limiting consumer good production, the high investment rate required restricting peasant cash incomes. Low peasant incomes, in other words, were the logical outcome of the development strategy China followed during the Cultural Revolution period.

The increase in production costs is perhaps the major immediate factor why gains in agricultural incomes fell far behind gains in agricultural output. Table 1 shows the increase and increase rate in some of the principal inputs between 1952 and 1978. Whereas costs of production in the late 1950s came to about 25 percent of gross output value, this proportion increased to about 30 percent on average in the late 1970s and over 40 percent in the highly mechanized communes.

The example of the Nanshunchun Brigade shows how heavy production expenses can depress member incomes despite rising yields. In addition to the rise in production costs, however, the extremely low price received for agricultural products has remained a sharp constraint on peasant incomes. It is true that the terms of trade have moved gradually back in favor of agriculture since the early 1950s, but until the sharp increases in prices implemented in March 1979, agricultural prices remained extremely low relative to the cost of inputs and other industrial products. Even after the 1979 increases, moreover, which increased the purchasing price index for farm and sideline products by 22.1%,[13] agricultural prices remained low relative to industrial prices. Further price relief for the agricultural sector will be necessary and the rise in the index by 7.1% in 1980 compared to a 4.4% rise in retail prices in rural areas indicates that adjustments are continuing.[14]

Thus, although grain output rose 2.4 percent per year

between 1952 and 1978, slightly in excess of population growth, and the real value of gross agricultural output as a whole grew by 3.2% per year in the same period,[15] incomes in the countryside have increased very little and living standards remain very low. This, again, is not to belittle the real gains in living standards not reflected in personal income, gains most notable in areas like improved access to medical services, but to set these gains within a broader perspective. For the country as a whole, per-capita grain output in 1978 was no higher than in 1957. One of the central questions which current policy must address is why the agricultural sector, aided by massive increases in material inputs and labor, and with the communes providing an institutional framework exceptionally well-suited to rapid development,[16] could register no better than a marginally satisfactory performance. There was, in other words, a policy failure during the Cultural Revolution period which must be explained.

The evidence on agricultural labor input suggests that while output per worker increased by about 10 percent between 1957 and 1975, output per labor-day declined sharply—from 15 to 36%—as the number of days worked per person increased sharply.[17] During this period, industrial output was rising about 10 percent annually, but some of the difficulties in the industrial sector paralleled those in the agricultural sector. Substantial increases in investment reflecting a rising incremental capital-output ratio were needed for the output gains, limiting the scope for increases in real wages in industry, which remained unchanged between 1956 and 1975.[18]

Table 1

Increase in the Production of Principal Agricultural Inputs

Item	Unit	1952	1978	Average annual increase rate, 1953–1978
Chemical Fertilizer	thousand tons	39	8,693	23.1
Large & Medium Tractors	thousands	0.60	557	30.0
Hand Tractors	thousands	—	1,373	—
Power-driven Drainage & Irrigation Machines	thousand hp	128	65,575	27.1

Source: Statistical Bureau, People's Republic of China, *Main Indicators, Development of the National Economy of the People's Republic of China (1949 1978)*. Beijing: 1979, pp. 1–3.

China's New Development Strategy

Soon after the Gang of Four fell, China announced an ambitious set of targets for rapid industrial expansion, including a doubling of steel output to 60 million tons by 1985.[19] It soon became clear, however, that the nation lacked the infrastructure to support such a program, and that imbalances between heavy and light industry, industry and agriculture, infrastructure and directly productive activities, saving and investment, and foreign exchange requirements and availability made the long-range plan impractical. Official announcements then stressed that the targets were being postponed, not abandoned, which is true, but this tended to obscure the fact that a radically different, balanced development strategy was being substituted for the initial crash program.

The target of China's new development strategy remains ''attaining'' the four modernizations—industry, agriculture, science and technology, and national defense—by the turn of the century, but the strategy itself has changed. A three-year period of adjustment, running from 1979 to 1981, was established at the outset of the new program; its main thrust was the correction of imbalances, especially in infrastructure. The major emphasis during the adjustment period was to be on power and transport, with priority given to coal mining, electricity, oil, transport and building materials industries.[20]

It soon became evident that the economic adjustment period would require much more than three years, especially when the meaning attributed to adjustment was broadened in a basic sense to include structural reform of the economy. As a consequence, the Sixth Five-Year Plan period (1981–85) has also been designated as a period of readjustment. The changes all point toward rationalization of the economy and creation of conditions for balanced growth. The lopsided development of heavy industry is to be corrected with a decline in investment and increase in consumer goods production. Improvements in technical levels and management are to be stressed at enterprises, which will be accorded greater autonomy, and the weak links in the economic structure—energy, transportation and utilities especially—are to be strengthened.[21] The plans for the Sixth Five-Year Plan period indicate a continuation and deepening of the new economic strategy that has emerged since Mao's death.

In sharp contrast to the Cultural Revolution period, official policy under the new strategy is stressing material incentives over moral exhortation or social and political pressure as a means of inducing productive effort, although the latter elements are still present in the overall incentive structure. The new emphasis on material incentives requires a sharply stepped-up production of consumer goods, and thus light industry is also being stressed in current investment policies. This is a two-edged sword, since the high profit rate in light industry will serve to help finance the overall investment program the four modernizations will require. The emphasis on material incentives also calls for increased agricultural production, especially of meat and animal products, since close to half of consumers' incomes is spent on food.

Although allocating increased resources to expanding consumer goods and agricultural production is an essential part of the new strategy, the issue is far more than one of aggregate resource allocation in itself. As noted above, industry was producing greatly increased quantitites of agricultural inputs throughout the Cultural Revolution period and was itself expanding about 10 percent per year. These results were achieved, however, at a cost of sharply rising investment requirements per unit of output in both industry and agriculture, limiting the resources that could be devoted to improving people's living standards. The new strategy seeks to improve the efficiency with which resources are used and thereby to free some for consumption purposes even while aggregate growth continues at a rapid pace. The aim, therefore, is to improve the efficiency of the economic system such that a lower investment rate, freeing resources to improve mass consumption, will sustain the same or a higher rate of economic growth. The challenge is magnified by the economic imbalances which are the heritage of the Cultural

Plastic sheets covering early crops at the Long March People's Commune, suburban Shanghai.

Revolution period, imbalances the correction of which will now require costly investments in the energy and transport sectors which typically have extremely high investment requirements per unit of output.

A wide range of pragmatic measures to improve efficiency has been introduced or is in the process of being introduced, but the most important among these is a limited insertion of market forces in the economic system and greater autonomy for decision-making units in agriculture and industry. Industrial enterprises are now being given greater say over the use of their profits and depreciation funds, and the role of profit as a success indicator is being strengthened. At the same time, enterprises are increasingly free to purchase their input requirements directly from other enterprises and to sell their output directly to other enterprises or even abroad, as well as to state commercial units. Further, under an experimental program begun in 1979 and expanded considerably in 1980, some enterprises have been able to accept new employees by examination rather than have them assigned by one of the state labor bureaus (although the labor bureaus still determine the pool of qualified applicants eligible to take the examinations).

In agriculture, output targets remain part of the planning system, but acreage targets are now supposed to be left to the discretion of the commune production units. Purchase prices have been raised sharply for grain and subsidiary products and the free markets for private-plot produce are flourishing, contributing to a sharp rise in peasant incomes. Income from collective labor rose from 65 *yuan* per capita in 1977 to 74 *yuan* in 1978,[22] 83.4 *yuan* in 1979,[23] and 85.9 *yuan* in 1980, with incomes from the private plots now adding an additional 30-40 *yuan* per capita to collective income. The long-term modernization plan for agriculture calls for its mechanization and the accelerated development of scientific agriculture.

The new development strategy incorporates as well a sharply stepped-up role for foreign trade and investment, decreasing the investment rate to allow increased consumption, and placing a greater emphasis on the acquisition of modern technology as a means of sustaining economic growth. The increased role of foreign trade means that exports must increase; since the products of agriculture and light industry constitute a major share of exports, and since light industry still depends mainly on agricultural inputs, the strategy accords agriculture a key role. Indeed, since agriculture remains the weak link in the economy, the overall strategy for balanced growth depends heavily on improvement in the agricultural sector.

The Prospects for Agriculture

It might be most helpful to consider the outlook for agriculture and for the communes in particular from the standpoint of problems which the new strategy may appear to raise. I would like to consider these under four main headings. First, as I have indicated, the agricultural sector provides employment for about 300 million people, about 75 percent of China's labor force (of these, some 28 million are actually employed in commune and brigade-level industry). The commune system has played a key role in China's ability to employ productively virtually its entire labor force, an ability which stands in marked contrast to the typical underdeveloped country in the capitalist world, whose combined unemployment-underemployment rate is nearing 30 percent.[24] In capitalist countries, potentially productive labor will remain unutilized if the wage rate is above the marginal product of labor, but the commune does not treat wages as a cost so there is nothing to be gained by allowing people to remain idle as long as there are useful things to do. If China proceeds with agricultural mechanization, however, as is clearly its intent, it might appear that that will create serious employment problems in the countryside and undermine the commune system.

Second, the entire process of industrial rationalization and standardization would also appear to create problems for the communes. The communes have been largely—although by no means absolutely—self-reliant units and, in many respects, self-sufficient as well. Local industry was based on using resources not substantial enough to warrant state investment. The new plans call for the standardization of parts for agricultural machinery and for specialization in production. Thus commune and county factories will increasingly be producing parts for agricultural machines rather than whole machines, and there is a question as to whether they can be competitive with urban-based industry on this basis. Further, relative self-sufficiency will also be broken down by the increasing concentration of agricultural production in the regions best suited for the various crops. Finally, since production will have to be justified on the basis of efficiency and cost, and since the cost per unit of output is usually higher in the smaller plants than in the larger, state-owned plants,[25] there appears to be a threat to commune-based local industry.

Third, the shift to material incentives on a national level appears to undermine the collective ethos and certainly undermines the Dazhai model from which the entire nation was exhorted to learn during the Cultural Revolution period. According to the Dazhai model, the shared belief that the collective, self-reliant transformation of the environment provided the only basis for individual prosperity was to be the basis of agricultural development. Confronting extremely unfavorable natural conditions, the Dazhai brigade members, relying primarily on their own labor, worked very hard in carrying out terracing, water conservancy and other capital construction

Greenhouse for vegetable-growing at the Long March People's Commune. (Lippit)

projects, greatly increasing the yield of the land.[26] The new stress on material rewards stands in marked contrast to this ethos. No longer is the system of mutual assessment used to determine work points in most of the communes but specific jobs accomplished (e.g., so many points for plowing a field). Production for the market on private plots is encouraged. Material disincentives are also being used; in one commune near Shanghai, families which have a third child have 10 percent of the income to which they would otherwise be entitled deducted. Thus the new policies might appear to undermine collective effort in the countryside and indeed the commune as a collective institution.

Finally, the impact of the new strategy on the relative position of agriculture must be clarified. The Cultural Revolution's stress on equality incorporated attempts to overcome the "three great differences," two of which, the differences between urban and rural areas and between industry and agriculture, bear directly on the relative position of agriculture. The Cultural Revolution period in general was marked by a stress on agricultural and rural development, as reflected in the spread of medical coverage throughout the countryside, the development of the "barefoot doctor" system, the settling of urban youths in the countryside and the marked increase in the production by industry of agricultural means of production. Since China has attempted to make agricultural development the cornerstone of its overall development program, the impact of the new development strategy on the material prosperity and cultural development of the countryside must be examined.

Employment and Mechanization

The first question concerning the new strategy is that of employment; how is agricultural mechanization to be reconciled with full employment in the countryside? It should be noted first of all that Chinese government officials are quite sensitive to this question, and that the mechanization program is by no means simply a labor-saving one. Rather, its form is to be tailored to the particular needs of different locales. In certain seasons or in certain regions, labor is indeed relatively in short supply, and under such circumstances, the use of labor-saving machinery is considered appropriate. Thus in the Northeast and Northwest, where this situation often prevails, the government plans to mechanize plowing and weeding first. Mechanization is also considered appropriate where the labor is especially heavy and where land productivity can be raised, often through making possible multiple cropping. Thus in the south, the government plans for mechanization focus on the transplanting of rice and drying it after the harvest. This will release labor, but the surplus labor power can be used productively. Near Shanghai, mechanization has released peasants to engage in finer, more meticulous farming, greatly increasing yields. Such labor can also be used in capital construction work or in the development of forestry, fishing, animal husbandry and sideline activities, including handicrafts. Finally, the development of commune and brigade enterprises is also expected to absorb labor.

It should be kept in mind that the demand for labor, a demand derived from the demand for agricultural products, can also be expected to increase with the four modernizations. Mechanization in remote mountainous regions, for example, will often focus initially on improving transport, thereby opening new markets. The planned development of intermediate-sized cities, the national improvement in transportation, the opening of export markets, the development of light industry and rising consumer incomes can all be expected to expand agricultural markets, raising indirectly the demand for labor. It is within this context that mechanization-modernization is being pursued in China, and it is clear that there is no lessened commitment to full employment on the part of the government. As development proceeds, the communes will increasingly become integrated agricultural-industrial-service organizations, absorbing labor through the diversified activities this integrated character makes possible.

Labor power released through mechanization could, in principle, be absorbed in new collective activities or in the private plots and sideline activities. Although modest expansion in private activities has clearly taken place, it is unlikely that this could continue to a point where serious inroads on collective labor would occur. Several factors are responsible for this. First, public policy recognizes private activity as spare-time activity, and people are not free to participate in the collective economy just to the extent that they feel like it. Both mass pressures—the good of the whole depends on everyone's participating—and the entire leadership structure of the commune, from the team-level to the commune-level, tend to insure conformity in this respect. Thus at the Malienhua Brigade, for example, a bell rings at 8 A.M. to signal the start of collective labor for the village and again at 6 P.M. to signal its end.

Second, incentives in the collective economy are geared to tasks completed. Each job is assigned a certain number of work points and less intensive efforts will reduce the number of points earned. The recent spread of the contract system links reward to effort even more closely. Under the contract system, small groups within the production teams contract with the team as a whole to farm specific fields. They must turn over to the team an agreed amount of the harvest and have the right to retain any excess. Finally, employment in non-agricultural activities within the commune is growing faster than that in agricultural activities, and workers in commune enterprises have even less leeway than those doing agricultural work to substitute private for collective activity.

Duck pond at the Long March Commune. (Lippit)

Industrial Rationalization

The rationalization of industry, like mechanization, poses no threat to the agricultural sector. It is true that an increased division of labor is in prospect, but the commune enterprises will be incorporated in that division rather than excluded from it. New opportunities are expected to open up for producing industrial parts under contract for state-owned enterprises. Public policy and the whole strategy of development require that the commitment to rural, small-scale industry be maintained. Communes are expected to pay for their own mechanization. The principal source of funds for this is the development of commune enterprises. The stepped-up pace of mechanization promises to release some labor for commune enterprises even while it requires their expansion for funding. The government is highly conscious of this need and is committed to developing rural industries where rural areas have production advantages or economies of scale are not very significant. Thus, for example, the transfer of sugar beet and cane processing from urban areas to the countryside is planned. Finally, it should be noted that one principal target of rationalization is lowering the cost of agricultural inputs, an objective which promises to raise rural incomes. All of these factors would lead us to expect public policy to support a vigorous expansion of commune, production brigade and production team enterprises. In fact, such enterprises produced an output value of 49,000 million *yuan* in 1978, about 25% more than in 1977, which in turn was 43.7% higher than the 1976 figure.[27]

Material Incentives

Third, the shift to material incentives is quite real, but it is not immediately evident that this will eliminate the collective ethos. It should be kept in mind that Dazhai was a model, and that the reality of most of the countryside has been poverty with people working longer and longers hours for miniscule gains in income. Under such circumstances, which tend to breed cynicism as the promise of collective agriculture remains unrealized, we may question whether the collective ethos had very much power. Now the situation has changed; people's incomes for working for the collective are rising (from 65 *yuan* per capita in 1977 to 85.9 *yuan* in 1980) and further gains are in sight. Rising prosperity in the countryside not only increases individual cash incomes for collective labor, it also increases social services the collective can provide. Starting in 1979, for example, the Long March People's Commune near Shanghai instituted a retirement system. The retirement age is 65 and the pension is 20-28 *yuan* per month. Although very few communes are prosperous enough to institute retirement programs, such programs are clearly the wave of the future; China is in the midst of an historic shift from the family providing material security in old age to the collective. But to provide material security, output and income must rise greatly. In this sense we can say that material incentives which help to raise output levels are not necessarily in conflict with the collective ethos.

If material incentives were emphasized to the exclusion of the development of socialist consciousness then it is of course possible that the commune as a collective institution would be undermined. It is also possible—although rather unlikely—that recent changes will ultimately lead in that direction. What must be emphasized at present, however, is that reasonably-implemented material incentives *per se* are not necessarily anti-collective or anti-socialist, and under current conditions may well be essential to the development of the commune as a collective institution. That is to say, a prematurely egalitarian emphasis on socialist relations of production may, by cutting short the development of the forces of production, ultimately forestall the realization of an egalitarian, socialist society.

Agriculture and Economic Priorities

Finally, the new strategy remains committed to overcoming the differences between urban areas and the countryside, between industry and agriculture. Investment in agriculture is now a much higher share of state investment than at any time during the Cultural Revolution period. The commitment to rural development has certainly been increased, purchase prices for farm produce have been raised sharply and peasant incomes have leaped upwards, increasing on the average more rapidly than worker incomes. In 1979, peasant incomes from the collectives grew by 11.4 percent compared to an average real wage rise for workers in state-owned enterprises of 7.6 percent.[28] The four modernizations strategy calls for balanced growth, and since agriculture has been a weak link in the economy, special efforts are being made to develop it. Thus the share of state capital construction devoted to agriculture increased from 10.7% in 1978 to 14% in 1979[29] and will increase further to a planned 18% by 1982–84[30] even while accumulation within the sector was (and presumably will be) promoted by the sharp improvement in the terms of trade and the successful development of smaller local industry.

Further, other aspects of the development strategy promise to provide complementary support to the agricultural sector. The modernization of science and technology includes agricultural science as one of its emphases. Moreover, in the efforts to rationalize industry and thereby reduce production costs of industrial products, particular emphasis is being placed on lowering the costs of inputs for agriculture as part of a self-conscious effort to improve the terms of trade for the agricultural sector.

The new development strategy, like any possible course of action the Chinese could choose, has its own pitfalls and contradictions. Many of these are associated with the new reliance on market forces, even though these are not given completely free rein. Allowing the market to play a greater role in allocation, for example, gave rise to strong inflationary pressures in 1980 especially, pressures which required strong remedial action (prices have been stabilized in the main since a State Council edict of December 7, 1980, calling for price controls[31]). Moreover, since prices are a mix of administratively set prices—some set long ago in a different economic environment—and market-influenced ones, it is clear that they cannot always send the right signals; the most profitable crop, for example, is not necessarily the socially most desirable one.

Further, material incentives have a logic of their own, and it is not immediately clear how an aspiring socialist society can escape the smooth progression from material incentives to materialistic culture that has accompanied the development of the capitalist West. In addition, the new strategy will tend to promote an elite status for those who are educated or technically trained. Finally, the new strategy has the potential to increase certain inequalities, especially if those regions most favored or possessing the most favorable initial conditions develop far more rapidly than other regions. (It should be noted here as well, however, that the Cultural Revolution's emphasis on self-reliance had a similar implication for intensifying initial inequalities.)

Indeed, concerns like those enumerated above underlay the whole Cultural Revolution effort to find a viable alternative strategy. However, the failure of the Cultural Revolution policies—expressed most notably in the failure of incomes to rise, the perpetuation of social hierarchy, the rigid censorship, the failure of educational reform in the critical area of the substantive content of education, and the inability of the direct producers to control their own workplaces or participate meaningfully in higher levels of social decision-making—left no alternative to seeking a new strategy. The emergence of the present strategy must be understood within this context.

According to the argument I have presented, China's new development strategy is both necessary and viable. Although problem areas do exist, the leadership is aware of these for the most part and has taken measures to minimize the problems. Nevertheless, a number of contradictions will inevitably intensify as the new strategy is implemented, and the successful resolution of these will be a critical issue in the transition to socialism in China. If certain regions are allowed to prosper first, will decisive measures be taken at the appropriate time, when increased resources can be channeled to the lagging regions to help them catch up? Will rising incomes lead to a materialistic culture or provide the basis for a fuller development of social consciousness? Critical issues like these will have to be confronted in the fairly near future, but the inevitability of the confrontation does not in itself negate the validity of the new strategy, which was made necessary by the failure of the old and the absence of viable alternatives. To say that the new strategy is necessary and viable, however, is not to say that it will succeed; the issue of success will be determined ultimately by the skill and insight with which its own emerging contradictions will be dealt.

Changes in the Communes

The favorable implications for agriculture of the new development program are reinforced at the commune level by a series of policies which promise to strengthen the commune as an institution. It should be noted first that communes are collectives rather than state-owned institutions; that is to say, members receive instead of wages a share of the income after costs of production, taxes and various fund payments have been deducted from gross receipts. Although collectives have been regarded as socialist in China, they have been regarded as distinctly second-class socialist institutions. In urban areas, collective members have been prohibited by explicit government policy from receiving wages and benefits comparable to those of employees in state enterprises, and in the countryside this attitude has been reflected in intermittent pressures to raise the level of distribution from the team to the brigade or even the commune, which could lead ultimately to making the commune comparable to a state farm or factory with members receiving wages.

Such pressures were reflected in making the commune level the basic unit of distribution when the communes were first formed, and even when this proved impractical it remained a target for the near future. Thus Mao wrote in 1960:

> *Within a certain number of years our people's communes will have to carry through the transformation from ownership by the basic team to ownership by the basic commune, and then into ownership by the whole people.*[32]

In the same year he also wrote:

> *The socialist state and socialist construction cannot be established for any great length of time on the basis of ownership by the whole people* and *ownership by the collective as two different bases of ownership.*[33]

Mao argued on the one hand that communes as collectives would stifle the development of the productive forces and therefore limit peasant consumption and agricultural growth,[34] and on the other that ". . . if we do not let collective ownership become people's ownership . . . present living standards will surpass those of the workers to the detriment of both industrial and agricultural development."[35]

Now Mao of course contradicts himself here—the communes as collectives won't do because they won't meet the peasants' material needs and they won't do because they will make the peasants too prosperous—but what is significant is that whatever the pretext, the communes are viewed as improper and unsustainable in their present form. Mao's analysis, however, overlooks some of the unique features of the communes.

As they are currently constituted, the communes offer much greater scope than state-owned enterprises for local initiative and community action, at least at the team and brigade levels. Charles Bettelheim argues that socialism is a system of control by the direct producers as a class over their conditions of existence, and in the first instance over their productive activity and products.[36] This appears to be a satisfactory first approximation. Since state factory workers in China have much *less* control over their work activity, environment and products than commune members, it is questionable whether changing the ownership system as Mao advocates will really mark progress toward socialism.

The new attitudes towards the communes and to the collective form in general are much more practical and less ideological than those which prevailed during the Cultural Revolution. In urban areas, collectives are viewed as an essential means of absorbing the substantial influx into the labor force in recent years. In 1979 more than 9 million people found urban jobs, an unprecedented figure, and of the net increase in the urban labor force of 4.68 million (subtracting those who retired or left the labor force from the newly employed), 2.26 million or almost half increased employment in the collective sector.[37] To promote the development of the collectives, policy restrictions limiting collective-sector employees' wages and benefits compared to state sector employees have been abolished. In the same vein, pressure for rapid change in the ownership system of the communes has abated. In other areas, however, basic changes in the communes have either taken place or are in store.

Changes

First, the fact that the new development strategy accords material prosperity a much higher priority is of great importance. The commune, we should recall, is an institution which mixes local autonomy with state power. When most people were getting by on less than 65 *yuan* per year, the material needs of the population were not being met satisfactorily and enthusiasm for collective labor may not have been quite spontaneous. At the same time, the commune level was firmly an organ of state power and it was not unusual to find, for example, labor requisitioned to carry out certain projects.

At present the commune level is still an organ of state power, but there have been important shifts in the way that power is exercised. "Commandism" has been criticized and it is no longer permissible to order people to do uncompensated labor; all work must be paid for. Commandism of course has been criticized before, but the criticisms taken on a special significance this time because they have been made in the context of a concerted effort to unleash economic initiative at the level of the production unit and of the direct producer. The institutional basis for this effort is being established by the limited introduction of the market system in a context of overall planning. Without the market, production must be guided by administrative decisions centrally made and handed down, making some form of commandism almost inevitable.

With regard to the structure of material incentives as well, an important shift has taken place: the carrot has been enlarged and the income available for successful performance has been increased substantially. In March 1979, state purchase prices for grain were raised by 20 percent with a 50 percent bonus above the new price for deliveries to the state in excess of the planning quotas, and the 18 principal farm and sideline product purchase prices were raised by an average of 24.8 percent.[38] Not only have all prices and bonuses for above-quota production been raised, the quotas have been lowered so that a larger share of output will qualify for the bonus payments. Furthermore, paying commune members according to work accomplished rather than according to the system of mutual assessment increases the maximum earning capacity of—and therefore the incentives for—the most productive workers. Thus state power is increasingly exercised within the commune indirectly through the structure of incentives rather than directly in the form of commands or ideological pressures.

This change is reflected also in the changes in the planning system. In the past, plans typically specified the acreage to be devoted to specific crops, and regional self-sufficiency was stressed, especially in the growing of grain. Now, plans for

Malienhua Brigade in suburban Beijing: plastic sheets covering early plantings at night. (Lippit)

agriculture continue to specify output targets, but land use is left up to the producing units. Further, specialization is being encouraged, so that communes well situated for growing cotton or others whose hilly terrain is more suited to fruit-growing than to grain cultivation have increasing latitude to use their land in the most productive manner. State policy still expects some degree of self-sufficiency in grain, but the requirements are less severe than in the past and the scope for local initiative broader.

The active encouragement of the productive use of the private plots and of the free markets for the sale of their produce marks another shift in policy. The policy has already led to substantial gains in peasant incomes—and in urban supplies of pork, eggs and other farm products. In 1979, household sideline production contributed 30 to 40 *yuan* per capita to peasant incomes, 36-48% of the average collective income of 83.4 *yuan*.[39] In the same year, state purchases of eggs rose 48.1 percent to a record 825,000 tons,[40] and the total output of pork, beef and mutton rose 24.1 percent to 10,624,000 tons,[41] with the private plots making a substantial contribution to these increases. The revival of the private plots is of course part of the broader policy of increasing the use of material incentives to stimulate the growth of production.

The shift to paying people according to work accomplished is perhaps the most significant change in this respect. At the Sino-Japanese Friendship People's Commune, for example, men could receive a maximum of ten work points for a day's labor and women nine under the mutual assessment system. Today those are the average number of work points earned, but some men earn as much as 15 in a day and some women as much as 13-14; the men generally earn more in heavy work like leveling land and loading, the women earn more in transplanting rice, picking fruit and so forth. If work is done collectively, the group leader within the team can adjust the number of points each member receives to reflect differences in quantity and quality of work as long as he or she stays within the total number of points allotted for the task. Five work points is the minimum for a day's work, and six is the standard for junior high school graduates working as apprentices for one year. The main practical consequence of the change in the work point system appears to be raising the upper limit on the incomes the most productive workers can receive from collective labor.

Although the "revolutionary committee" structure is still to be found in the communes, the committees have become basically ordinary administrative bodies. Like many other local institutions in China, the communes increasingly use formal democratic procedures, as in the election of team and brigade leaders. Some commune-level cadres may increasingly be elected in the future as well, but we should expect most commune leaders to be appointed from above for quite some time to come, for that is the way the party-state assures itself that the communes will adhere to public policy. The role of the state has become less direct but no less significant because of that; public policy remains committed to the modernization of agriculture and the party continues to see a need for cadres to carry out that policy. Although the state is trying to interefere less with local production activities and to stimulate local initiative, its planning at an aggregative level has if anything been increased. China is trying to establish twelve regions within the country as areas of high, stable yields which can provide a dependable grain surplu for urban areas and to serve other purposes; these areas will receive priority in mechanization and supplies. Other areas will specialize increasingly in cotton and other industrial crops according to their natural advantages. China's agriculture remains very much a planned operation, and although agricultural purchase prices are likely to be raised further in the future, the market is not basically replacing planning in agriculture but serving as an adjunct. Under these circumstances, the basic structure of the commune is not likely to be altered.

Stepping up the pace of agricultural modernization, however, will have important consequences for the communes. The initiation of pensions is of outstanding importance among a range of social services that increased material prosperity will make possible. At the same time, the accelerated diversification of commune activities that modernization will simultaneously require and lead to promises to speed the transformation of the Chinese countryside. The outlook is not only for a narrowing of the differences in the nature of productive activity as well. Over the long run, China's unique development strategy points toward a balanced growth of industry and agriculture in a "civilized" countryside, with the commune as its institutional core.

Notes

1. *Beijing Review* (hereafter *BR*), May 18, 1981, p. 20.

2. The descriptive materials on particular communes were gathered on a trip to China made by the author in April 1980 to investigate economic conditions.

3. *BR*, August 18, 1980, p. 4.

4. This and subsequent Ministry of Agriculture estimates were provided to the author by senior Ministry officials in April 1980.

5. *BR*, May 11, 1981, p. 25.

6. *BR*, May 18, 1981, p. 19.

7. *BR*, May 18, 1981, p. 17.

8. The following account of the Nanshunchun Brigade is based on information provided to the author by a former Vice-Chairman of the Nanyang People's Commune.

9. Information provided in the personal discussions with the author.

10. Data provided by officials of the Ministry of Agriculture.

11. Information provided to the author in a discussion with a member of their family.

12. *BR*, December 21, 1979, p. 10.

13. *BR*, May 18, 1981, p. 17.

14. Ibid.

15. State Statistical Bureau, People's Republic of China, *Main Indicators, Development of the National Economy of the People's Republic of China* (1949–1978). Beijing, 1979.

16. For a discussion of the role of the commune in Chinese development see my article, "The Commune in Chinese Development," *Modern China*, Vol. 3, No. 2 (April 1977), pp. 229-255.

17. Thomas Rawski, "Economic Growth and Employment in China," *World Development*, Vol. 7, Nos. 8/9 (August-September 1979), p. 777.

18. Nicholas Lardy, *Economic Growth and Distribution in China* (Cambridge: Cambridge University Press, 1978), p. 175.

19. Robert F. Dernberger and David Fasenfest, "China's Post-Mao Economic Future," in U.S. Congress, Joint Economic Committee, *Chinese Economy Post-Mao* (Washington, D.C.: U.S. Government Printing Office, November 9, 1978), p. 6.

20. A rather full discussion of the logic of the three-year adjustment policy appears in Shi Zhengwen, "Readjusting the National Economy: Why and How?" *BR*, June 29, 1979, pp. 13-23.

21. *BR*, May 11, 1981.

22. *BR*, August 18, 1980, p. 4.

23. *BR*, April 21, 1980, p. 17.

24. The reference here to productive employment is not meant to suggest that productivity is high; the truth is quite to the contrary as the data in the text on income levels and declining labor productivity should make clear. Despite low productivity, however, people in China are employed and are making a net contribution to output. A major task for economic reform in China is to raise productivity without generating unemployment. The contrasting datum for the capitalist world is from Michael P. Todaro, *Economic Development in the Third World* (New York: Longman, 1977).

25. Jon Sigurdson, "Rural Industrialization in China," U.S. Congress, Joint Economic Committee, *China: A Reassessment of the Economy* (Washington, D.C.: U.S. Government Printing Office, July 10, 1975), pp. 411-435.

26. An excellent account of the Tachai model appears in Neville Maxwell, "Learning from Tachai," *World Development*, Vol. 3, Nos. 7 & 8 (July-August 1975), pp. 473-495.

27. *BR*, September 28, 1979, p. 4.

28. *BR*, May 19, 1980, p. 18, and July 7, 1980, p. 6.

29. *BR*, July 20, 1979, p. 9.

30. *BR*, March 24, 1980, p. 17.

31. *BR*, May 18, 1981, p. 21.

32. Mao Tse-tung, *A Critique of Soviet Economics* (New York: Monthly Review Press, 1977), p. 34.

33. Ibid., p. 53.

34. Ibid., p. 54.

35. Ibid., p. 68.

36. Charles Bettelheim and Paul Sweezy, *On The Transition to Socialism* (New York: Monthly Review Press, 1971), p. 35.

37. *BR*, May 19, 1980, p. 23.

38. *BR*, July 20, 1979, p. 8.

39. *BR*, July 7, 1980, p. 7.

40. *BR*, January 28, 1980, p. 7.

41. *BR*, May 12, 1980, p. 14.

Post-Mao Changes in a South China Production Brigade

by Victor Nee

With the opening of possibilities for field work in China, we can anticipate a new stage in the systematic study of Chinese society. Previously, sociologists and anthropologists were limited in their quest for social data to refugee interviews, deciphering Chinese newspapers, and reports filed by visiting delegations and journalists. Although relatively sophisticated methods were developed by researchers to compensate the "data problem,"[1] the field maintained a defensive stance when challenged on the reliability of its data.

In this report I shall discuss the findings of a recent field work project which brought me to a village that I had studied from afar through informant interviewing.[2] The field work was conducted in a rural county in southwestern Fujian province, from March 17 to April 18, 1980. A month would not have been adequate for a serious sociological study had it not been that prior to my visit, I had completed an interview project with former educated youths who lived in the village from 1969–1975. The interview project, carried out at Cornell University from December 1977 to September 1979, produced unusually rich data, about 1,500 pages of detailed text and diagrams about life and social structure in the village. My visit to the village allowed me the opportunity to conduct an independent study to check the reliability of the data I had gathered from afar, as well as to learn about changes and developments subsequent to my informants' departure in 1975. Methodologically, therefore, the study can be seen as a bridge between the earlier works based upon refugee interviews and the new studies of Chinese society being conducted in the field by sociologists and anthropologists. The report discusses the impact of recent changes in national agrarian policies, the current birth control campaign, youth discontent, and evidence of consolidation of the local elite in light of the data gathered from interviewing former educated youths.

Yangbei Production Brigade is a single surname settlement, with a population of 2,400, located in one of the three Hakka counties bordering Guangdong and Jiangxi provinces. It is a two day bus ride from Xiamen, along winding mountain roads. In modern times these counties experienced major peasant uprisings. In 1929 Yangbei villagers, together with peasants from neighboring villages, organized a peasant movement and succeeded in establishing a soviet government in the Xiangdong market town. The area continued to support an active guerrilla movement after the defeat of the Xiangdong soviet government and the fall of the base area. Survivors of the peasant movement recall seeing Mao Zedong at Gutian, a day's walk from the village, during the Gutian Conference in December 1929. These counties continued to be regarded as a poor hinterland area by provincial authorities in Fuzhou. Economic development and standard of living remained lower than the national norms. In 1979, per capita income in Xiangdong People's Commune was 68.10 *yuan,* whereas that for Fujian province was estimated at 80 *yuan*. Per capita grain consumption in the commune was cited at 523 *jin,* whereas national per capita grain consumption is about 600 *jin*. After the departure of the last educated youths from Yangbei in 1977, there have been few visitors from the coastal cities.

From Radicalism to Market Socialism.

Peasant morale, according to my original informants, was low in the early 1970s, during the resurgence of rural radicalism associated with the ultra-left phase of the Cultural Revolution. They had told me that during the "learn from Dazhai" campaign, the village moved from team to brigade accounting. The village adopted the Dazhai workpoint system, stressing political, rather than material incentives. Better-managed "rich" teams were called on to assist the poor teams. This was accomplished both through direct labor contribution, and through a type of economic subsidy accomplished by brigade accounting, which leveled workpoint value between rich and poor teams. As in the abortive Great Leap Forward, peasants were mobilized to contribute labor for local construction projects. The free market was tightly controlled through the imposition of regulations that restricted the sale of pork and grain and discouraged peasants from engaging in handicrafts and other household sidelines. The size of free plots was cut back by 40 percent. Reminiscent of the Great Leap Forward, though on a minor scale, there was a drop in grain production, a shortage of fresh pork in the free market, and a thriving black market in grain. Villagers grumbled to the educated youths that they didn't have enough to eat, and that their present standard of living was lower than before the Great Leap.

At the time of my early interviews, the description of declining standard of living and peasant discontent seemed to me too much like the stereotypical refugee account. Certainly

Table 1

Yangbei Production Brigade: Per Capita Grain Consumption

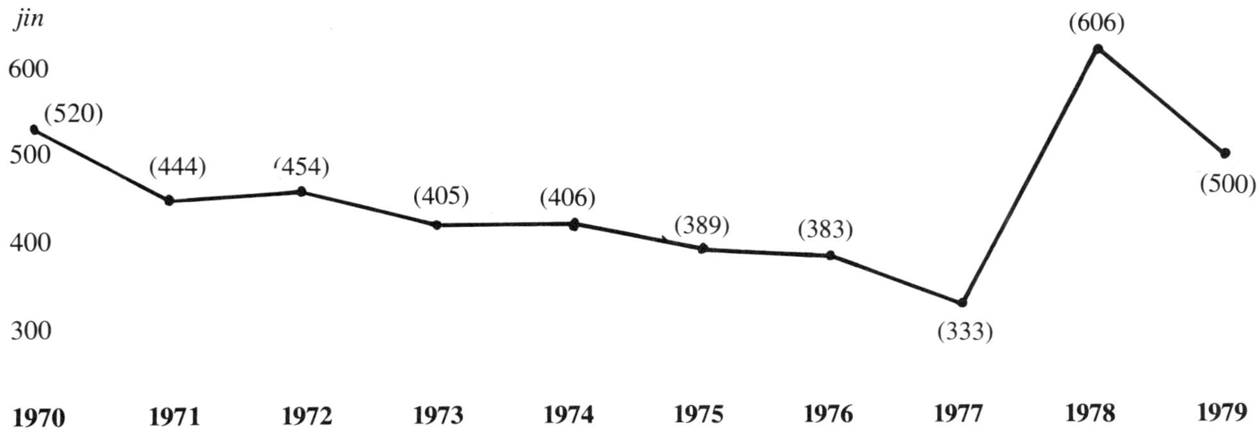

people have been known to complain even when their conditions were actually improving bit by bit. Without concrete data on consumption patterns over time, it was impossible to assess the validity of claims that radical policies had depressed the rural economy enough to lower the living standard in the village below that which was achieved on a per capita basis in the 1950s.

Informal conversations with villagers early in my field work this spring revealed that villagers felt their standard of living had improved markedly since the mid-1970s; but older villagers still maintained that per capita consumption was not up to par with the level attained in the 1950s before the Great Leap Forward. As table 1 reveals, the data on per capita grain consumption supported the villagers' statements of improved living standard. There was a dramatic increase in per capita grain consumption from the low of 333 *jin** in 1977 to 606 *jin* in 1979, followed by a dip to 500 *jin* in 1979 due to a serious spring drought that year. A poll of older peasants revealed estimates from per capita grain consumption for 1955–57 ranging from 575 *jin* to 600 *jin*, markedly higher than the per capita grain consumption between the years 1970–77, confirming the data from the educated youths. I concluded, then, that the dip in consumption in 1979 from the high in 1978 accounted for the perception that the living standard in the mid-1950s was still slightly higher. I emphasize grain consumption as a key indicator of living standard because of its importance to the peasant household economy. With an adequate grain supply, exceeding what is needed for human consumption, the peasant can increase production of pigs and poultry, the main source of cash income. The recent increases in grain supply thus was reflected in the abundant supply of fresh pork and poultry at the free market.

As a result of the recent improvement in living standard, there was a noticeable optimism among villagers at the time of my visit. The mood was reflected in the numbers of new homes in the process of construction, in comments suggestive of increased enthusiasm for working in the collective sector, and in the general belief that grain production would continue to increase. Villagers attributed the sharp increase in grain production to changes in the management of the team economy and the restoration of a more pragmatic rural policy. Although the experiment with brigade accounting was terminated in 1973, it was not until the four modernizations campaign was launched that reforms were carried out in the village. These reforms were reminiscent of those associated with Chen Yun during the recovery years after the Great Leap Forward.

The brigade party secretary's comment on the direction of reforms reflects the liberalized climate of thinking in regards to management and incentives. He remarked that "because of the strong tradition of individual household production, the closer we can approximate individual household production while still maintaining the collective system of ownership, the higher the productivity we can expect to achieve." This candid appraisal reflected the change in sentiment away from the radical emphasis on increasing the size and scale of agricultural organization to a belief that smaller units of production were more efficient and capable of achieving higher productivity. Villagers felt that smaller teams were easier to manage and that people could identify more with the fruits of their labor, whereas the redistributive aspect of brigade accounting made it less rewarding for people in richer teams to work hard. Since 1978, there was a rash of team fissions in the brigade; from an original 11 production teams, there were twenty-one teams, with the smallest team comprising only 7 households. When asked whether there were villagers who preferred to return entirely to individual household production, villagers said there were those who felt this way. When asked what were the advantages of collectivized agriculture, team cadres replied that it was realized in a better division of labor and in an economy of scale. Villagers said that only the production team could purchase chemical fertilizer, insecticides, and power tillers, whereas individuals could not; moreover, only the teams qualified for the low interests credit from the state for purchases of modern inputs. Also, while a few households strong in labor power might prefer individual farming, households that were short on labor power and on skilled farmers, who had sufficient breadth of experience to feel they could handle the entire cycle of agricultural production, (such as female-headed households or households of cadres or soldiers who worked outside), did not anticipate

*All grain figures are for unhusked rice.

Table 2

Yangbei Production Brigade: ratio of $\frac{\text{gross income}}{\text{production costs}}$

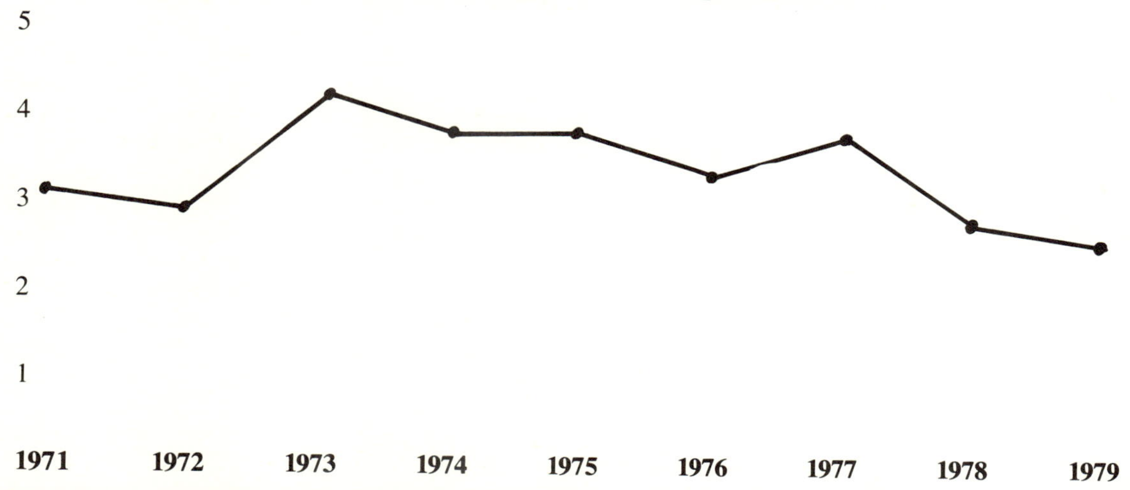

advantages in individual farming. Nonetheless, it was clear that the trend was towards smaller units of production. Before my departure from the field, a team cadre told me that he felt there were soon to be further team fissions.*

Accompanying the trend towards smaller production teams was the concern of villagers to implement incentive systems that reward individual effort within the context of collective farming. There was a decisive shift away from non-material incentives to a reward system that tied workpoint allotment directly to performance. As a result, the frequency of meetings held to evaluate and assign workpoint value to an individual's performance increased, with some teams doing this as often as once a month; by contrast, when the educated youths lived in the village, workpoint assignments were made once a year, and at times every other year. With teams empowered to decide on the most appropriate incentive system suited to their needs, there has been a tendency for teams to approach incentives on a tentative, experimental basis, emphasizing pragmatic considerations. Accordingly, there was a mix of incentive systems being used by different teams in the brigade. Some teams had recently adopted the "baogong daozu,jiafen daotien" system of dividing tasks among the team's small groups and assigning workpoint value to a specified plot or task. Villagers felt the advantage of this system was that it rewarded on the basis of a specified task or plot of land without limitation of time, thus those who completed their task earlier would be given the same workpoints as others who took longer to complete a similar task. While this system tended to reward speed, villagers who didn't use this system pointed to its disadvantages: quality of work tended to drop, as villagers rushed to complete their work so that they could leave earlier and tend to their household sidelines. The teams that employed this system asserted that the problem of quality control could be corrected by an alert team leader and group pressure. These teams, however, were among the affluent teams, with a history of good management and strong collective discipline. The more commonly used incentive system was the system called "dingchan daozu" which assigned production quotas to small groups based upon previous years' production. If the small group succeeded in surpassing the quota, 50 percent of any surplus production was divided among small group members as bonus. The strength of this system, villagers said, was that it rewarded the quality of performance and actual results; however, they also pointed out that there was an element of luck involved since grain production fluctuated from year to year according to climatic conditions, a factor beyond their control.

While villagers believed that the trends towards smaller teams, more effective incentives and greater team autonomy have contributed to higher morale, there was yet another factor responsible for the increases in grain production of the past years. This has been the very sizeable increase in modern inputs utilized by the production teams. Since 1975, when most of the educated youths left the village, the number of power tillers owned by production teams increased from three to seventeen; recently the brigade acquired a large, second-hand tractor which it utilized primarily for transport purposes. The amount of chemical fertilizer and insecticide available to the teams also increased dramatically.

In fact, there was a close correlation between the increase in application of chemical fertilizer and grain production; grain production virtually doubled following the sharp increase in chemical fertilizer application in 1978. However, the increasing use of modern inputs raised the cost of production significantly, resulting in a declining ratio between income and production costs. Thus, while grain production increased sharply since 1977, per capita income from the collective sector increased only slightly, reflecting the declining profit margins.

As a result of mechanization, the amount of time required of villagers to work in the collective sector declined in recent years by almost 30 percent. Whereas a strong laborer worked approximately 280 days a year a few years ago, today he or she might work only 200 days; moreover, the workday shortened by more than two hours during the non-busy season in the collec-

*A recent letter from the village (January 1981) reported that the process of team fission had resulted in an apparent breakup of collectivized agriculture with new teams in the natural village now as small as two households. How this came about and the implications of this breakup will be the focus of a planned revisit to Yangbei during the summer of 1981.

tive sector. The opening up of more free time and the declining profit margins in the collective sector led villagers to focus more of their time and effort in developing their household sideline production. Increased per capita grain allotment stimulated hog and poultry production, the basis of the household sideline economy, yet it has been difficult for villagers to start new sideline production. In the mountainous area where rural industrialization proceeded very slowly, the possibilities for sideline income outside of the exploitation of natural resources such as resin, bamboo shoots and mushrooms appear to be limited by a shortage of capital and experience in handicraft production. Nonetheless, it appeared that villagers were concentrating more effort and time into raising their household sideline production. As one villager said, "If I don't use the extra time, then there isn't any income to make up for the fewer workpoints we make each year." Although the value of workpoints increased, villagers understood that effective use of time in increasing household sideline income was the best way for them to increase their overall family income, at least in the short run. Thus, villagers were planning to dig ponds to raise fish, opening up new land on the hillside, which according to the new policy could be used by the household for its own sideline production, and trying to think up other possible sideline productive schemes.

In balance, the increases in grain production did not lead to a comparable increase in income from the collective sector due to increasing production costs. But because more families overdrafted in the last two years, per capita grain consumption increased substantially. This, in turn, brought in more cash income from the sale of hogs and poultry. There was an increase in per capita consumption, in household sideline income; but overall, these increases appeared not to have resulted in a living standard higher than what was achieved during the mid-1950s.

Birth Control

Underlying the apparent lack of increase in per capita income over the past two decades was a village population that grew from 1346 in 1954 to 2202 by 1979, an increase of 61 percent. On the basis of the informant data, I had predicted that the birth rate in the village would continue to be high relative to urban areas, despite the government's concerted effort to bring about a rapid decline in population growth. According to my data, there were strong economic and social incentives for villagers to continue to have large families. Villagers preferred families ranging from five to three children, with four children the ideal; having two sons seemed to many villagers to provide adequate insurance in the event that one fell ill or died of an accident. Despite the government's policy encouraging late marriages, marriages were performed early in the area with women marrying between the ages of 18 and 21 and men 20 and 22. It was the custom for couples to have their first child soon after the marriage, followed by successive children spaced relatively closely behind each birth. Having children was for villagers an investment for future security and even prosperity. Male children provided family continuity and support for parents in old age. Among the most impoverished and pathetic villagers were elderly couples without adult offspring, object lessons for villagers who failed to have sons.

Female children were also seen as providing benefits for the family, although daughters, who would marry out (in most cases to other villages), were seen as merely temporary members. A daughter could help out with household tasks and, during the teenage years, she contributed to the family economy through the workpoints she earned. An unmarried teenage girl was considered among the best workers in the team. Although villagers felt that they were likely to experience a period of economic difficulty when their children were young, there was the expectation that once they came of age to work, the family could begin to prosper. Moreover, the economic burden of having small dependent children was minimized by the policy of allowing families to overdraft on their income from the collective economy. Overdrafts were like interest-free loans which allowed villagers to defer payments until their children were old enough to work in the team economy, thus paying off the cost of their upbringing. There was also the positive incentive of having children in a time of grain shortage, such as the one which was experienced in the early 1970s. Villagers calculated that the grain ration alloted each child was more than adequate for the child's minimal needs, thus leaving a small surplus for adult consumption. In addition, each child was given a free plot allotment by the team. Families with few children generally were compelled to purchase high priced rice on the black market when their rations ran short, whereas families with many children often sold rice on the black market to raise additional cash income. Villagers felt it was better to have children than to have to purchase rice on the black market, because in the end you have something to show for it.

In the early 1970s the county government initiated a birth control campaign which, for a brief period, put pressure on villagers to practice planned parenthood. Brigade cadres were mobilized to take the lead in accepting sterilization. Prizes and bonuses were offered to women who agreed to sterilization. The county birth control office sent its cadres to the communes and villages to educate local cadres and villagers to the importance of birth control. The county sent a female gynecologist to the commune hospital as a permanent staff member to take charge of the local birth control program. For a brief period, there were a number of women in the village who aborted pregnancies and accepted sterilization. Once the campaign was over, however, villagers realized that the government was not going to enforce its strict sanction, which had stipulated that families that gave birth to more than two children had to open up an extra *mu* of land for cultivation. According to the educated youths, some women who aborted their pregnancy regretted having done so, and proceeded to get pregnant again. There was a general sense among villagers that sterilization was bad for the health, weakening them; men felt that it undermined their masculinity. Villagers gossiped that ever since the party secretary was sterilized, he seemed less vigorous and masculine. Another cadre attributed his wife's leaving him for another man to his sterilization. The educated youth reported that other means of birth control such as the pill and I.U.D. were not available, and the sole means of birth control appeared to have been abortions and sterilization. It seemed from the educated youth's account, therefore, that the birth control program in the commune was relatively ineffectual. For these reasons I anticipated a continuing high rate of population increase.

During my field work, I conducted a house to house survey in four production teams to administer a birth control census based upon one which had been implemented in Taiwan. The census revealed that most villagers still preferred 3 to 4 children, stating that the ideal was two sons and a daughter. Virtually all villagers believed that it was necessary to have at least one son.

Photos of Yangbei by Victor Nee.

Yet despite these attitudes, there was a general agreement among villagers that birth control was necessary, which was reflected by the fact that 87 percent of fertile married women in the sample were practicing birth control. The number of sterilizations in this sample was high, at 55 percent of fertile married couples. Couples not practicing birth control were young recently married villagers. My prediction of continuing high birth rates thus was supported by the fact that the desire to have more than two children was prevalent in the village. However, I had not accounted for the strictness with which new birth control regulations were being enforced by the county and commune governments.

The objective of the new birth control regulations was to limit young peasant families to two children. Although in urban areas the goal was a one-child family, in rural areas, the State, while encouraging one-child families, only hoped to achieve within the short term the acceptance of the two-child family. It was clear from talking with villagers that they felt the new campaign was more serious and concerted than any previous birth control program. Each level of local organization, from the production team to the commune, had its birth control cadre or representative. Birth control was made a top priority issue for local cadres and there was no question about the commitment of the State to achieving a rapid decline in population growth. But what most impressed villagers were the strict sanctions for having more than the permitted number of children. After the birth of the first child, the mother was required to agree to the installation of an I.U.D. at the commune hospital upon registration of the baby's birth. Refusal to comply meant the baby could not be registered, thus denying the family the alloted grain ration, free plot assignment and other coupons for the additional family member. After five years the couple could apply to the commune for permission to have the I.U.D. removed for a second pregnancy. After the second birth, the husband or wife are required to agree to sterilization, or to a contract with the State that if they choose to use another form of birth control, an accidental pregnancy will have to be aborted. Likewise, failure to comply meant the child could not be registered. In the way of positive incentives, couples who agreed to sterilization after the birth of the first child are given in lump sum a sewing machine by the commune, 30 *yuan,* and 50 *jin* of rice. It would appear unlikely that, if many peasants agreed to limiting their families to one child, local government could afford to provide such generous grants.

The combination of sanctions and incentives seems to have had impressive results in lowering population growth in the area. Population growth in the county dropped from 3.1 percent in 1975 to 1.4 percent in 1979, with the 1980 objective set slightly below 1 percent. This trend towards lower population growth was paralleled in Yangbei brigade which showed a resumption of higher birth rate after the birth control campaign of the early 1970s faded, followed by a dip in 1974–75 and a steady decline after 1976. Commune officials said that Yangbei had the highest birth rate in the commune in 1979, which they attributed to the large numbers of recently married couples, who, they pointed out, were having their first births. They were confident, however, that Yangbei would in the next few years experience a futher decline in birth rate, bringing it down to the level of the commune as a whole, which was 1 percent in 1979. It is interesting to note that the new sanctions effectively undermined the past economic incentives for having more children. Villagers said that while they strongly preferred to have more than two children, the prospect of raising a child without the benefits of additional rice ration and free plot was economically too heavy a burden for them. Nonetheless, there were a few households in the four teams surveyed that were adept at taking advantage of the fact that I.U.D. proved to be only about 80 percent effective by going ahead and having a child in the case of an accidental pregnancy.

Youth and the Closure of Social Mobility.

One of the striking changes from the early 1970s was the higher attendance of both boys and girls in the village elementary school and commune lower middle school. Whereas the educated youths reported a low level of interest in schooling among parents and young people in the early 1970s, there has been an apparent change in sentiment. According to the principal of the village school, nearly all of the school age children in the village are attending the elementary school, and a surpris-

ingly high percentage, 95 percent are now continuing on to complete lower middle school education, with an accompanying increase in the numbers that go on to upper middle school. In the early 1970s, there were very few in the village among the youth that continued to upper middle school, and while the trend was towards higher male attendance in the lower middle school, there were few female students who went on to lower middle school. Instead the tendency was for parents to withdraw their daughters before graduation from the elementary school so that they could contribute more directly to the household tasks and enter the work force earlier. It was felt, however, that a boy needed more schooling as preparation for his becoming head of the household, to properly manage the family sideline production. By 1980, it appeared that there was a significant change in parental attitude towards their daughters' education, reflected by the fact that female attendance in the elementary school was as high as male, and by the increasing numbers of village girls continuing their education to the lower-middle school level. In interviewing parents, moreover, a common response was to say that a girl ought to continue her education as far as her ability could take her. The village teachers felt that students were much more serious and diligent in their studies, and pointed to the fact that every school night the study room which the school kept open was filled with students preparing their lessons.

It is difficult to account for the change in attitude towards schooling, other than a vague belief villagers have that education provided a means to get ahead. Certainly some parents harbored the hope that their children might be able to avoid the hard work of farming. Certainly among the young villagers who spent their evenings studying in the elementary study hall were boys and girls who dreamed of passing the entrance examination for one of the county's universities or technical college. Yet, the chances of their doing so seemed terribly limited, if the record of the past few years is any indication of the prospects for a young villager to gain admission to an institution of higher education. The commune reported only one student in the past three years who was able to pass the entrance examination for a technical middle school in the district capital, Longyan. Apparently, the new competitive entrance examinations and the superiority of urban schools have resulted in a sharp reduction of students from the villages in universities and technical institutes. Faculty at the province's major universities, Xiamen and Fuzhou universities, were concerned that rural applicants scored significantly lower on college entrance exams and were being admitted in much fewer numbers.

Upon graduation from lower and also upper middle school, virtually all young graduates can expect to return to the village to join the production teams and work along side their parents. The State does not assign work for rural youth in the public sector as it does for urban youth. In fact, villagers pointed with some bitterness to the givernment's regulation that restricted people with village registration from employment in State-managed enterprises. The former brigade party secretary, an old guerrilla activist, quoted a saying in the village that reflected discontent and cynicism: "Urban youths don't even need technical skill to get assigned to a good job, but a rural youth who has technical skill still can't get ahead." A few lucky middle school graduates were selected each year for recruitment in the People's Liberation Army, an honor that most village young men still aspire to. But, whereas in the past returned army men could look forward to State Assignments in the public sector, mainly as local cadres, in recent years such assignments have been more difficult to get. Instead, returned army men since the early 1970s appeared to have taken positions as cadres in the brigade, a non-State job.

The seeming paucity of opportunity for mobility faced by a generation of village youth, born after 1949 and far better educated than their parents, has inevitably created a problem of adjustment for these youths. An upper middle school graduate discovers upon his return to the village that his education has not helped him to be a better farmer, and that he must learn skills which his peers who dropped out of high school earlier have already mastered. His initial workpoint assignment, therefore, might be lower than the other, more experienced team members. But expenses have increased for a young villager, If he hopes to marry, he must be able to save money towards the marriage expense, which has been increasing, and towards eventually building his own home. Yet, all he can expect to earn in a day's work is from .50 –.70 *yuan,* depending on his team

Table 3

Yangbei Production Brigade: Per Capita Income from Collective Sector

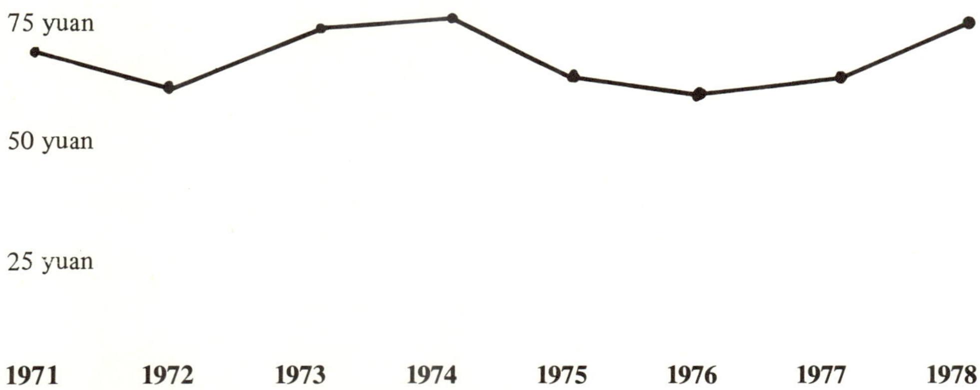

and workpoint assignment. Young villagers felt that this is a small amount of money for the amount of labor that it requires, just enough to cover living expenses, with little left for saving. Young villagers said that all they think about was how to earn more money, how to get ahead, and become established. While they voiced dissatisfaction with their lot in being ordinary peasants, and hoped for jobs with a salary, "eating state grain," they were realistic enough to know that this was a dream not likely to be fulfilled, and that their future almost certainly would be as farmers. As one youth said, "there is no way out." Older villagers acknowledged the problem, that the youth did not look forward to a life on the farm, had higher expectations, and felt frustrated. They sympathized with their aspirations for work as factory workers or state personnel, and readily admitted that the present regulations preventing rural youths from gaining access to these jobs were unfair. There was complaint about what they described as the *buyuan* system, reinstituted in recent years, whereby parents working in the state sector, whether as factory workers, teachers or cadres, can upon retirement pass on a job in the same field or organization to a daughter or son. Villagers felt that this system sealed off any hope for their children to get salaried jobs, and sealed their fate from generation to generation on the farm. They questioned whether the *buyuan* system was compatible with the spirit of socialism, pointing to the inequity of young people getting jobs not on the basis of merit, but because their parents happened to have worked for the State.[3]

Data from the educated youth hinted at the problem of rising expectation and discontent among village youth, but at the time there were fewer young villagers with education whose hopes and imagination reached out beyond the confines of village society. Perhaps the presence of urban-educated youth in the village had the lasting effect of influencing the present generation of peasant youth to want more in life than what their parents wanted, and to yearn for opportunities outside the village. One county official expressed concern about the possibility that mechanization and higher educational achievement, in the absence of rapid economic growth in the province, might produce the conditions for instability in the future. With more free time and higher expectations, he said, there was no telling what thoughts might go on in people's minds. The fact that the "problem of youth" has emerged as a major concern among China's new leadership, is suggestive that such worry has also been on the minds of policy makers in Beijing.

Consolidation of the Local Elite

Data from the informant interviews provided evidence of a trend towards the consolidation of a local elite, firmly entrenched in the local bureaucracy, extending from the county government down to the production brigades. The core of this local elite apeared to be the old guerrilla fighters who participated in the struggle to liberate the county, land reform and collectivization activists, and returned People's Liberation Army soldiers, with a sprinkling of graduates from upper middle school who were recruited into the bureaucracy in the 1950s and 60s.

In the early 1950s the county government was staffed heavily by "outside" cadres from North China who came south with the army during the Liberation War. In the period following the liberation of the county there was a shortage of qualified local cadres due to the low literacy rate among guerilla fighters and land reform activists. Those who were literate, however, were quickly promoted from the basic levels to help staff the growing local government bureaus. A favored source of cadres recruitment were returned People's Liberation Army soldiers. In the army, a young peasant could take literacy courses, engage in organized political study, participate in a large organization whose ethos of disciplined service to country was expected to broaden the peasant's outlook and range of experience, making him less susceptible to localist values and interests. Moreover, the army provided excellent opportunities for a young peasant to join the Party. Increasingly, during the late 1950s and 1960s local cadres were recruited into the county government and the newly established people's communes; among them were large numbers of returned soldiers.

One institution in particular became the virtual retirement grounds for returned soldiers, the militia. According to my informants, during the Cultural Revolution commune militia commanders were propelled to dominant positions in the communes when they were called upon by the PLA garrison in Longyan District to take control of newly established revolutionary committees. As chairmen of the county and commune revolutionary committees, these militia commanders formed a cohesive elite group of local men. Their common years of service in the army provided a strong sense of camaraderie which was cemented in years of attending meetings and frequent communications as local commanders of the commune militia organizations. Though accountable to the Party bureaucracy, militia commanders nonetheless had deep roots in the villages. There were three commune militia commanders from Yangbei, the most powerful of whom was the militia commander of the commune which straddled the county town. Yangbei also boosted a number of important county cadres, one of whom was a leading cadre in the county public security organization.

What was the fate of the militia commanders in the post-Cultural Revolution period? It seemed that they were more vulnerable than the other local cadres to displacement because they came to power when Lin Biao's influence was at its peak. To my surprise, *none* of the Yangbei cadres had been purged after the fall of the Cultural Revolution radical leadership in Fujian, a stronghold of the so-called "gang of four." The three militia commanders were still leading cadres in their respective commune administrations, holding joint positions either as vice-Party secretary or vice-chairman of the commune revolutionary committee. Like the militia commanders, the other cadres from Yangbei were also able to retain their positions in the local bureaucracy. A county cadre who worked in the important grain department was transferred back to Yangbei during a campaign to strengthen grass roots leadership, but after a brief tenure as brigade party secretary, he was transferred to the commune to be its vice-chairman. The core leadership group in the brigade during the Cultural Revolution period was similarly transferred to the commune administration where they occupied important middle level positions. These transfers strengthened the control of local people in the commune administration. If Yangbei was typical of the county, the stability of the local elite was impressive in light of the dramatic changes in national and provincial politics in recent years.

At both the county and commune level, the leading cadre is an "outsider" from either another county or, at the commune level, another commune in Wuping county. This policy conforms to the traditional rule of avoidance of the Chinese bureaucracy, The bureaucrats who staff local government in China today have a higher official status. According to local cadres interviewed in Wuping county, the staff of the county and commune bureaucracy exercise considerable defacto control. A number of local cadres said that an "outside" cadre must be very attentive to cultivating good ties with local cadres to gain their support. When an "outside" cadre arrives on a new assignment, he enters a complex society where, without the support of local cadres, he is "like a blind man," who can "accomplish little." Local cadres on the other hand have a deep familiarity with local society and can mobilize long established networks of relationships to get things done. Moreover due to the greater size of local government now as compared to imperial times, the staff of local people is considerably larger in the Communist bureaucracy. Local cadres claimed that, if an "outside" cadre antagonized local sentiment, they might actively work to undermine the "outside" cadre by going behind his back and isolating him or her. They might also bring their complaints to cadres from the locality who work in the county government, who in turn can bring them to the attention of the county leadership. If complaints were persistent and serious, the county might send a work team down to investigate the problem. Thus the local cadres with their extensive links in the community and bureaucracy would make formidable opponents. Local cadres I interviewed readily admitted that personal ties were important in getting things accomplished in the local government. As a cadre told me, "if you have a good relationship with another cadre, you can go to him and personally ask him for help." County cadres from the locality said that they were eager to lend a helping hand to their village as long as requests were within the bounds of propriety. With the ascendency of local cadres in the county and commune bureaucracy, localism has become a structural problem and can be expected to assert itself in the years ahead.

In Yangbei (V. Nee).

Discussion.

Although I was able to gather a considerable amount of new data from my field work in Yangbei, some of the main findings of which were highlighted in this report, the primary value of the field work, in terms of the study as a whole, was to enhance my confidence in the reliability of the original data from educated youth interviews. This was accomplished through matching up "key indicators" such as household composition, consumption patterns, material possessions, prevalent attitudes, events and even gossip to check for any discrepancies. In cases where discrepancies were discovered, I sought to account for them through further questioning. For example, I had anticipated that the birth rate, on the basis of interviews with the educated youth, would remain high in the village. Yet, my census of four production teams revealed that in fact, birth control had been successfully implemented, as reflected in the overall decline of birth rate in the brigade in recent years. The discrepancy was attributed to changes in State policy, and not to any unreliability factor in the educated youths' account.

Likewise, the discrepancy between the low morale of peasants of the early 1970s and the more positive attitudes expressed during my visit was also explained by changes in State policy. The fact that older peasants still maintained that, in terms of food consumption, the 1950s was better than the present period not only provided evidence supporting the educated youths' report, but it also was consistent with the statistical data on food consumption gathered during the 1970s. Social structural data gathered in my brief field work in the village closely corroborated the information provided by the educated youths. This was true not only for kinship pattern, household composition, norms and custom, but also of data on local elite and politics. Even attitudes could be validated on sensitive issues such as youth discontent. The educated youths hinted at the problem of closed avenues for mobility for young villagers. My research in the field confirmed this problem and uncovered a further aggravation of the youth frustration as more village youth continued their education to middle school but found jobs in the State sector scarce.

Notes

1. See, for example, Andrew Walder, "Press Accounts and the Study of Chinese Society," *China Quarterly*, Vol. 79, September 1979; and the methodological note in William Parish and Martin Whyte's *Village and Family in Contemporary China* (Chicago: University of Chicago Press, 1979).

2. This study was funded by a postdoctoral research grant from the Social Science Research Council 1980–81. The study will be published in book form at a later date. I am appreciative of the helpful comments I received from Carl Riskin, William Parish, Edward Friedman, and Mark Selden.

3. Interviews in Fuzhou and Beijing confirmed the existence of the *buyuan* system. Urban people seemed to feel that the system was developed to provide further social security upon retirement. Although the stipulation was that the child upon his or her parent's retirement was entitled to a job in the same general area of employment, in practice the child was able to get jobs in the same organization, often in the same specialization. Apparently in Shanghai, experienced workers were retiring early in order to allow a son or daughter to get a job in the factory resulting in a problem of a reduction of the skilled work force in exchange for inexperienced young workers with lower technical qualification.

Surplus Transfer and Economic Development in Taiwan and Shanghai

by James E. Nickum

We learn by comparing. Yet reality presents us with few clear-cut comparisons. There are almost always mitigating factors. Nowhere is this more evident than in the comparison of economic and political systems. For example, the average citizen of the Soviet Union is poorer and politically more inhibited than a counterpart in the United States; but is this the inevitable consequence of Marxism(-Leninism), or is it because the Soviet citizen lives in a system descended from czarist serfdom, always relatively poor, always oppressed?

The situation is equally complex if we try to compare living standards or development patterns in Taiwan with the remainder of China. They are two vastly different entities. Taiwan is much smaller and more compact, with fewer problems of coordination and control. At the time of division three decades ago, it had a better educated populace and a more advanced capital infrastructure, especially in agriculture. It had a well-articulated market structure, both internally and externally, stimulated purposefully by the Japanese in fifty years of occupation.

Nonetheless, a comparison of some sort between the market-oriented and directive plan-oriented portions of China should yield important insights. My original interest in this topic arose out of concern with the difference in living standards as a possible stumbling block to reintegration. It seemed most appropriate to choose an advanced political-economic unit within the PRC to match against Taiwan to see how living standards differ in practice. Shanghai, as the most advanced, was a logical choice.

The matchup turned out to be quite close in a number of ways, allowing for more than a simple comparison of living standards.[1] By observing two entities which share a number of common "environmental" characteristics, it is possible to see very clearly two quite different paths of economic development.

Shanghai Municipality, established in its present boundaries in 1958 (including ten rural *xian),* is smaller than Taiwan in land area but similar in population. Both had 10 million residents in 1958. The number has diverged since, as Taiwan's has grown past 17 million, while Shanghai's did not grow at all until quite recently (now about 12.5 million). They have nearly identical urban-rural population mixes (about 50-50 in 1974). Shanghai's economy is well-integrated and tied to exchange-oriented production. Even thirty years ago it had a good economic base in place, centered around foreign trade and the textile industry. As with Taiwan, Shanghai's development was dominated by foreign presence. Both agricultures are based on rice, and although Shanghai has only 40 percent of the cultivated area of Taiwan, it has 70 percent of the irrigated acreage. Also, quite importantly, the data are, by PRC standards, both good and abundant for Shanghai.

Even with good units of comparison, I have acquired few definitive insights on the problem of reintegration. Those that I have are at the end of this piece. What I have discovered, and what I wish to discuss here in the main, are two quite different paths to economic development, determined by the larger economy within which each is imbedded.

I focus on the period from 1965 to 1974, as the data are relatively abundant for these two years for Shanghai. In addition, 1965 was the year when U.S. economic aid to Taiwan was terminated; and after 1974, Shanghai became a focal point of the succession struggle for two very abnormal years.

Ordinarily, it might be considered curious if not downright improper to compare a municipality imbedded within a nation-state with an economic entity which deals with the rest of the world as a *de facto* nation, for the latter usually encounters greater "transactions costs" in making its external economic exchanges. Except for labor market conditions, however, this does not seem to be a serious problem in the present case. On the one hand, Shanghai's lack of market barriers to external trade is counterbalanced by the hindrances of self-intitiated exchange imposed by the PRC's "planned" administrative, non-market methods of economic coordination. On the other hand, despite barriers, both systems maintain extensive external economic relations. Taiwan has one of the highest foreign trade turnover rates in the world, with exports and imports each roughly half its gross national product. In some years (1972, 1973, 1976, 1977, 1978) its total foreign trade exceeded that of the entire PRC. Over 80 percent of Shanghai's industrial products are sent elsewhere, and the municipality has even exported whole factories (including workers) to interior provinces.

Of course, the nature of external economic contact differs. Separate exchange mechanisms are in operation, and each has a

Figure 1

Direction of Net Resource Transfer: Taiwan

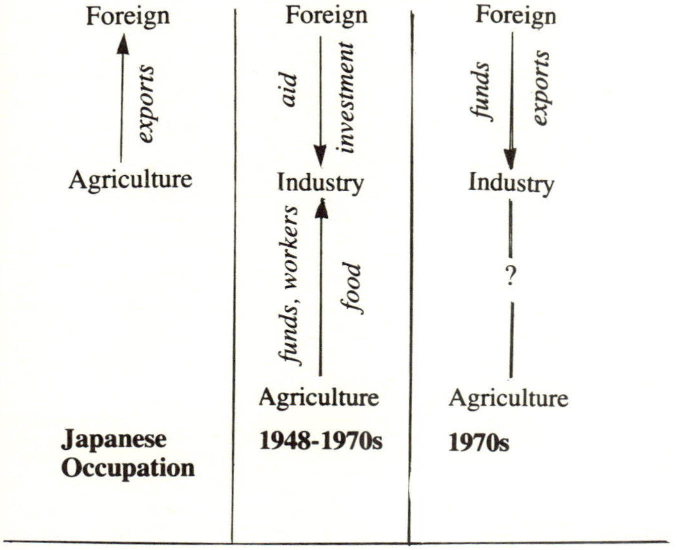

very different kind of reference group with which to market its goods: Taiwan trades, as do most who trade, with the rich; Shanghai sends much, probably most of its economic output to the relatively poor. These interactions in turn are related to the nature of the economic system.

How do the economic systems differ? Briefly, in Shanghai: (1) The means of production and distribution, and the financial system are owned either by the state or, especially in the countryside, by a collective; (2) The principal resource allocation mechanism, especially for the means of production, intermediate goods, and goods for foreign trade, is the state plan. In the PRC, this entails varying degrees of centralization, and a connection with the larger economy based upon directives and national policy guidelines rather than upon market signals; and (3) The state controls the labor market. Wage scales in state industry (which predominates) are set by high levels of the state. In addition, unlike in the Soviet Union, virtually all urban workers are assigned jobs by the state, and mobility is severely restricted unless authorized at a fairly high level.

In Taiwan: (1) Although the bulk of the means of production were originally in state hands, private ownership has been encouraged and now predominates; (2) The market is the principal means of allocating resources and determining what will be produced, including especially the foreign market; and (3) Wages tend to be set by the interplay of market forces as well. The unions are placid and there is no explicit state regulation of wages or restrictions on the movement of workers from job to job.

A multisectoral scheme highlights some of the most essential characteristics of the economic development process (see Figs. 1 and 2). For Taiwan, the principal sectors considered are the agricultural, the industrial, and the foreign. For Shanghai, "foreign" is replaced by the "rest of China." This does not mean that the foreign sector is unimportant to Shanghai's economy; rather, it is subsumed under the same central control that determines all exchanges outside the municipality.

I focus here on the general direction of net resource transfer between the various sectors and, to a lesser degree, on the accompanying claims of laborers to the fruits of their toil. In so doing, I am assuming that, at least here, the real world is one in "disequilibrium," with unrequited (and fairly obvious) resource (or "surplus") transfers made on the basis of essentially political (including monopoly) decisions. Since the Marxist paradigm deals more specifically with the issue of the generation and transfer of "surplus value," I shall attempt (not altogether confidently) to make use of this Marxist as well as more standard neoclassical economic concepts.

In twentieth century Taiwan, the foreign sector has tended to predominate over the domestic economy. Under the Japanese and the early Guomindang, exports were mostly agricultural, especially rice and sugar. Agricultural output was expanded through a nearly classical (Marx) mechanism of exploitation. Peasant income from field crops was maintained at a static, "subsistence" level, while the surplus value generated by increased production was transferred elsewhere—under the Japanese, mostly to Japan, and under the Guomindang, to the industrial sector. Increases in output came from improvements in the means of production—through infrastructural investment such as irrigation facilities, and through technological change (especially in seeds).

This pattern was maintained through the early 1960s. Instruments such as taxes and the manipulation of the terms of trade between industry and agriculture were used to transfer resources out of the rural sector. Population growth, combined with more intensive exploitation of the household, produced a reserve army of low-paid agricultural labor, which in turn could be used to keep industrial wages down. Agricultural productivity increased through improvements in capital and technology.

Industry for its part specialized in labor-intensive production tied to the export market. According to Johnston and Kilby, large-scale firms "insured that every commercially feasible possibility for substituting labor for capital was exploited," while small firms made use of finely differentiated market wage

Figure 2

Direction of Net Resource Transfer: Shanghai

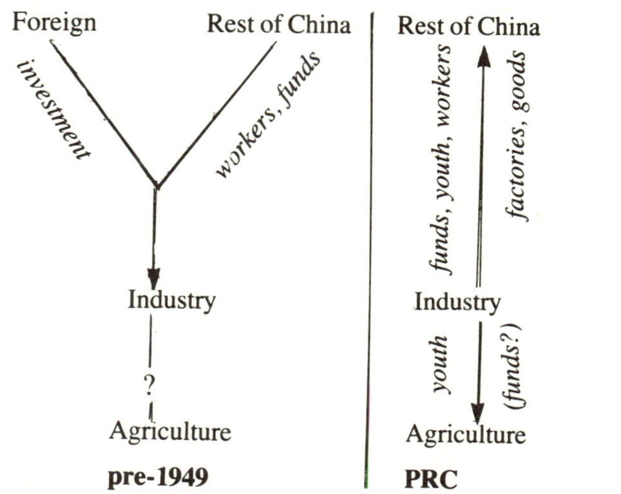

Note: The transfer of youth has not been entirely deleterious to the urban-industrial economy, although it may have contributed to a decline in the service sector. Also, the transfer was often a mixed blessing to the "beneficiaries."

rates to siphon low cost labor out of the household and, on a part-time basis, out of agriculture.[2]

Since the early 1960s, however, important structural shifts have taken place. The most marked manifestation of this has been a braking of agricultural growth. According to Y. T. Wang, the Secretary-General of the Chinese-American Joint Commission on Rural Reconstruction (JCRR), "The annual growth rate of agriculture averaged only 2.2% for 1969-72, the period of the fifth Four-Year Economic Development Plan, and it went down further to 1.2% for 1973-75, as compared with the average of more than 5.0% for all previous Plan periods."[3] This was *following* the promulgation in 1969 of a new agricultural policy designed to counter the downturn in growth of the previous few years.

In addition, recent agricultural growth has been unevenly distributed. Production of the basic field crops, rice and sugar, which originally fuelled Taiwan's agricultural growth, has stagnated. Rice output peaked in 1968, rebounding only in 1976. Sugar cane did not regain its 1965 level until 1977. The production of sweet potatoes, mainly used as hog feed, with the second largest acreage, grew rapidly until 1967, but has fallen precipitously since. The overall multiple cropping index began to decline in 1969, with notable decreases in the sown area of winter crops such as sweet potatoes.[4]

Farm output growth between 1965 and 1974 was due almost entirely to increases in livestock and commercial crops such as fruit, vegetables and mushrooms. Although land ownership is quite egalitarian by world standards, these cropping shifts probably have not benefited the median rural family, which has relied since 1970 on nonfarm receipts for any increase in its income. This increase has been quite substantial, so that the average "rural family" now receives less than half its income from farm operations. Those families who do receive relatively more from farming tend to have higher incomes, but rural family incomes appear to have become slightly more equal. The income disparity between rural and nonrural families widened significantly, however.[5]

Why has agricultural output stagnated? Yields are high, but they are still below the most advanced world levels. There has been some encroachment on agricultural land by the cities and industry, but that does not explain the decline in the cropping ratio on the remaining farmland. Land holdings are small and fragmented, often on slopeland, hindering certain kinds of mechanization, but again this does not appear to be the principal bottleneck.

The most compelling reason for the decline appears to be the very success of the previous policy of extraction, especially of labor. Since about 1962, Taiwan's rate of labor absorption out of agriculture has outpaced population growth. One consequence of this was that the real wage rate in industry, which had been stable, began to increase. Another consequence was that the countryside began to feel the effects of being stripped of its labor, especially but not exclusively that of its youth. Farm household population began to decline in absolute terms in 1969. Particularly marked was the decrease in the number of part-owners and tenants, from 33 percent of the total farm household in 1967 to 21 percent in 1974 and 17 percent in 1976.[6] Labor intput into rice production, in workdays, was less in 1974 than it was in 1952.[7] Matters were not helped by the maintenance, until recently, of a policy of low producer prices for farm products, especially rice, through government dominance over the supply of critical inputs, notably chemical fertilizer.

In the earlier Guomindang years, Taiwan's industry was promoted not only by extraction from the countryside but also by a transfer of funds from abroad in the form of overseas Chinese remittances and U.S. aid. During the 1950s, over half of Taiwan's net domestic investment was attributable to the latter. Because of external financing, Taiwan was able to support a rate of investment greater than domestic savings for 9 of the 13 years between 1952 and 1964. After 1963, the rate of domestic savings increased rapidly, rising within a decade from 20 percent of national income to 35 percent and taking up much of the slack left by the end of U.S. aid. Private consumption, although increasing in absolute terms, fell steadily from 68 percent of GNP in 1961 to 52 percent in 1973. Although much diminished since 1965, external finance has continued to flow into Taiwan on a net basis, much of it in the form of direct private foreign investment. In recent years, Taiwan has also contributed to the net flow of funds inward from abroad by running balance of trade surpluses.

The results, in terms of industrial output, have been quite impressive. The increase in industrial and mining production value (IMPV) of 15.1 percent per annum between 1965 and 1974 is higher than the growth in gross value of industrial output (GVIO) (a roughly comparable category) reported for any of the 29 PRC province-level administrative units except the smallest three: Ningxia, Tibet, and Qinghai. (Hebei, Shandong, and Beijing, all of comparable economic size to Taiwan, had annual GVIO growth rates above 14 percent, however.)[8]

Turning to Shanghai (fig. 2), we see quite a different picture. Shanghai before World War II was the principal beneficiary of foreign investment and of much domestic Chinese investment funds as well. In addition, the rest of China provided a reservoir of subsistence wage labor, especially women and children, for modern industry.[9] While the net impact of the foreigner on China is highly controversial, scholars agree that the effect on Shanghai's industrial output was, to put it mildly, stimulating, both directly and in eliciting domestic industrialization efforts.[10]

The rural agricultural *xian* now incorporated in Shanghai have been less important a source of surplus than was Taiwan's farm sector. Although quite productive in land yields, the suburban areas have historically been unable to provide sufficient foodstuffs for the city dwellers or cotton for the textile industry which formed the original core of Shanghai's manufacturing.[11]

With the establishment of the PRC, Shanghai's economic role has changed considerably. While still mandated to increase its industrial and agricultural output, Shanghai has become a major source of "surplus" of various kinds for the remainder of the PRC. Financial transfers are the most remarkable. From 1950 to 1976, funds provided the center by Shanghai accounted for 41.9 percent of the national capital investment budget. Of the total remitted by Shanghai, only 7.6 percent was returned in the form of capital construction grants.[12] Indeed, data released by the PRC indicate that the net outflow of funds has amounted to approximately the entire value added in industrial production. This is the sort of figure which makes one suspect the statistician, but it does indicate an enormous unrequited outpouring of funds, one which may have become a political pawn in the struggles of 1974-1976, when Shanghai "failed" to meet its revenue targets.

Another prominent characteristic of Shanghai's development, until 1979, was the apparent lack of population growth since the establishment of the present municipality in 1958. This is clearly a conscious policy, which is implemented through the transfer of personnel out of Shanghai, especially middle school graduates but also workers, who are often transferred to the interior with their factories. Over 100 textile mills alone have been shipped out. This outward transfer, especially of educated youth and workers, has slowed down considerably, and possibly reversed since the Third Plenary Session of the 11th Central Committee of the Communist Party in late 1978.

Shanghai's urban labor force increased from 2.4 million in 1957 to 3.0 million in 1975, but all of this increase came from greater participation, from 40.3 percent of total population in 1957 to 52.6 percent in 1975. Almost half of this increase was due to the mobilization of housewives.[14]

Yet despite the strict restraints of funds and labor and the turmoil of the Cultural Revolution, Shanghai's GVIO increased at a respectable 9.2 percent per annum between 1965 and 1974. Increases in output were due to three factors: the transfer of workers from nonindustrial production to industrial; a shift from consumer goods (mainly textile) to capital intensive (especially producer goods, e.g., petrochemical) industry; and the introduction of labor-saving technology into existing production processes. The real wage rate appears to have changed little, unlike what one would expect in a closed market system with a similarly tight labor market. Thus the vast bulk of per worker increases in output was converted into surplus value. Recently, we have witnessed another phenomenon that, at least on the surface, moves counter to a free market solution: an increase in urban unemployment at the same time that wages have increased.

Like the rest of the PRC, Shanghai's rural areas have benefited from transfers from the municipality's urban industrial sector. The suburban counties are not an important source of workers for urban industry, although *rural* industrialization has become increasingly significant in recent years. The labor power remaining in the countryside, already with a heavier proportion of young adults than in Taiwan, has been augmented with the infusion of roughly 40 percent of Shanghai's one million rusticated educated youths.

It is difficult to determine the net flow of non-labor surplus, because basic field crops (grain and cotton) are subject to state procurement pricing (and a nominal tax) held low to keep urban wages down and urban-generated surplus high. On the other hand, prices of inputs to the farm collective such as chemical fertilizer are held low by the state, often leading to administrative allocation or distribution via waiting list.

The urban grain ration is used to control migration rather than consumption, which appears to be more than adequate. Indeed, increases in procurement prices of grain over the past decade or two have not been offset by higher urban sales prices. This has led to growing financial losses to the state on the exchange. Even the recent (November 1979) increase in urban food prices maintained grain prices at the same level.

It is therefore not clear that state price setting is more exploitative to the farmer than in a market system, despite the continual calls to shift the flow of funds towards agriculture by lowering the "scissors" ratio of the prices of industrial inputs purchased in the countryside to those of farm outputs. Indeed, it would appear that farmer price incentives to produce field crops, while not outstanding, have been better than in Taiwan, at least until the recent price rises for grain in both systems.

Mechanization of Shaghai's extensive collective fields has raised labor productivity. Ninety percent of the 360,000 hectares cultivated in 1976 were machine-plowed and 98 percent were irrigated by electric pumps.[15] This has permitted the introduction of new crop strains and new cropping systems. The acreage under triple cropping increased from 20 percent of the cultivated acreage in 1965 to 56 percent in 1974. Specific acreage figures indicate an increase in the multiple cropping index from roughly 180 to 216. Grain output increased by 51 percent in the same period. By 1974, Shanghai had a higher grain yield per crop (3.7 T./ha. cf. 3.1 T./ha.) and per capita (222 kg. cf. 160 kg.) than Taiwan, producing almost as much total grain (2.4 million T. cf. 2.6 million T.) with only 40 percent of the latter's total cultivated acreage and three-quarters of its sown acreage.

I have dwelt on agriculture in both systems, partly out of my own interest in the area, but also because the differing nature of surplus generation and transfer is particularly highlighted in its effect on the two countrysides. In the case of Taiwan, what is shown is the power of the previous extractive policy begun by the Japanese and adapted by the Guomindang to the service of the urban-industrial sector, which has only recently become nearly self-sustaining. Agriculture, once dynamic, lagged, as the old growth strategy became increasingly inadequate. Incomes in the countryside increased, though not as rapidly as in the cities, principally from an increase in non-agricultural employment.

Taiwan as a whole is a closed system with respect to its labor supply, so the tightening of the labor market has led to considerable increases in real wages and consumption levels. These increases have continued to lag behind the pace of economic growth, causing the rate of savings and domestically funded capital accumulation to continue to increase as a proportion of GNP.

Shaghai's rural sector, like the rest of the PRC, has benefited from the restraints on and transfers from the urban-industrial sector. Clearly, despite what available data indicate, Shanghai invests a great deal—heavy industry does not come cheaply—but the net flow of funds and labor has definitely been outward, under the direction of a superordinate central plan. Viewed as a closed system, Shanghai's labor market is even tighter than that of Taiwan, yet real wages do not appear to have increased at all during a period of nearly 10 percent industrial growth per annum. Obviously this did not sit well with a sizeable portion of the labor force, as evidenced by recent press disclosures and wage increases. It is also clear, however, that despite restrictions on the movement of labor, Shanghai's workers operate within the larger context of the PRC. This wider, poorer reference group helps restrain wages (especially when there *is* some possibility of being transferred into that group). This restraint appears to have generated a surplus large enough not only to support Shanghai's industrial and agricultural growth but to lay some golden eggs for the rest of the country.

Does the comparison between Taiwan and Shanghai over the period of the late 1960s and early 1970s contain any lessons for a possible future reintegration of Taiwan and mainland China? Perhaps, but no simple ones. *Prima facie,* it would seem that if a "Shanghai solution" were to be adopted for Taiwan, the island's urban population would be held in check, wages would increase slowly if at all and much of the urban-generated surplus would be siphoned off to benefit relatively backward areas. The industrial growth rate might slow down a bit but would not grind to a halt, as new technology would continue to be introduced. The decline in agricultural output might be held in check through a continuation of the reversal of urban-rural surplus transfer and greater fixity of the rural labor force in the villages. Rural industry and commerce, already well developed, would certainly translate easily into a Shanghai-style rural development strategy, though a change to collective ownership might be required for consistency.

Yet it would be facile in the extreme to assume that such a Shanghai solution would actually be adopted. First of all, the conditions of reintegration, if it ever happens, might preclude the imposition of the controls and changes in ownership structure necessary to make the Shanghai way work. Secondly, the Cultural Revolution Shanghai model may not serve well for Taiwan in a united front "four modernizations" future — the aspects of the principal contradiction have changed considerably. Finally, the current trend of events points to a convergence of paths. Indeed, Shanghai, as other urban areas, seems to be moving toward a "Taiwan solution" with more mobility of labor, the development of an urban collective (i.e., quasi-family) economy to abosrb surplus labor and boost the service trades, the solicitation of funds from abroad and the establishment of direct trade relations with foreigners, and increasing wages in the state industrial enterprises. There are, as always, mitigating factors, but the analogy is intriguing.

Notes

1. A detailed analysis of comparative living standards may be found in James E. Nickum and David C. Schak, "Living Standards and Economic Development in Shanghai and Taiwan," *China Quarterly*, No. 77, March 1979, pp. 25-49. Our conclusions were much as to be expected: although she or he produces much less per capita, the average Taiwan resident, urban or rural, has in most respects a higher material standard of living, although perhaps a less secure and more male-oriented one.

2. Bruce F. Johnston and Peter Kilby, *Agriculture and Structural Transformation* (New York: Oxford University Press, 1975), p. 315. See also Teng-hui Lee, *Intersectoral Capital Flows in the Economic Development of Taiwan, 1895-1960* (Ithaca and London: Cornell University Press, 1971), for a detailed economic analysis of the transfer of surplus out of agriculture.

3. Y.T. Wang, "Chinese-American Joint Commission on Rural Reconstruction (JCRR): Its Organisation, Policies and Objectives, and Contributions to the Agricultural Development of Taiwan," *Agricultural Administration*, 4, July 1977, p. 187.

4. Directorate-General of Budget, Accounting & Statistics, Executive Yuan, The Republic of China, *Statistical Yearbook of the Republic of China 1977* [SY 1977], pp. 86 and 99; and Yu-kang Mao, "Effects of Changes in Agricultural Structure on Farm Management in Taiwan," *Industry of Free China*, 42, December 1975, p. 31.

5. Marcia L. Ong, Dale W. Adams and I. J. Singh, "Voluntary Rural Savings Capacities in Taiwan 1960 to 1970," Economics and Sociology Occasional Paper No. 175, Department of Agricultural Economics and Rural Sociology, The Ohio State University, 8 February 1974, p. 10; and Wan-yong Kuo, "Income Distribution by Size in Taiwan Area — Changes and Causes," *Industry of Free China*, 45, January 1978, pp. 21, 35.

6. SY 1977, p. 96. Many of these may have become full owners. (I owe this insight to William Lavely.) The decline in part-owners and tenants reflects the tendency to equalization among those remaining in the countryside.

7. Kuo-ting Li, "Strategy for Rice Production in Taiwan," *Industry of Free China*, 47, February 1977, p. 6.

8. R. M. Field, N. R. Lardy and J. P. Emerson, *Provincial Industrial Output in the People's Republic of China: 1949-75*, Foreign Economic Report No. 12 (Washington, D. C.: U. S. Dept. of Commerce, September 1976), pp. 10-11; and Nickum and Schak, p. 27.

9. Victor D. Lippit, "The Development of Underdevelopment in China," *Modern China*, 4. July 1978, pp. 251-327.

10. *E. g.*, Lippit; and Robert F. Dernberger, "The Role of the Foreigner in China's Economic Development," in Dwight H. Perkins, ed., *China's Modern Economy in Historical Perspective* (Stanford: Stanford University Press, 1975), pp. 19-47.

11. Rhoads Murphey, *Shanghai: Key to Modern China* (Cambridge: Harvard University Press, 1953), pp. 146-153, 171-172.

12. Peng Chong, "Chongfen liyong he jiji fazhan Shanghai gongye, wei shixian sige xiandaihua gengda gongxian," *Renmin Ribao*, 8 December 1977, p. 1.

13. Nicholas R. Lardy, "Centralization and Decentralization in China's Fiscal Management," *China Quarterly*, No. 61, March 1975, pp. 55-59; and Nickum and Schak, p. 30.

14. Paul E. Ivory and William R. Lavely, "Rustication, Demographic Change, and Development in Shanghai," *Asian Survey*, 17, March 1977, pp. 440-455.

15. "Shanghai," handout, n.d., n.p., pp. 4-5. Obtained in the PRC in 1978 by Harry Harding.

Dilemmas of Socialist Development: An Analysis of Strategic Lines in China, 1949–1981

by Peter Van Ness and Satish Raichur*

. . . how to build this future—which is not something to be received by men, but is rather something to be created by them.

—*Paulo Freire*

The end is the means by which you achieve it. Today's step is tomorrow's life.

—*Wilhelm Reich*

Chairman Mao has been officially laid to rest, and the process of leadership transition begun at his death in 1976 appears to be largely completed. The Central Committee of the Chinese Communist Party at its meeting in June 1981, on the 60th anniversary of the Party's founding, both chose a new Party Chairman, Hu Yaobang,and approved a 35,000-word resolution evaluating Mao Zedong's contributions and mistakes during the period of his rule.[1] The new Deng Xiaoping leadership, comprised principally of Mao's opponents from the Cultural Revolution, has adopted a new design for development in China and has proposed new methods for achieving socialist construction. The time seems ripe for an evaluation of socialist development to date under the People's Republic of China.[2]

The purpose of this article is to identify, to describe, and to analyze the implications of the principal alternative strategic lines of socialist development which have been attempted in China during the first thirty-two years of the People's Republic, from 1949 to 1981. In our view, there have been three such lines (*luxian*), each of them a distinctly different approach to socialist development conceived in terms of its own particular logic and basic theories, and implemented in China during a particular historical period. We have labelled them: Strategy A (the strategic design for the First Five Year Plan, 1953–57); Strategy B (the Great Leap Forward, 1958–60); and Strategy C (so far only partially implemented under the Four Modernizations, 1978–present).[3]

Each strategic line is familiar to students of comparative socialist development. Strategy A is the Stalinist model which emphasizes centralized bureaucratic planning and resource allocation, or what Western economists have called "command economy." Strategy B is a social mobilization approach, based on Party-directed mass movements to create a communist "new man." And Strategy C or "market socialism" is an effort to build a market mechanism into a socialist planned economy in order to increase productivity, to achieve greater economic efficiency, and to stimulate the intiative of workers and managers through material incentives.

In our judgment, the first two strategies have failed for different reasons as systematic attempts to achieve socialist construction in China, and the third is fundamentally flawed. We will try to explain how and why.

In the theoretical and comparative literature on socialist development, a number of authors, both Marxists and non-Marxists, have identified alternative strategies of socialist development approximately in terms of what we are calling Strategies A,B, and C. For example, Sweezy in his debate with Bettelheim[4] describes three alternative roads very similar to what we have found in the case of China. Another example is Eckstein.[5] Eckstein died before the Chinese leadership began systematically to implement a market-socialist strategy in 1978, but he, like Sweezy, identified the same three alternative approaches. Eckstein recognized, even in the readjustment and recovery from the Great Leap period in China, 1961–65, how decentralizing decision-making to production units, emphasizing material incentives, and increasing the scope of the market all seemed to fit together as one potential approach to socialist

* We are grateful to the following for their criticisms and suggestions for revision of earlier drafts of this paper: to members of the University of Denver's FGOD Seminar, especially Xu Ming and Huang Fanzhang; to participants in the Center for Chinese Studies Regional Seminar at the University of California, Berkeley, to which this paper was presented in March 1981, especially Irma Adelman and Laura Tyson; and to the reviewers for the *Bulletin of Concerned Asian Scholars*. In addition, we would like to thank the students over the years in our seminar on the Political Economy of the PRC with whom we have investigated most of the central problems addressed in this paper.

development — a market socialism approach (our Strategy C) which was later adopted by the Deng Xiaoping leadership in 1978 under the so-called Four Modernizations.

Clearly there are a number of parallels between the Chinese experience and that of other socialist countries. For example, the Soviet Union under Stalin attempted to impose Strategy A, the Stalinist model, on virtually all socialist countries that Moscow could influence; and, therefore, most socialist countries have had a significant experience with that strategic line. Regarding Strategy B, the social mobilization model, there are some striking parallels, for example, between Cuban policy during the period 1966–70 and China during the Great Leap Forward, 1958–60.[6] And, finally, the present Chinese leadership has been studying and emulating certain aspects of the Strategy C, the market socialism model, drawing on the experiences of Yugoslavia and Hungary.[7]

In order to maximize opportunities for cross-socialist country comparisons, when analyzing the Chinese experience, we will describe the three models which have been attempted in China in terms which could be applied to any other socialist society. See, for example, our Figure 1 and Table 2 below.

Franz Schurmann provides the best clue to the historical relationship among these three approaches to building socialism when he characterizes them as: centralization-(Strategy A), decentralization II (Strategy B), and decentralization I (Strategy C).[8] As Schurmann's labels suggest, Strategies B and C—two different kinds of decentralization—are both reactions to an initial experience with Strategy A, the centralized Stalinist model. They are micro answers to problems created as a result of the macro preoccupations of Strategy A (stifling of initiative and enthusiasm at the production unit level, economic sector imbalance, low productivity of labor and capital, etc.). Strategy B, by means of social mobilization, proposes a more political solution to these problems; Strategy C, through use of the market and material incentives, suggests an economic solution. To our knowledge, the best descriptions of each of these general strategic lines which are available in English are: for Strategy A, Stalin's *Economic Problems of Socialism in the U.S.S.R.*;[9] for describing Strategy B, Mao Zedong's *A Critique of Soviet Economics*;[10] and, finally, with regard to Strategy C, a book by the Czech economic theorist of the "Prague Spring" in 1968, Ota Sik, *Plan and Market Under Socialism.*[11]

As an interpretation of China's development history, our analysis differs markedly from interpretations that have characterized PRC history in terms of "pendulum swings" alternating between radical and pragmatic phases, or, for example, from the Skinner and Winckler model (1969) which has interpreted PRC history as essentially cyclical, involving little or no qualitative change.[12] Our analysis also differs from those who interpret the Cultural Revolution period, 1966-76, as reflecting a significant departure in development strategy.[13] Instead, we argue that the Cultural Revolution is better understood as a struggle in the realm of so-called "superstructure," an intra-Party leadership conflict which became a mass movement in the years 1966–69 but which did not involve important innovations in development strategy.

Definition of Terms

We use the term strategic *line* to mean a conceptual model for development. It is a systematic design which spells out both the ends and the means for purposeful action. Strategic lines, if adopted by a ruling communist party, are implemented by specific development *policies*. If the policies are thought to be successful and if they are sustained over time, they create a particular *social system*, a social order and way of life which has its own characteristic division of labor, culture and social values, and form of political rule. Thus, the Strategy A line was successfully implemented in terms of the policies of the First Five Year Plan, which in turn created a social system in China characterized by a centralized, bureaucratic command economy. Subsequently, the mass mobilization line of Strategy B was attempted during 1958–60 under the policies of the Great Leap Forward and the communes, but it was never successfully implemented. In 1961–62, the basic policies were changed in order to reverse the economic downturn of 1959–61. Finally, the third alternative, Strategy C, the market socialism line, to date has only been partially implemented under the policies of the Four Modernizations, and the results so far are mixed.

The term *socialism* has been used in many different ways. For the purposes of this analysis, socialism is understood to be a process of basic societal transformation, an historical period of planned transformation from capitalism to communism, undertaken in a society ruled by a communist party. We assume that the various communist party leaders and planners will often have very different notions about what socialism in concrete terms means and what the central characteristics of socialism as a process of transformation should be, but they all agree that communism is the end and that all of them are trying to achieve it. Hence, proponents of different strategies of socialist development may disagree about the means, socialism; but we assume that they agree about the end, communism. Quite frankly, we feel that much of the debate concerning which communist party-ruled countries are "socialist" and which are not has been unproductive. One of the main reasons for our decision to define socialism as a process is to emphasize the importance of focusing on the direction of social change produced by the implementation of each of the three strategies as a basis for evaluating the different approaches.[14]

There is no textbook definition of *communism* in the classical Marxist literature. Here, we assume that the proponents of the various strategies of socialist development would all agree on a definition limited to three characteristics; ownership of the means of production, the process of production, and distribution—the less ambiguous characteristics of communist society. Hence, we define a communist society as one in which: 1) the means of production are owned by the whole people (e.g., in Mao Zedong's terms, the means of production have been redistributed to all the people); 2) the production process is fully socialized; and 3) distribution of that which is produced is on the basis of "need" rather than an individual's "work"—commodities are no longer produced for exchange but rather products are allocated on the basis of need. We will limit our definition to these characteristics. Communist party leaders and planners might well disagree about other defining characteristics of communism: for example, what level of social output in production is essential to provide the material basis of support for communist society; what the disappearance of social classes might mean in concrete terms; or what procedures would replace the state and perform the continuing necessary functions of organizing production, allocating that which is produced, and regulating social interaction in a communist society.

Finally, the debate—or, more accurately, the struggle—among proponents of the different strategic lines of socialist development is carried out within the conceptual context of Marxist economic theory. The advocates of all three different strategies of socialist development similarly conceive of the process of achieving communism as one requiring the concurrent development of both *forces of production* and *relations of production* in order to create the material conditions required for a transition from socialist to communist society. They identify the main contradictions in the socialist historical period as those between the forces of production and the relations of production, and between the superstructure and the economic base.[15] The forces of production have been defined as "the relation of society to the forces of nature, in contest with which it secures the material values it needs," and relations of production as "the relations of men to one another in the process of production."[16] The forces of production include labor, the means of production (land, tools, or machinery, and raw materials), and technology. Relations of production essentially comprise the ownership of the means of production, the social organization or administration of production, and the distribution of that which is produced. In terms of Marxist theory, the two together (the forces of production and the relations of production) constitute the *economic base* or material foundation of any society. The *superstructure* of society, which includes government and other social institutions, legal systems, culture and ideology, is usually conceived of as a reflection of the economic base—i.e., the economic base of any society is thought largely to determine the structure of classes, government, and prevailing ideology.

Preliminary Comparisons: Theoretical and Historical

Figure 1 depicts the three strategies of socialist development in China in terms of the contradiction between relations of production and forces of production. Forces of production constitute the horizontal axis and are specified in terms of a continuum indicating changes in capacity to produce "use values" (i.e., the productive capacity of the economy) running from subsistence to affluence. Changes in relations of production, indicated on the vertical axis, are specified on the basis of the main characteristics of different kinds of societies: feudal, capitalist, and then classless society under communism. The northeast corner of Figure 1, towards which all three strategies are directed is "communism."

The three strategies are compared in Figure 1. The pattern depicted for each strategic line represents *the logic* of the strategic design, *not necessarily the actual performance* of the strategy when it was implemented in China. Strategy A, implemented during the First Five Year Plan, 1953–57, conceived of a fairly linear relationship between the development of forces of production and relations of production. An initial period of sharp changes in relations of production (e.g., the takeover of state capitalist enterprises, the establishment of joint state-private enterprises, and the collectivization of agriculture) would be followed by a consistent pattern of planned incremental changes—initially intended to cover three five-year-plans, 1953–67—in both relations of production and forces of production moving toward communism. By contrast, Strategy B, Mao Zedong's design for the Great Leap Forward, 1958–60, sought to achieve qualitative leaps in relations of production as a part of a dialectical process leading to more rapid development of both relations of production and forces of production. During 1958, for example, the hope was often expressed that this approach could significantly shorten the road to communism. Finally, Strategy C, the present Four Modernizations development strategy, places great emphasis on the development of the forces of production or economic capacity through retrenchment with respect to relations of production (e.g., by seeking to combine market with plan, encouraging foreign private investment in China, and emphasizing individualized material work incentives). Although the characteristics of Strategy A and Strategy C are very different, the two strategic lines are similar in envisaging a continuous pattern of incremental change, rather than the dialectical pattern described by Strategy B.

Table 1 places the three strategies within the thirty-two year history of the People's Republic. It is our contention that the alternative approaches which we have labelled Strategies A,B, and C were the principal strategic lines of socialist development attempted during this time in China.

The first period in the economic history of the PRC, 1949–52, was essentially a time of rehabilitation. For over a century (since the first Opium War in 1839–42), China had experienced the agonies of foreign invasion and domestic turmoil. Worst of all had been the Japanese invasion of China (1937–45) and the subsequent four years of civil war between the Guomindang government of President Chiang Kai-shek and the revolutionary movement led by the Chinese Communist Party. Once victorious in 1949, the CCP's principal tasks were to establish order under CCP rule, to resume production in industry and agriculture, and to carry out a basic land reform in the rural areas of China. As the prominent Chinese economist Xue Muqiao pointed out in a recent interpretation of the PRC's economic history, "By the end of 1952 the work of agrarian reform and economic recovery had been successfully completed."[17]

Having consolidated their regime and achieved a level of production comparable to pre-1949 peak years, the CCP leadership in 1953 was prepared to launch its first major effort to achieve socialist construction in China. This was the First Five Year Plan, 1953–57, and Strategy A. Although the Chinese leadership never completely copied the Stalinist strategic line (especially with regard to the collectivization of agriculture), many aspects of Strategy A were borrowed from Soviet theory and the U.S.S.R.'s development experience. Moreover, Soviet economic support and technological assistance were central factors in the design and success of the First Five Year Plan. Xue

Figure 1

Strategies of Socialist Development: Compared in Terms of Relations of Production and Forces of Production

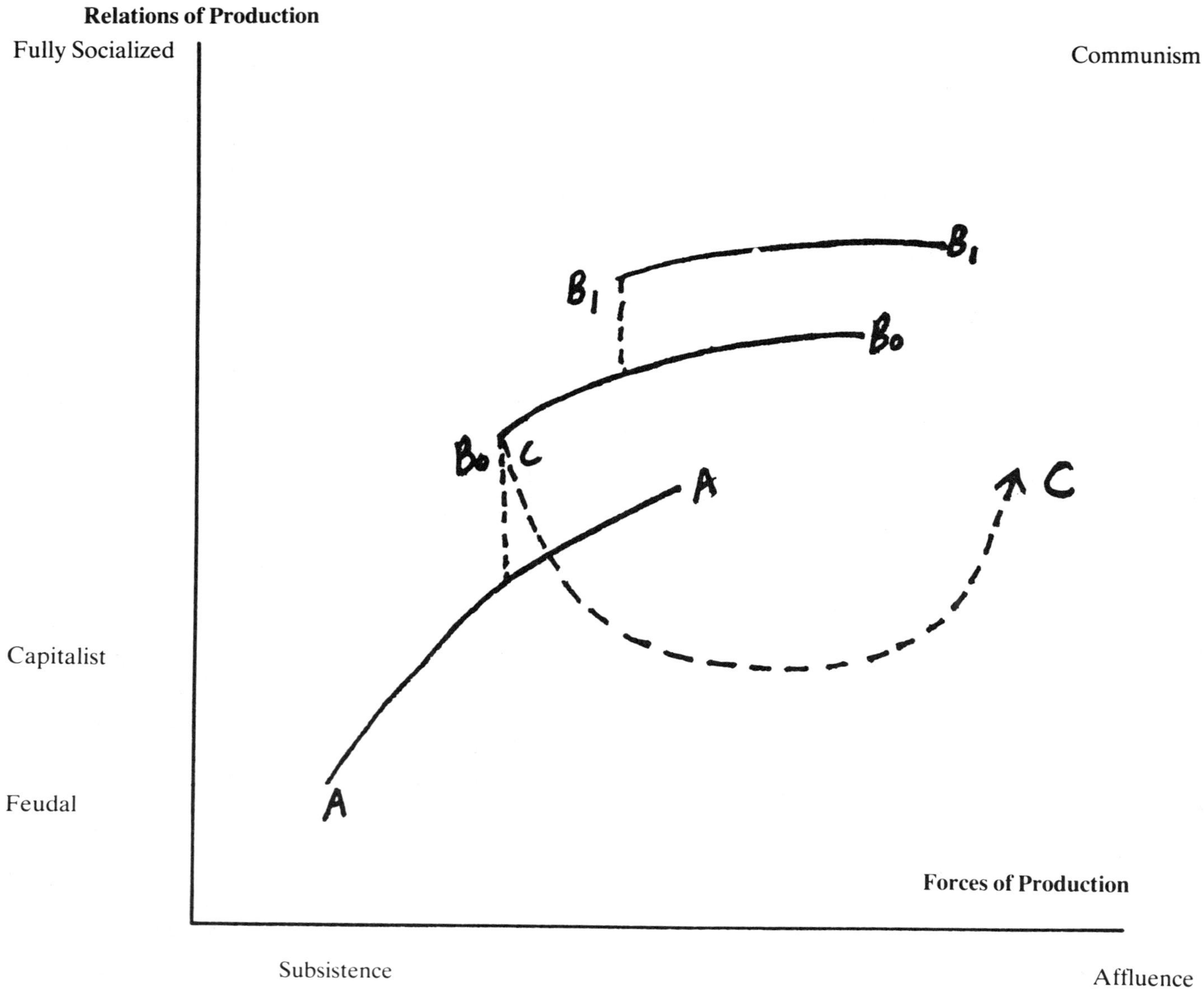

Muqiao, in his review of Chinese development, comments:

> *In the First Five Year Plan we emulated the Soviet Union and implemented a policy of giving priority to the development of heavy indsutry. With the help of the Soviet Union, China carried out the construction of 156 key projects (mainly heavy industries) to lay the initial foundation for socialist industry, and the achievement was colossal.*[19]

Although there was continuing debate in China regarding many aspects of this first effort at socialist development, it seems that all of China's top Party leaders agreed that it was the correct approach. Mao Zedong as well as the comrades with whom he would later disagree profoundly (e.g., Liu Shaoqi, Deng Xiaoping, and Peng Dehuai) all favored the Strategy A approach at that time.

By 1956, however, Mao with his speech, "On the Ten Major Relationships," began to press for an alternative approach. The Great Leap Forward, 1958–60,and the people's communes constituted his design for achieving a faster transition to communism by employing an approach, Strategy B, built upon ideas proven to be successful during China's struggle against the Japanese during the Yanan Period. Rejecting reliance on heavy industry, Mao called for simultaneous development of agriculture and industry to be combined with a massive social mobilization to release the productive energies of the Chinese people. A new kind of social organization, the people's commune, would be the vehicle for resolving the contradiction between

Table 1

Periods in PRC Economic History & Strategies of Development[18]

	Policies	Strategies
1949–52	Rehabilitation of the economy	
1953–57	First Five Year Plan	Strategy A
1958–60	Great Leap Forward and Communes	Strategy B
1961–65	Readjustment and Recovery	
1966–76	Great Proletarian Cultural Revolution	
1976–77	(CCP leadership transition: deaths of Zhou Enlai, Zhu De, and Mao Zedong; and defeat of the "Gang of Four")	
1978–present	Four Modernizations	Strategy C

China's two economies (the collective agricultural economy and state-owned industry) and serve as the institutional basis for the transition from socialism to communism. For Mao:

> *The characteristic of the people's commune is that it is the basic level at which industry, agriculture, the military, education, and commerce are to be integrated in our social structure. . . . The commune is the best organizational form for carrying out the two transitions, from socialist (the present) to all-embracing public, and from all-embracing public to communist ownership. In the future, when the transitions have been completed, the commune will be the basic mechanism of communist society.*[20]

The Great Leap failed. Publicly, three reasons were given: 1) natural disasters; 2) the abrupt cutoff of Soviet aid and the withdrawal of all Soviet technicians in the summer of 1960; and 3) a rather ambiguous category of organization and administrative problems having to do with the implementation of the Great Leap approach. During 1959–61, China experienced a decline in output comparable in magnitude to the American Great Depression of the 1930s—but in a country having a material standard of life which was only a fraction of that enjoyed in the United States. CIA economists estimate that China's agricultural production dropped thirty-one per cent from the peak year of 1958 to the bottom of the economic decline in 1960. Industrial production is estimated to have dropped forty-two per cent in just one year, from 1960 to 1961.[21] Such sharp economic reverses caused great hardship throughout China. Party policies sought to equalize food consumption among the population in order to avoid large-scale starvation.

The Party leadership divided over its interpretation of what went wrong and what should be done. Most courageous among those who opposed Mao Zedong was Peng Dehuai, Defense Minister and long time associate of Mao, who circulated a "letter of opinion" criticizing the Leap at the Lushan plenum of the CCP Central Committee in July 1959.[22] Mao subsequently attacked Peng, and the meeting passed a resolution dismissing him from office.

By 1961–62, the Party had agreed upon a number of expedient measures to readjust the economic system in order to halt the decline and to restore economic growth. These measures constituted a substantial retreat in relations of production from the surges in a communist direction attempted during the Great Leap Forward.[23] For example, in agriculture, the 25,000 large-scale communes of 1958–59 were reorganized into 75,000 smaller communes (about the size of the *xiang* or administrative village); the production team (approximately the size of a small village) was made the basic accounting unit; and peasants in the collective economy were once again permitted "private plots" on which to raise crops for household consumption and even for sale.[24] This structure of collectivized production has remained largely the same since 1962, in spite of efforts at different times during the decade from 1966 to 1976 to alter it.

The policies of readjustment during 1961–65 were successful, and economic recovery and the beginning of a general pattern of growth of output ensued. However, the consensus within the Party leadership that expedient policies should be undertaken in the short run to deal with the economic decline began to break down once a pattern of substantial economic growth had again been restored. Many CCP leaders had opposed Mao's Strategy B concept of development as early as 1955–56 when he first pressed for its implementation. After the collapse of the Great Leap and the extreme price that the Chinese people paid for its failure, presumably many others were determined not to permit another such experiment in social change in China. But Mao would not remain content with the status quo. Precisely at the time that the policies of economic readjustment were being formally adopted as Party doctrine, Mao Zedong sought to reverse the retreat from socialism in the relations of production and superstructure in China by launching a Socialist Education Campaign. By means of education and propaganda, the campaign was designed to build on the poor and lower-middle peasants in the countryside, revitalize the class struggle, and to press Chinese society once again in a communist direction.

Differences about the correct road for China's future came to a head in 1965 and 1966. The Great Proletarian Cultural Revolution became a struggle over policy and power, each side convinced that its approach to socialist construction was the best for China, and that the opposition's strategy would lead to disaster. In June 1966, Mao Zedong and Lin Biao, frustrated by Party obstruction and sabotage of their initiatives, turned the Cultural Revolution into a mass movement to remove their opponents from power. "Bombard the Headquarters" was their motto as student Red Guards besieged government and party offices. Mao, Chairman of the Chinese Communist Party, had gone to the streets to recapture control of his own party organization. Cadres at all levels were thrown out of office between 1966 and 1969, and head-of-state Liu Shaoqi and CCP General Secretary Deng Xiaoping were singled out as the most prominent "persons in authority taking the capitalist road." The Cultural Revolution focused largely on superstructure, and it had surprisingly little effect in reshaping the economic base of Chinese society.[25] It was a struggle which remained unresolved for ten years, 1966–76, and which resulted in no fundamental and consistent new direction with respect to Chinese development. Hence, for the purpose of this analysis, the Cultural Revolution does not represent a separate strategic line of socialist development.

The Ninth Party Congress in April 1969 seemed to signal at least a limited victory for the cultural revolutionaries, but it was followed by further struggles—especially between Mao and Lin Biao. Ultimately, Lin died under mysterious circumstances in a plane crash in September 1971, and was charged with having attempted a military coup d'etat.[26] Struggles within the Party over policy and power continued until Mao's death in September 1976.

Looking back over the period from the beginning of the Cultural Revolution in 1966 to Mao's death in 1976, the present leadership tends to lump together the entire decade as ten years lost to Cultural Revolution. The inconsistency of the policies implemented during this ten years is explained by some as due to virtually continuous struggles within the top Party leadership resulting in no agreement about a clear new strategy, and by others as reflecting popular resistance to policies that did not make any sense. In autumn 1979, Ye Jianying, in his speech celebrating the thirtieth anniversary of the founding of the People's Republic, analyzed the impact of the so-called Gang of Four and concluded: "In everything they did they set themselves against the overwhelming majority of the people in the Party and country." The ten years, according to Ye Jianying, were "an appalling catastrophe suffered by all our people."[27]

The traumatic year for China was 1976. First, in January, came the death of Premier Zhou Enlai, and later, in April, the Tian An Men demonstrations (now usually called the April 5th Movement) in support of Premier Zhou and against the policies and power of Jiang Qing (Mao's wife), Zhang Chunqiao (a Deputy Premier), and others in the group which would later be called the Gang of Four. During the summer the old veteran and acting head-of-state Zhu De died, and one of the most destructive earthquakes in history killed 240,000 people in Tangshan. Finally, in September, Chairman Mao died, and the final stage in the process of leadership succession began. In October, the Gang of Four was arrested, and during the following year, a new leadership was formed around Hua Guofeng, supposedly chosen by Mao to succeed him; Ye Jianying, a veteran cadre closely linked to the military; and Deng Xiaoping, once again rehabilitated to become the mainstay of the new regime.

After the new leadership had consolidated its power in 1977, a new strategy of socialist development began to take shape. The Four Modernizations—a plan to turn China into a powerful socialist country with modern agriculture, industry, national defense, and science and technology by the year 2000—had its roots in Premier Zhou's report to the First Session of the Third National People's Congress in 1964 (before the Cultural Revolution) and the Fourth National People's Congress of January 1975. But the Four Modernizations as an approch to socialist construction was not duly adopted as policy until after the First and Second Sessions of the Fifth National People's Congress and the Third Plenum of the Eleventh Central Committee of the CCP—meetings held in 1978 and 1979. Even today, certain aspects of the strategy are still being debated in China, and much of what apparently had been decided has not yet been fully implemented.

Nonetheless, the general patterns of the new strategy are fairly clear. The Deng Xiaoping leadership has proposed a combination of market mechanism with state plan, more autonomy for production units, a strategy which overwhelmingly emphasizes the development of productive forces, and an appeal to workers based on greater material rewards and consumer benefits. In 1979, Zhao Ziyang, more recently elevated to the Standing Committee of the Party Politburo and the position of Premier, defined socialism as having two central principles: 1) public ownership of the means of production, and 2) distribution on the basis of "to each according to his work." "With these two principles as the prerequisites," Zhao Ziyang asserted, "we should adopt whatever system, structure, policy and method are most effective in promoting the development of the productive forces."[28] In other words, according to Zhao, if those two principles are kept inviolate, almost anything else might be attempted in China in an effort to develop the economy.

Logic and Implementation

Table 2 identifies the key differences among the three major strategies of socialist development which have been attempted in China. Our analysis will focus on comparing Strategy B and Strategy C, but let us begin with a brief description of Strategy A to set the scene in concrete terms for the subsequent discussion of the other two strategic lines. Rather than analysing the separate dimensions of the strategies (i.e., reading Table 2 horizontally, across the three alternatives), we will emphasize the integrating logic and how the separate dimensions fit into a logical whole as a strategy of development (i.e., reading down the three columns).

Strategy A

The Chinese never fully adopted even those ideas that were proffered by the Soviets during the First Five Year Plan, so Strategy A in its implementation was always a mixture of Soviet advice and the dynamic of the CCP experience up to that point. Soviet influence was greatest in the heavy industry sector during the first ten years of the People's Republic, and pervasive as well in military organization and science and technology. However, in agriculture (from which seventy per cent of output was derived in 1949), the CCP kept its own counsel, and the success of the collectivization of Chinese agriculture between 1953 and 1956 was in no sense due to Soviet advice but was rather the result of tried and tested CCP mobilization strategies from pre-1949 and the initial land reform program.

As has been mentioned, the First Five Year Plan was originally intended as the first of three five-year-plans, to be implemented in connection with a comprehensive program of Soviet economic and technological assistance to China. Soviet aid commitments were part of a combination

Table 2
Strategies of Socialist Development: Dimensions

	Strategy A	Strategy B	Strategy C
1. strategy focus:	social system (country-wide infrastructure)	individual ("new man")	production unit (management of enterprises)
2. structural point of policy initiative:	center	intermediate level (commune in China)	production unit
3. economic base/super-structure emphasis:	relations of production & forces of production together	relations of production & superstructure	forces of production
4. economic sector emphasis (assuming that "balance" and integration of sectors is always important):	heavy industry	simultaneous development of industry & agriculture	agriculture and light industry (consumption emphasis)
5. strategy implementation:	plan	social mobilization within plan	plan-market combination
6. work incentive emphasis:	individual, material incentives	moral plus material incentives on group basis	individual, material incentives
7. international economic relations:	integration with Soviet Union and socialist camp economies	self-reliance[29]	integration into the world market economy
8. role of the communist party:	centralized rule from top down	social mobilizer in process of "continuous revolution"	contradiction between economic decentralization and Party political power

of military security and assistance pacts negotiated by Chairman Mao himself in Moscow from December 1949 to February 1950. These negotiations came at a time when the Cold War was reaching fever pitch and only shortly before the outbreak of the Korean War in June 1950. Chinese intervention came in October-November to help defend North Korea after the United Nations forces crossed the 38th parallel in an American-led rollback operation. Already in June 1949, Mao Zedong had put forth the policy of "leaning to one side," cooperating with the socialist countries against the imperialists. By the end of 1950, the CCP had little alternative since the American reaction to the outbreak of the Korean War included efforts to clamp a global embargo on trade with the People's Republic and to isolate it diplomatically. The CCP had no choice after 1950 but to rely on their Soviet and East European comrades.

In this sense, Strategy A for China was an imposed system, especially as it affected heavy industry. The Soviet Union provided approximately $1.5 billion in credits to China during the 1950s, and thousands of Russians and East Europeans worked in China as technical advisors in positions critical to China's economic modernization.[30] Soviet planning concepts, patterns of industrial and scientific organization, and a wide variety of technologies had important influences in China during these years. Strategy A—a "command economy"—gave clear priority to developing central planning; it emphasized heavy industry in an effort to build a country-wide industrial infrastructure; and the strategic design was one which seemed to assure a roughly proportional concurrent development of relations of production and forces of production in the direction of communism (see Figure 1).

Initially, Strategy A was tremendously successful as a design for achieving economic growth and modernization. For example, during the five years from 1953 through 1957, industrial production increased by 128.6% and agricultural production by 24.8%. Heavy industry increased an annual average of 25.4% during these years, and light industry an annual average of 12.9%.[31]

Strategy B

By the mid-1950s, the international situation had changed. Stalin had died in March 1953, and a negotiated conclusion of the Korean War had been reached soon thereafter. Gradually China had broken out of the American-imposed diplomatic isolation, especially after the successful Bandung summit conference of Afro-Asian states in 1955. Domestically, the First Five Year Plan had been successful in laying the material foundations for socialist construction in China, and internationally, conditions were shifting, it seemed, in favor of the socialist camp. Prompted by the Soviet launching of the first earth satellite in October 1957, Sputnik I, Mao Zedong put forward a new interpretation of global politics using the metaphor of East Wind over the West Wind.[32]

By 1955–56, Mao had apparently concluded that the time was ripe for building socialism—socialism on a Chinese design fitted to China's concrete conditions—and that the Soviet-style First Five Year Plan should not be continued. Indeed high rates of economic growth and an immense development of heavy industry had been achieved, but at the same time, differences between mental and manual labor, city and countryside, and worker and peasant were growing greater. Building socialism for Mao was a dynamic, mass-participant process, not simply the imposition of a centralized social system which gave directions to the populace. It has been a working assumption among many American political scientists, especially since the Cultural Revolution, that the state system in China is fundamentally unstable. On the contrary, for Mao in the mid-1950s, the PRC state system was seen to be too stable, too centralized, too rigid, and too given to running the country by issuing commands from the Center.

The logic of Strategy B, which in our view is best represented in the approach attempted during the Great Leap Forward, begins with a particular epistemology and emphasizes transforming individual citizens as both the means and the end of socialist construction. For example, compared with the logic of Strategy C or market socialism, Strategy B as a concept of socialist development is different in many fundamental ways, especially regarding epistemology or how one attempts to understand the world, assumptions about human motivation, and theories about how societies change.

The Strategy B approach, which is conceptually founded on dialectical materialism, begins with the proposition that contradictions exist in all things and that life should be understood as a dialectical process. There are "laws" which govern the evolution of human affairs, but these laws are different for the various countries because of the particularities of the concrete conditions of each. Thus, a strategy for socialist development (like a struggle for national liberation or any other purposeful collective action) must be undertaken as a process of discovery. No one knows in advance what the objective laws are. Hence, the correct strategy must be discovered through experience. According to Mao:

> *At the beginning no one has knowledge. Foreknowledge has never existed. If you want to know the objective laws of the development of things and events you must go through the process of practice, adopt a Marxist-Leninist attiude, compare successes and failures, continually practicing and studying, going through multiple successes and failures; moreover, meticulous research must be performed. There is no other way to make one's own knowledge gradually conform to the laws. For those who see only victory but not defeat it will not be possible to know these laws.*[33]

For Mao, "Human knowledge and the capability to transform nature have no limit."[34] We are limited only by our capacity to understand. Therefore, those who aspire to achieve socialist construction must work in the unknown to discover those laws of transformation which apply in the particular conditions of any country. Socialist transformation is not achieved by anyone's imposing a system. Transformation, by definition, is anti-system.

In Mao's view, the Chinese Communists would have to be as inventive and imaginative in designing strategies for socialist construction in a non-industrialized country as, for example, Marx was original in his analysis of capitalism in the middle of the 19th century. They would have to find ways of doing what had never been done before.

People must liberate themselves, Mao insisted—they must transform themselves. For example, land was not given to peasants in China during the period of land reform. Rather, under the leadership of the Party, they waged a class struggle to take the land away from the landlords.

Mao argues that contradictions are the motive force in the development of socialism, and that "a thoroughgoing socialist revolution must advance along the three fronts of politics, economics,and ideology."[35] In his view, "no line of development is straight; it is wave or spiral shaped. . . . The development of all things is characterized by imbalance."[36] According to Mao Zedong, in a process of socialist construction, changes in relations of production must be closely linked to changes in forces of production, and the impact of superstructure is also important in creating the ideological and political bases for intitiatives in the transformation of the economic base of the society.[37]

The Great Leap approach clearly draws on an analogy with the successful mass mobilization strategies of the Yanan Period during the war against Japan. In socialist construction, as in waging revolutionary war, Mao assumes that the key to success is a motivated population. Party-led efforts to mobilize and to sustain support should be designed to tap the basic enthusiasm of the people through the implementation of the "mass line." It is not a matter of moral *versus* material incentives for Mao Zedong, but rather political mobilization to achieve greater collective efforts in which all will benefit. In terms of the logic of Strategy B, those who "serve the people" also serve themselves as the collective effort moves forward both relations of production and forces of production at an unprecedented rate. At a micro level, as has already been mentioned, the commune was for Mao the basic social unit of socialist transformation, and the creation of the "new man" in China was in a sense both the means and the ends of Strategy B. The success of the Maoist concept of socialist development during the Great Leap depended on individual Chinese making a commitment to work selflessly and energetically for the collective good. If such mass attitudes could be inculcated and such behavior sustained, both the productive energies needed to develop productive forces and the ideological and political prerequisites for communist society could be attained simultaneously.

Strategy C

Finally, let us turn to Strategy C, the market socialism approach.[38] Although there are a number of different thinkers contributing theory to the Four Modernizations strategy of socialist development (e.g., Chen Yun, Hu Qiaomu, Xue Muqiao, Deng Liqun, and Ma Hong) and there are some disagreements among them, it seems to us that the strategy as a general line is fairly clear and consistent. Moreover, Chinese economists confirm that the ideas underlying the Four Modernizations are largely in agreement with the theoretical argument made in Ota Sik's *Plan and Market Under Socialism*. Therefore, Sik can also be helpful in illuminating this approach.

The Strategy C concept seems to assume that the laws for the development of socialism are fairly well understood. Unlike Mao, who calls for *discovering* laws of development, Hu Qiaomu has written an important article calling upon the people of China to *observe* economic laws.[39]

In the minds of the theorists of Strategy C, these laws call for an overwhelming emphasis on the development of forces of production. They condemn the policies of the Great Leap as utopian and conceived on the basis of idealism rather than concrete materialist analyses of the potentialities of Chinese society. Unstated in their arguments—but clearly implied—is the understanding that to reconsolidate Chinese society after the ten lost years of Cultural Revolution, 1966–76, Chinese development strategy must make a short term retreat from socialism in relations of production (see Figure 1) in order to get the economic system running efficiently after such prolonged dislocations—attributed to the Gang of Four (and Mao Zedong).

In order to increase efficiency and economic output, Strategy C calls for the combination of a market mechanism with state plan; the competition of production units within a given industry; much greater autonomy to be permitted to individual enterprises; and appeals to Chinese workers to produce more and better quality products in return for individual material rewards. The production unit is the focus of this strategy, and improving enterprise management is one of its principal tasks.

The pattern of development envisaged by Strategy C is continuous and incremental, not wave-like as in Strategy B, on the assumption that after certain levels in the development of productive forces are achieved, somehow changes in the relations of production moving sharply in a more communist direction would take place. One problem here is that there is no theory as yet spelling out how or why that would take place. On the contrary, Xue Muqiao, for example, is theorizing about how the collective economy should be expanded as one way of dealing with unemployment, rather than designing ways to transform the collective economy into the more socialist form of ownership by the whole people.[40]

Underlying Strategy C is the assumption that human beings are basically motivated by individual material interests, and that the best way to increase efficiency and productivity is to encourage competition among workers and enterprises through promises that those which produce most will be rewarded most. This, it would seem, is the main intended function of the market and the concept of distribution on the basis of "to each according to his work."[41] In evaluating the Four Modernizations approach as it is implemented in China, some of the central theoretical and empirical questions which should be considered, we think, are: 1) the role of "law of value" in both circulation and production; 2) treating means of production as "commodities" and what implications follow from that for the principle of public ownership of the means of production (especially in light of Mao's notion of the redistribution of the ownership of the means of production as one of the key elements in a process of socialist transformation); and 3) greater enterprise autonomy combined with distribution based on "to each according to his work" and their influences on worker income differentials, social stratification in Chinese society, and the politics and socialist consciousness of a socialist society.[42]

Finally, with regard to international economic relations, Strategy C calls for China to become integrated with the world market system for the purpose of gaining access to foreign capital and technology—in a manner parallel to international economic relations under Strategy A which call for integration with the economies of the U.S.S.R. and the socialist camp. Strategy A, "leaning to one side," is based on economic integration with the East; Strategy C, leaning toward the other side, seeks integration with the West. Both differ markedly in this regard from the "self reliance" policy of Strategy B.[43] At year end 1981, international economic policies that were anathema under Mao Zedong's rule were being pursued by the Four Modernizations leadership: establishing joint ventures in China with multi-national corporations;[44] joining the International Monetary Fund and the World Bank, the two key multilateral institutions linking the capitalist industrialized countries with the Third World; accepting long-term foreign loans; building a tourist industry;[45] importing foreign consumer goods for sale to Chinese citizens; and sending thousands of Chinese students and scholars abroad for academic training in capitalist countries.

Implications and Evaluation: Dilemmas of Socialist Development

Only one of the three approaches to socialist construction considered here, Strategy A, has ever been completely implemented in China in the sense of a strategic *line* being translated into public *policies* which ultimately transform the structure of society into a particular kind of *social system*. In fact, in terms of its fundamental characteristics, the social system of China in 1982 was still that which was created during the First Five Year Plan, 1953–57: i.e., a centralized command economy, under the political regime of a "dictatorship of the proletariat." Hence, the evidence available is only sufficient for an empirical evaluation of Strategy A. With regard to Strategies B and C, we must rely more on the implications of the conceptual design and on evidence from the experiences of other socialist countries. For example, "market socialism" strategies have been implemented for a number of years in both Yugoslavia and Hungary. Evidence from the economic history of these two countries can suggest implications for the implementation of the Four Modernizations approach in China. To our knowledge, Strategy B, the mass mobilization line, has never been successfully implemented in any country. We will return to this point.

Strategy A

The successes of the Stalinist model in China were: 1) establishing an infrastructure for industrial development; 2) achieving high rates of economic growth, especially in heavy industry; and 3) bringing about significant social change, principally the nationalization of industry and the collectivization of agriculture.

With regard to the shortcomings of Strategy A, probably the most telling criticisms are those made by Mao

Zedong and Ota Sik, both proponents of alternative development strategies.[46] Critics find that, economically, Strategy A: 1) produces economic sector imbalances and bottlenecks through its emphasis on heavy industry; 2) leads to irrational resources allocation and production priorities, because of the inefficiencies of administered allocation; 3) stifles the enthusiasm and initiative of workers and enterprise managers; and, over the long run, 4) leads to low rates of capital and labor productivity.

Politically, the critics say, the social system created by Strategy A becomes a dictatorship by the ruling communist party in the "new class" sense of Milovan Djilas[47] or what some Poles during the strikes of 1980–81 were calling the "red bourgeoisie."[48] Applying Lenin's *State and Revolution* to the analysis of socialist societies under Strategy A, one can argue that the communist party having established a "dictatorship of the proletariat" does not *own* but comes to *control* the means of production and emerges as a new ruling class, enjoying tremendous power through their centralized bureaucratic direction of the economy under state planning, and their formal monopoly of political power. As a result, the initial process of social transformation toward communist society begun under a Strategy A-type social system *stops*, because of the vested interest developed by the "new class" in the established order. In addition, it would seem that such a system has a tendency to stratify into privileged and less privileged groups, and to rigidify under bureaucratic rule.

If socialism is understood as we have defined it in this paper—i.e., as a process of basic societal transformation and an historical period of planned transition from capitalism to communism—then, under Strategy A, the term "socialist state" becomes a contradiction in terms. "Socialism" calls for basic social transformation, but the "state" stands for defense of the established order. Empirically, in contemporary history, it seems that the principal function of *any* state has been to preserve the established order, and those leaders who hold state power (including revolutionaries who have won state power by force) develop an interest in preserving that order which sustains them in power. From this perspective, it should not be surprising to find that in socialist societies, state officials and economic planners do not write theory of socialist transformation. Instead, they write designs for the development of productive forces—strategies to achieve wealth and power which do not threaten the established order. One wonders, therefore, how under a Strategy A social system there can ever be a successful *socialist* state in the sense of those who hold state power directing a process of basic social transformation which must ultimately undermine their own power.

Strategy B

In these terms, however, Strategy B is an exception. Of the three strategic lines, it is the only one designed to produce repeated attempts to achieve social transformation toward the communist-society ideal. Significantly, the communist party leaders who write Strategy B theory and call for mass mobilization strategies of development are the original leaders of the struggle for state power, men like Mao and Castro, who apparently retain in their minds a vision of the ideals for which the revolution was made in the first place, and for whom, unlike most of their Party comrades, achieving state power and the privileges that go with it are not enough.

Mao Zedong believed that the two objectives of social transformation (continuing fundamental change in the relations of production) and economic modernization (the rapid development of productive forces) were congruent objectives which could both most rapidly be achieved through strategies of social mobilization. Unlike the theory of Strategy C which conceives of a trade-off relationship between the two objectives at least in the short run (see Figure 1), Strategy B theory argues that the key to socialist development is to achieve both goals simultaneously by means of social mobilization.

In fact, however, the Great Leap line in China, 1958–60, failed to achieve *either* sustained social transformation *or* economic modernization. Instead, the Great Leap Forward resulted in a sharp economic downturn and widespread hardship for the Chinese people. Moreover, social mobilization strategies have never been successful in achieving both objectives over a sustained period of time in any other socialist country either.

In China after Mao's death, the prevailing view was obviously that the theoretical design of Strategy B was fundamentally wrong, that it was an "idealist" notion inappropriate to the objective conditions (the present stage of the development of productive forces) in China,[49] or even that it was a theory contrary to human nature. At least one senior member of the CCP has concluded that Mao Zedong "was never a Marxist."[50] Yet, Mao's concept of mass mobilization did indeed succeed as a strategy during the struggle for state power before 1949. Why did it fail as a design for socialist construction in the late 1950s?

In the critics' view, the Great Leap failed because the Chinese people would not support it. For example, some argue that the Yanan analogy, which Mao invoked, was at best inappropriate. During the Yanan Period, the Chinese people were fighting for their lives against invading Japanese, and later fighting to overthrow a corrupt and rapacious Guomindang government before it exterminated them. Radical solutions, they argue, were appropriate to the radical problems of the time. But by the late 1950s, conditions were very different. The people of China felt relatively secure from foreign attack and had become concerned with the more prosaic problems of increasing their material living standard, planning careers, and aspiring to brighter futures for their children. Radical policies of mobilization and continuous remobilization failed, therefore, to gain necessary popular support.

Another way of trying to understand the contrast between Mao's success during the struggle for state power and his failure during the Great Leap Forward might be to compare the importance of popular support for the CCP leadership before and after 1949. During the struggle for state power (both against the Japanese and the Guomindang government), the Party's survival was at stake. If the Party's mass mobilization policies were not successful in winning the support of the Chinese people, the CCP leadership as well as its followers would be destroyed. However, after gaining state power, the Maoist Party, although it still needed the support of the people it governed like any modern state leadership does, no longer depended to such a great extent on popular support for its own survival. Popular support as the critical test of the success of Party policies was no longer so important. Perhaps inevitably, Mao and the Party leadership became less responsive to the desires and demands of the Chinese people, and more likely to engage in "commandism"—ordering things done, rather than designing policies responsive to the people's concerns and requirements. In China today, people joke that Mao's approach after the mid-1950s was not so much based on the "mass movement" (*qunzhong yundong*), as "moving masses" (*yundong qunzhong*)—i.e., Party leaders manipulating the Chinese people for their own selfish purposes.

The actual reasons for the failure of the Great Leap and other Strategy B attempts remain, in our view, an open empirical question—a question of critical significance for the hope of socialist transformation under any of the established socialist systems in the world today. Empirical research in China and Cuba, for example, will have to determine the reasons for the failure to implement successfully the Strategy B approach to socialist development. We suggest, however, that the answer to this question should be sought not only in investigations of the appropriateness of the theory to existing conditions and the willingness of citizens to support policies of radical transformation, but also in research on the resistance and possible sabotage by a communist party "new class" fearful of losing its privileges and power.

Strategy C

As we have seen, advocates of the Strategy C approach criticize the inefficiencies of centralized state planning and the emphasis placed by the Stalinist model (Strategy A) on achieving rigid output quotas, arguing that such a system does not produce what is needed and desired by consumers and that the system stifles both workers' enthusiasm and managerial initiative. By combining socialist planning with a competitive market system, they say, a Strategy C approach can inspire enthusiasm among workers and managers, and reverse the pattern of low productivity and inefficiency. Enterprises should be required to compete against each other within the market, and they should earn material rewards on the basis of comparative efficiency and profitability. Workers, similarly, should be compensated for the quantity and quality of their work as measured by the market, thus directly linking production performance to material reward.[51]

The market is the heart of this design for socialist development. Moreover, a market is not something that can be turned on today and off tomorrow. It is a structural phenomenon which must be permitted to function according to its own dynamic in order to produce the promised economic benefits. The market mechanism is intended to reshape individual and institutional expectations and behaviors, and ultimately, the success or failure of Strategy C is dependent upon the implementation of a market mechanism.

Politically , it seems, especially from the experience in Yugoslavia, that under Strategy C, there arises an almost inevitable contradiction between the communist party's formal monopoly of political power and the economic power enjoyed by production units under this kind of decentralized economic system. Hence, the implementation of Strategy C would seem to challenge the customary notion of the communist party's leadership role under the "dictatorship of the proletariat." At the same time, however, Strategy C may provide the best available means to date of democratizing the Stalinist social system—the economic power of worker-managed enterprises increasingly cutting into the centralized political power of the Party. The struggle over implementing market socialism reforms in China during 1980 and 1981 seems to have been principally a struggle between Strategy A and Strategy C adherents—the advocates of Strategy A fearful, among other things, of the threat to the power of the Party and State Center represented by Strategy C efforts to decentralize economic decision-making.[52]

Economically, market systems do seem, through competition, to force upon production units requirements for greater efficiency, and therefore, we should expect a fully implemented Strategy C to result in higher rates of productivity.[53] However, the incorporation of a market mechanism in a socialist planned economy can also lead to new problems for communist-party planners—especially inflation and unemployment. For example, Yugoslavia, the socialist country having the longest experience with market socialism, illustrates some of these problems. Yugoslavia registered a record balance of payments deficit in 1980, and was suffering from significant unemployment and a perennial foreign trade deficit. Furthermore, the September 1980 cost-of-living in that country was 35.8% higher than the 1979 average.[54] Reports from China in early 1981, where Strategy C has thus far only been partially implemented, indicate that the Deng Xiaoping leadership is reevaluating China's economic reforms because of similar problems: government budget deficits, inflation, overcommitment in contracts for major purchases of plant and equipment from abroad, and failure to complete successfully foreign plants in China or to bring them into production as designed.[55]

Ultimately, the central problem regarding Strategy C as an approach to socialist development, in our view, is that no matter how economically successful it may turn out to be, market socialism inevitably involves a serious reversal in the relations of production. It leads away from development toward communist society without offering any immediate prospect that these trends will be changed. To be blunt, Strategy C in both its domestic and international characteristics amounts to "taking the capitalist road."

Once implemented by government policies, the strategic line of market socialism creates its own particular kind of social system, through reshaping both the social structure and people's way of life. For Mao Zedong and many communists, the heart of socialist culture is the collective spirit represented in the slogan "serve the people." By contrast, the culture of a market system enjoins each to "serve thyself." Strategy C in its practical implications is not a design for socialist construction but rather a formula for restoring the central structural characteristic of a capitalist economic system, the market.

Notes

1. *Renmin Ribao*, June 30 and July 1 and 2, 1981.

2. For comprehensive data on economic performance under the PRC, see the following sources: Joint Economic Committee, Congress of the United States, *Chinese Economy Post-Mao*, Vol. 1, (Washington, D.C.: U.S. Government Printing Office, 1978); the nine-volume study by the World Bank, *China: Socialist Economic Development*, June 1, 1981 (Report No.3391-CHA) (*The Economist*, June 20, 1981, pp. 44-45 summarizes and comments on the World Bank report); and the annual reports of the PRC State Statistical Bureau on the economic performance of the previous year (e.g., "Communique on Fulfilment of China's 1981 National Economic Plan," *Beijing Review*, May 17, 1982, pp. 15-24).

3. Those years since 1949, other than the time periods specified here as representative of Strategies A, B, or C, were, as we will argue below, years of rehabilitation, readjustment, or intra-Party struggle. See Table 1 below.

4. Paul M. Sweezy and Charles Bettelheim, *On the Transition to Socialism* (New York: Monthly Review Press, 1971).

5. Alexander Eckstein, *China's Economic Revolution* (Cambridge: Cambridge University Press, 1977). For a somewhat different but provocative perspective, see also Charles E. Lindblom, *Politics and Markets* (New York: Basic Books, 1977).

6. See Carmelo Mesa-Lago, *Cuba in the 1970's* (Albuquerque: University of New Mexico Press, 1978), pp. 2-3.

7. For example, Luo Yuanzhen, Deputy Director of the Institute of World Economy of the Chinese Academy of Social Sciences, is head of a national society in China for the study of Yugoslav political economy, *Nansilafu Jingji Yanjiu Hui*.

8. Franz Schurmann, *Ideology and Organization in Communist China* (Berkeley: University of California Press, 1968 edition), pp. 175-178.

9. Beijing: Foreign Languages Press, 1972 (first published in 1952 in Russian).

10. Translated by Moss Roberts; New York: Monthly Review Press, 1977. This is a collection of translations from *Mao Zedong Sixiang Wansui* (Long Live the Thought of Mao Zedong), 1967 and 1969. For concepts related to Strategy B, see also: Mao, *On the Correct Handling of Contradictions Among the People* (Beijing: Foreign Languages Press, 1957); Mao, *Four Essays on Philosophy* (Beijing: Foreign Languages Press, 1966); and Stuart Schram (ed.), *Chairman Mao Talks to the People, Talks and Letters: 1956-1971* (New York: Pantheon, 1974).

11. Translated by Eleanor Wheeler; White Plains, New York: International Arts and Sciences Press, 1967. Regarding Strategy C and its justification and implementation in China, see also Xue Muqiao, *China's Socialist Economy* (Beijing: Foreign Languages Press, 1981).

12. G. William Skinner and Edwin A. Winckler, "Compliance Succession in Rural Communist China: A Cyclical Theory," in Amitai Etzioni (ed.), *A Sociological Reader on Complex Organizations* (New York: Holt, Rinehart, and Winston, 1969). See, also, Andrew J. Nathan, "Policy Oscillations in the People's Republic of China: a Critique." and Edwin A. Winckler, "Policy Oscillations in the People's Republic of China: a Reply" both in *China Quarterly*, December 1976.

13. For example, see Suzanne Paine, "Balanced Development: Maoist Conception and Chinese Practice," *World Development*, 1976, No. 4, pp. 277-304; and David Mamo, "Mao's Model for Socialist Transition Reconsidered," *Modern China*, January 1981, pp. 55-81.

14. For a contemporary Chinese notion of treating socialism as a process, see Xue, *China's Socialist Economy*, p. viii.

15. For example, *ibid.*, pp. v-viii.

16. Stalin, *Economic Problems of Socialism in the U.S.S.R.*, p. 64. Marx in *Critique of Political Economy* writes:

> *In the social production of their life, men enter into definite relations that are indispensable and independent of their will,* relations of production *which correspond to a definite stage of development of their material* productive forces. *The sum total of these relations of production constitutes the economic structure of society, the real foundation, on which rises a legal and political superstructure and to which correspond definite forms of social consciousness. The mode of production of material life conditions the social, political, and intellectual life process in general. It is not the consciousness of men that determines their being, but, on the contrary, their social being that determines their consciousness. At a certain stage of their development, the material productive forces of society come in conflict with the existing relations of production, or—what is but a legal expression for the same thing—with the property relations within which they have been at work hitherto. From forms of development of the productive forces these relations turn into their fetters. Then begins an epoch of social revolution. With the change of the economic foundations the entire immense superstructure is more or less rapidly transformed.*

David McLellan, *Karl Marx: Selected Writings* (London: Oxford University Press, 1977), p. 389.

17. Xue Muqiao, "Thirty Years of Hardship in Building Our Country," *Hongqi*, 1979, No. 10, p. 40.

18. See footnote number 3.

19. Xue, "Thirty Years," p. 44.

20. Mao, *A Critique of Soviet Economics*, p. 134. For further discussion of Chinese hopes for the commune during this period, see the documents collected in Robert R. Bowie and John K. Fairbank, *Communist China 1955-1959: Policy Documents with Analysis* (Cambridge: Harvard University Press, 1965), pp. 389-529. See, also, "Sixty Points on Working Methods—A Draft Resolution from the Office of the Centre of the CCP," (London: Oxford University Press, 1970), pp. 57-76. And, finally, for internal criticism of the communes and the Great Leap, especially from Peng Dehuai, and the discussion surrounding it, see Union Research Institute, *The Case of Peng Teh-Huai 1959-1968* (Hong Kong: Union Research Institute, 1968).

21. Joint Economic Committee, Congress of the US, *Chinese Economy Post-Mao*, p. 208.

22. Union Research Institute, *Case of Peng Teh-Huai*, pp. 7-13.

23. See the seventy articles regarding industrial policy and the sixty regulations for the people's communes in *Documents of the Chinese Communist Party Central Committee, September 1956-April 1969* (Hong Kong: Union Research Institute, 1971), pp. 689-725.

24. James Townsend, *Politics in China* (Boston: Little, Brown, 1980), Table 1, pp. 120-121.

25. However, the Cultural Revolution did have some impact on the economic base in some parts of China in the following ways: some factories were sent to the countryside; some collectives in the cities, especially in service industries (e.g., restaurants and laundries), were put under state ownership; in some rural areas, attempts were made to make the brigade rather than the team the basic accounting unit; and the policies of "politics in command" in both industry and agriculture sometimes reshaped the organization of production and patterns of distribution. For example, Parish and Whyte in their study of rural Guangdong Province found significant changes undertaken beginning in 1968-69 due to implementation of the Dazhai work-point system and a different system for the distribution of grain. William L. Parish and Martin King Whyte, *Village and Family in Contemporary China* (Chicago: University of Chicago Press, 1978), pp. 63-66.

26. See: Michael Y. M. Kau (ed.), *The Lin Piao Affair: Power Politics and Military Coup* (White Plains, New York: International Arts and Sciences Press, 1975); and, more recently, *Beijing Review*, December 22, 1980, pp. 19-28.

27. *Beijing Review*, October 5, 1979, p. 19.

28. *Beijing Review*, November 23, 1979, p. 3.

29. The Great Leap Forward did not begin with an emphasis on self-reliance in 1958. Self-reliance was only adopted as policy later, after 1960 when the Soviets cut off their aid to China. Nonetheless, theoretically, self-reliance fits very well the general logic of a Strategy B approach to socialist development.

30. John Gittings, *Survey of the Sino-Soviet Dispute: A Commentary and Extracts from the Recent Polemics, 1963-67* (London: Oxford University Press, 1968), pp. 130-132.

31. Xue Muqiao, "Thirty Years of Hardship," p. 44.

32. Donald S. Zagoria, *The Sino-Soviet Conflict, 1956-1961* (Princeton: Princeton University Press, 1962), Chapters 4 and 5.

33. Mao, *Critique of Soviet Economics*, p. 72.

34. *Ibid.*, p. 137.

35. *Ibid.*, p. 48.

36. *Ibid.*, p. 80.

37. *Ibid.*, pp. 67-68.

38. It should be noted that a number of socialist countries are presently experimenting with varieties of the Strategy C model, including Vietnam. See, for example, *Far Eastern Economic Review*, February 27-March 5, 1981, pp. 28-34; and June 19, 1981, pp. 56-57.

39. "Observe Economic Laws,Speed Up the Four Modernizations," (a three-part article) appearing in *Peking Review*, November 10, 17, and 24, 1978. Some other useful Chinese-language sources for identifying the basic ideas of Strategy C in China are: Xue Muqiao, *Shehuizhuyi Jingji Lilun Wenti* (Theoretical Problems of Socialist Economy) (Beijing: People's Publishers, 1979); Ma Hong, "The Reform of the System of Economic Management and the Expansion of Enterprise Autonomy" *Hongqi*, 1979, No. 10, pp. 50–58; and Deng Liqun, *Tantan Jihua Tiaojie he Shichang* (A Discussion on Planning Regulation and Market Regulation) (Beijing: People's Publishers, 1979).

40. *Renmin Ribao*, July 20, 1979, p.2.

41. See, for example, "Implementing the Socialist Principle 'To Each According to His Work,'" *Peking Review*, August 4 and 18, 1978. One Chinese economist, Huang Fanzhang, has suggested that the market mechanism and "consumers' sovereignty" should be central elements in a socialist economy in order to mediate the different economic interests which inevitably would develop among different enterprises and individuals. The market, according to Huang, would permit those who serve China's consumers better to earn more, and those who serve badly to earn less. Moreover, such a mechanism would encourage Chinese producers in the aggregate to be more productive and efficient. Huang Fanzhang, "Comment on 'Consumers' Sovereignty,'" *Jingji Guanli* (Economic Management), 1979, No. 2, pp. 25-27.

42. Irma Adelman, for example, has commented that based on her investigations of other economic systems, she could not see how a successful implementation of Strategy C could avoid increasing income inequality at least in the short run (comment at the Center for Chinese Studies Regional Seminar, University of California, Berkeley, March 21, 1981).

43. See Peter Van Ness, "China and the Third World," *Current History*, September 1974, pp. 106-109 and 133.

44. *Beijing Review* of April 5, 1982 (p. 11) reports: "More than 1,000 joint ventures and co-operative and compensatory trade items with foreign businesses, totalling 2,900 million US dollars in investment, have been approved by the Chinese Government since the adoption of the open-door policy and the promulgation in 1979 of the Law Governing Joint Ventures with Chinese and Foreign Investments."

45. China's State Statistical Bureau reports that during the year 1981: "The total number of foreigners, overseas Chinese and Chinese compatriots from Xianggang (Hong Kong) and Aomen (Macao) coming on tours and visits and for trade, sports, scientific and cultural exchanges reached 7,767,000, a 36.2 percent increase over the previous year. Included were 675,000 foreign tourists, a 27.6 per cent rise over 1980. Annual foreign exchange income was 1,380 million yuan Renminbi, 49.7 percent increase over 1980." *Beijing Review*, May 17, 1982, p. 22.

46. Ota Sik's *Plan and Market Under Socialism* contains the most thorough critique of the economics of the Stalinist model that we are aware of. However, it is important to note that given certain historical conditions, Strategy A does seem to provide very substantial economic benefits for a time. See, for example, Sik's distinction between "extensive" and "intensive" development of production (pp. 49-51).

47. Milovan Djilas, *The New Class: An Analysis of the Communist System* (New York: Praeger, 1957).

48. New York *Times*, September 5, 1980.

49. For a parallel critique of Strategy B in general terms, see Ota Sik, *Plan and Market*, pp. 361-364.

50. Personal conversation in Beijing, December, 1980.

51. For a good example of Strategy C reforms in both theory and practice, see the articles describing changes undertaken in 417 enterprises in Sichuan Province, in *Beijing Review*, April 6, 1981, pp. 21–29. See, also: Nicholas H. Ludlow, "Who's the Boss? After Ten Years They Still Don't Know," *China Business Review*, January-February 1981, pp. 14-16; and Thomas H. Pyle, "Reforming Chinese Management," *China Business Review*, May-June 1981, pp. 7-19. Regarding agriculture, see David Bonavia, "China Rediscovers the Family Farm," *Far Eastern Economic Review*, June 19, 1981, pp. 56-57.

52. See, for example, Martin Weil, "The Collapse of Construction Projects," *China Business Review*, January-February 1981, pp. 9-13.

53. Xue Muqiao writes that in China, "Six times more workers are needed in light industry and 11 times more in heavy industry to produce the same quantities of goods as in developed capitalist countries" (*China's Socialist Economy*, p. 201). Xue argues that "The transition from socialism to communism requires a level of productive forces much higher than what is already attained in developed capitalist countries. . . . If we fail to develop the productive forces or raise our labour productivity much higher than that under capitalism, the final victory of communism will be out of the question" (p. 307).

54. Associated Press in *Rocky Mountain News*, October 31, 1980, p.75.

55. By the end of 1980, Strategy C reforms had been undertaken in 6,600 enterprises in the state-owned economy in China which together in 1980 accounted for sixty percent of total industrial output value and seventy percent of profits turned over to the state. However, because of problems arising from the effort to implement a Strategy C model, the Deng Xiaoping leadership decided at a December 1980 work conference of the CCP Central Committee not to extend the reforms. Instead of "reform," it was decided that "readjustment" would be the central task of the Sixth Five Year Plan (1981-85). For a summary, see *Beijing Review*, May 11, 1981, p. 3.

Contributors

Marc Blecher is an Associate Professor of Government at Oberlin College. He is the co-author of *Micropolitics in Contemporary China: A Technical Unit Before and After the Cultural Revolution* (1979) and the coordinator of a group project which conducted field research in China on urban/rural development in a Chinese county.

Peer Moller Christensen is a researcher at the Institute of East Asian Studies, University of Aarhus, Denmark, and a freelance writer and consultant on Chinese politics and economics. He studied at Fudan University, Shanghai, in 1979-80.

Ralph Croizier is an Associate Professor of History at the University of Victoria, British Columbia. He has written many papers and reviews in the fields of Chinese medicine and history, and he is the author of *Koxinga and Chinese Nationalism: History, Myth, and the Hero (1977).*

Bruce Cumings is an Associate Professor of International Studies at the University of Washington. He is the author of *The Origins of the Korean War: Liberation and the Emergence of State Regimes, 1945-47* (1981) and the editor of *Child of Conflict: Korean-American Relations, 1945-53* (forthcoming).

Jorgen Delman is a researcher and consultant in the China Information Service of the Institute of East Asian Studies, University of Aarhus, Denmark. He has written on China's modern history, political economic theory, and education, and he was a student at Beijing University in 1977-78.

Edward Friedman is a Professor of Political Science at the University of Wisconsin. He is the author of numerous works on modern and contemporary China and U.S.-Asian relations, including *Backward Toward Revolution: The Chinese Revolutionary Party* (1974). He is currently completing a collaborative study, *Wugong: A Chinese Village in a Socialist State*, growing out of field research in China in 1978 and 1980.

Victor Lippit is an Associate Professor of Economics at the University of California, Riverside. He is the author of *Land Reform and Economic Development in China: Institutional Change and Development Finance* (1974), the co-editor of *The Transition to Socialism in China* (1982), and a major contributor to *The Development of Underdevelopment in China* (1980).

Mitch Meisner has taught Chinese and comparative politics at the University of California at Santa Cruz and at Michigan State University. A long-time student of the national agricultural model, he is the author of articles on China's rural development and contemporary politics. He is presently in law school at the University of Michigan.

Victor Nee is an Associate Professor of Sociology at the University of California, Santa Barbara. He is the author of *The Cultural Revolution at Peking University* (1969), co-author of *Longtime Californ': A Study of an American Chinatown* (1973), and co-author and co-editor of *State and Society in Contemporary China* (forthcoming). He is currently completing a book on peasant life in contemporary China.

James Nickum teaches economics at Cornell University and is a consultant on China's water problems to the World Bank and the United Nations University. He is the author of *Hydraulic Engineering and Water Resources in the People's Republic of China* (1977) and the editor of *Water Management Organization in the People's Republic of China* (1981).

Satish Raichur was an Associate Professor of Economics at the University of Denver. He is the co-author of *Special Bibliography in Monetary Economics* (1976) and *Multilateral Aid Activity in Latin America* (1976) and co-editor of *The Politics of Aid, Trade, and Investment* (1976). He was Chairman of the Department of Economics at the University of Denver at the time of his untimely death in June 1980.

Peter Van Ness is an Associate Professor in the Graduate School of International Studies, University of Denver. He is the author of *Revolution and Chinese Foreign Policy: Peking's Support for Wars of National Liberation* (1970) and the forthcoming *Civilizer States: America and China in the Modern World*.